Ending Intimate Abuse

Ending Intimate Abuse

Practical Guidance and
Survival Strategies

Albert R. Roberts and
Beverly Schenkman Roberts

OXFORD
UNIVERSITY PRESS

2005

OXFORD

UNIVERSITY PRESS

Oxford University Press, Inc., publishes works that further
Oxford University's objective of excellence
in research, scholarship, and education.

Oxford   New York

Auckland   Cape Town   Dar es Salaam   Hong Kong   Karachi
Kuala Lumpur   Madrid   Melbourne   Mexico City   Nairobi
New Delhi   Shanghai   Taipei   Toronto

With offices in
Argentina   Austria   Brazil   Chile   Czech Republic   France   Greece
Guatemala   Hungary   Italy   Japan   Poland   Portugal   Singapore
South Korea   Switzerland   Thailand   Turkey   Ukraine   Vietnam

Published by Oxford University Press, Inc.
198 Madison Avenue, New York, New York 10016

www.oup.com

Oxford is a registered trademark of Oxford University Press

Library of Congress Cataloging-in-Publication Data
Roberts, Albert R.
Ending intimate abuse : practical guidance and survival strategies /
Albert R. Roberts and Beverly Schenkman Roberts.
p. cm.
Includes bibliographical references and index.
ISBN-13 978-0-19-513547-3
ISBN 0-19-513547-4
1. Abused women—United States.   2. Family violence—United States.
3. Family violence—United States—Prevention.
I. Roberts, Beverly Schenkman.   II. Title.
HV6626.2.R6 2005
362.82'92—dc22   2004016316

1 3 5 7 9 8 6 4 2
Printed in the United States of America
on acid-free paper

To our wonderful son Seth and to Beverly's loving parents,

Edith and Jerry Schenkman, and to the loving memory

of Al's parents, Evelyn and Harry Roberts.

To all resilient survivors of domestic violence—may the

ways in which they ended the battering relationship serve as

an inspiration for all women in violent relationships.

If you are currently in a violent intimate relationship and need help,
please call the toll-free National Domestic Violence Hotline:
1-800-799-SAFE (7233) or
check the directory of over 500 statewide and local domestic hotlines at
the back of this book.

Preface

The impetus for this book grows out of my 25 years of research in the field of domestic violence, in which I studied crisis intervention programs, emergency shelters, prosecutor-based victim/witness assistance programs, and criminal justice intervention programs for perpetrators of domestic violence. The book is based on a study of 501 formerly battered women conducted between 1993 and 2001. My early research interest began in 1978 when I was an assistant professor of social work and sociology at Brooklyn College of C.U.N.Y. At the time, I was shocked to learn that one of my most intelligent, conscientious, and outspoken students had been violently battered by her first husband, a middle-class and seemingly nonviolent plumber when he proposed marriage. She was living with her older sister and brother-in-law, and she had met her husband by formal introduction since he was a neighbor and friend of her brother-in-law.

When I later wrote about this student's horrendous experiences, and the new life she was able to enjoy once she left the batterer, I gave her the pseudonym "Millie" to protect her confidentiality. Millie was first assaulted two weeks before her wedding, when her fiancé punched her. Afterward, he apologized, and she forgave him, since she was only 18 years old and believed that love could really conquer all. Millie was also in total shock from the first battering incident since her fiancé had appeared to be the perfect gentleman. He had not tried to have sexual intercourse with her until two months of steady dating had taken place. In sharp contrast, Millie indicated that most other dates tried to have sex on the first or second date. Surprisingly, however, by the third year of their marriage, Millie's husband had become a drug addict and chronic batterer.

Not only did I learn about domestic violence from Millie; I also learned about the enormous personal growth and success that is achievable when one is able to end a violent marriage. After leaving her abusive husband, Millie went to college and became a social worker. (Millie's experiences are not included in the 501 cases that are discussed in this book because she told me about her transformation from battered wife to energetic college senior in the late 1970s, decades before this study was undertaken.)

In 1979, I was also responsible for placing social work student interns in the newly opened emergency shelters for battered women in Brooklyn and Manhattan, at Maimonides Hospital and Long Island College Hospital social work departments in Brooklyn, at National Save-A-Life League in Manhattan, and at the Victim Information Bureau in Hauppauge, New York. Since battered women's shelters were just emerging in the late 1970s, no scholar or practitioner had conducted a national survey on them. So, in 1979, my coauthor and wife, Beverly Roberts, and I conducted the first national survey on the organizational structure and functions of 89 shelters for battered women and their children. The survey was published as a book, *Sheltering Battered Women: A National Study and Service Guide,* in 1981. It was one of the first in Dr. Violet Franks's Focus on Women book series. In 1984 Dr. Lenore Walker's classic *Battered Women Syndrome* was also published in this book series.

In 1984, I directed the National Institute of Justice–funded research project on the effectiveness of crisis intervention with violent crime victims at the Victim Services Agency (VSA), which had neighborhood offices in the five boroughs of New York City, and learned a tremendous amount about violent crime victims, crisis intervention, and victim services from interviewing victims at the neighborhood offices of VSA, as well as police precincts. In 1989, I completed a national organizational study of 184 prosecutor-based victim/witness assistance programs, the first of its kind. The Honorable Deborah Daniels, assistant attorney general for the U.S. Department of Justice (formerly chief counsel for the Marion County Prosecutor's Office in Indianapolis), provided valuable technical assistance with my earlier prosecutor-based victim/witness assistance study.

For more than 25 years, I have been conducting research and publishing articles and books on different aspects of domestic violence, but the earlier publications have been geared primarily to a clinical or scholarly audience. This book is decidedly different from them in that its primary target audience is professionals, parents, and the abused adolescent and young adult women themselves. These are the women who—if confronted by a violent boyfriend or husband—can end the violent relationship quickly by knowing what steps to take. The goal of this book is to provide case studies of women who have been abused by their boyfriends or husbands so that we can learn from them and *prevent* similar abuse in the lives of those who come to us for help. In addition, we hope this book will serve to heighten the awareness of the steps that are necessary to halt such violence quickly, if it does occur. Finally, we believe that the positive outcomes shared by so many of the women discussed in this book will offer hope and comfort to women who are in an abusive relationship and to their parents—as they plan for brighter days when the violent relationship is behind them.

Beverly Roberts is a social worker and a health advocacy program director for women with disabilities at The Arc of New Jersey. With 25 years of professional experience, she has had many positions serving the community: as a vocational evaluator and rehabilitation counselor at Sinai Hospital in Baltimore; as program development specialist with the Bureau of Residential Services of the New Jersey Division of Youth and Family Services; as assistant director and project officer at Queens College of the C.U.N.Y. Grants and Contracts Office; as consultant and evaluator with the Community Service Council of Greater Indianapolis; and currently as health advocate and director at the Mainstreaming Medical Care program and as the editor of the newsletter *Healthy Times* at The Arc of New Jersey. Because of the encouragement of our editor, Joan Bossert, we teamed up to write this book.

This book has two primary purposes. (1) We present profiles of abused women, indicating characteristics of those women who are and are not able to end the cycle of violence, drawn from a study of 501 abused women who were grouped in five different levels of severity and duration of woman battering. We describe the successful short-term cases in which women who were abused by their boyfriends or partners were able to end the relationship quickly, in contrast to a group of married women with children who were victimized for many years. (2) We provide practical guidelines for professionals to offer to young women, as well as their parents, closest friends, and siblings, describing the benefits and limitations of the agencies that have developed services to aid abused women: criminal justice agencies, mental health services, hospitals, hotlines, shelters for battered women, legal aid and private attorneys, and social service agencies. Warning signs, clues, behavioral patterns, and characteristics of men who hit women are thoroughly explored. We include a personal safety plan; a seven-stage crisis intervention model; a directory of national and local 24-hour domestic violence hotlines and resource centers for abused women; and a glossary of domestic violence, criminal justice, and legal terms.

Most previous studies have focused on the most visible battered women —namely, those who came to shelters, hospital emergency rooms, and police departments. The short-term battering cases, in which the women are able to end the dating relationship shortly after the violence begins, have received very little public attention. These young women who permanently break off the abusive relationship after one to three incidents are usually hard to find. We used a snowball sample in which 30 of my graduate and undergraduate college seniors interviewed close friends, acquaintances, or siblings who had been abused in the previous three years. Each student was trained in interviewing techniques by me and used a 39-page interview schedule of both stuctured and open-ended questions.

This book offers a bird's-eye view of dating relationships that have gone awry, from the perspective of older adolescents or young adult women who were able to end the relationship soon after the violence began. We believe that there are clear-cut warning signs that women in either dating relationships or recently married need to know (see chapters 1, 2, and 3). In contrast, we also provide the perspective of women at the opposite end of the continuum—those who ignored the early warning signs and, as a result, have suffered many years of violence (see chapters 4–6).

Paying attention to the stories of women who were able to permanently end a dating or marital relationship after just one or a small number of physically abusive acts will, we hope, help teens and young women nationwide. If we understand the critical factors or sequence of events that enable women to walk away from violence, we can begin to eliminate the domestic violence that is prevalent throughout the United States.

A Note on the Research Design: the study we draw on in this book was a qualitative, exploratory study using a structured, standardized interview format. The nonrandom sample consisted of 501 battered women purposefully drawn from four different populations in New Jersey. Because the design sampled battered women in only one location (New Jersey), the study findings are not generalizable to the population of all battered women in other regions of the United States. The sample consisted of battered women found at

- A New Jersey state women's prison who had killed their partners (105)

- Three suburban New Jersey police departments (105)

- Three battered women's shelters in New Jersey (105), or found through

- a convenience sample of formerly abused women living in New Jersey (186)

While the primary audiences for this book are family members and social service professionals who counsel women in dating and marital relationships, we also hope members of the clergy, teachers, high school guidance counselors, prevention specialists, nurses, health educators, attorneys, judges, college student services advisors, college counselors, residence counselors in dormitories, and domestic violence advocates, as well as their close friends, female roommates, classmates, and coworkers, will find this book useful in understanding batterers and their victims. I especially hope that all high school, college and university, and public libraries will place a copy of this work in their collections where those in need may find it.

Albert R. Roberts, Ph.D.
Rutgers University, Piscataway, N.J.
November, 2003

Acknowledgments

The most important acknowledgment goes to all of the women who agreed to be interviewed, sharing their experiences and the suffering and emotional anguish they had endured as well as the positive turning points that led to ending their violent relationships. This book would not have been written without the conscientious and responsive help of all of the senior author's former student interviewers. Special appreciation goes to the following students who completed approximately 10 to 30 interviews each: Lt. James Brady, M.A.; Lisa Cassa, J.D.; Sgt. Patricia Cassidy, J.D.; Shara Corrigan, J.D.; Patricia Dahl, B.S.; Beth Feder, J.D.; Kimberly A. Huangfu, J.D.; Vicki Jacobs, J.D.; Juliette Murphy, B.S.; Connie Nelson, B.S.; Colleen O'Brien, M.A.; Patrice Paldino, J.D.; Gina Pisano-Robertiello, Ph.D.; Wanda Garcia, M.S.W.; Donna Gilchrist, M.S.W.; Joanne Gonsalez, J.D.; Chandra L. Rainey, B.S.; Jeannie Saracino, J.D.; Katherine Stott, J.D.; and Lisa Trembly, J.D.

Two esteemed faculty members who had served on the Rutgers Universtiy Committee on Research with Human Subjects deserve special acknowledgment for suggesting several additional questions for the interview schedule: Professors Maurice Elias and Helene White. We would also like to express our deep sense of gratitude to consulting editor, Lisa Schwartz, who wrote an early draft of chapters 2–5; Professor Elizabeth Plionis whose incisive, skillful, and thorough editorial suggestions strenghtened all 11 chapters; Professor Karel Kurst-Swanger who wrote and rewrote chapter 10 on police and court guidelines for abuse victims; Professor Karen Knox and Eileen Kelley who cowrote chapter 11 on drug facilitated date rape; and our niece; and Evelyn Roberts Levine who cowrote the detailed glossary.

Our appreciation also goes to several faculty and former faculty colleagues at Rutgers University—Professors Miriam Dinerman, Gloria Bonilla Santiago, Michael J. Camasso, Lennox S. Hinds, and Edward Lowenstein. The sage advice of the late Dr. Robert Nevin from Indiana University School of Social Work helped us to realize the significance of critical incidents in childhood and adolescence on healthcare research. Dr. Bonilla Santiago provided invaluable assistance early in the study by coleading two focus groups in which we pretested and expanded the interview questionnaire. Dr. Camasso has gone far beyond the call of duty in preparing the codebook for the data analysis, supervising the student coders, and most importantly discussing the predictive power and implications of the factorial analysis. Dr. Camasso was also a major catylst to conceptualizing the continuum of the duration and severity of woman battering.

We are especially grateful for the advice and support of Captain William Flynn, M.A. (New Brunswick Police Department), Chief Thomas Finn, M.P.A. (Director of Public Safety, East Brunswick Police Department), and Chief William Spain, M.A. (East Windsor Police Department).

Special thanks go to Joan H. Bossert, Associate Publisher and Vice-President at Oxford University Press for her sage guidance, editorial insights, and long-term commitment to publishing original and timely books on medicine, psychology, public health, and social work. Without Joan's valuable advice our book would never have been published by Oxford University Press. Thanks also to the dedicated staff at Oxford University Press including Maura Roessner, Jessica Ryan, and Norman Hirschy.

Contents

I

The Study of 501 Abused Women

1

Proceed with Caution

Activating a Zero Tolerance Policy and Warning Signs of Male Batterers

Sonia, a 20-year-old college student, at the time of the interview, had met Brad the summer after she graduated from high school. Brad was the first boyfriend she had who took her to expensive restaurants and college fraternity parties. He was very polite to her parents and younger sister. Sonia believed that she was very much in love with Brad. Sonia was a virgin when they started dating; six months into the relationship, they had sexual intercourse for the first time. Describing the night when she lost her virginity, Sonia said that Brad was very romantic and the wine she drank put her in the mood. Shortly thereafter, however, Brad thought that Sonia was looking at his friend Tony and was so jealous that he slapped her for the first time. The next day, Brad brought Sonia flowers and apologized, blaming his slapping her on the liquor and his love for her. She forgave him.

Sonia was completely unprepared for the rapid escalation in violence that occurred several months later. Brad became furiously jealous and violent after a male coworker of Sonia played a practical joke on her. When Brad was finished, Sonia's lips were bleeding, the inside of her gums were torn up, and she had a swollen face. Sonia said that she was in a state of shock after the beating and questioned whether she would be able to trust another boyfriend in the future. Sonia's circumstances are described in more detail later in this chapter.

Christy, a 24-year-old college graduate who was now managing a restaurant, was physically abused and stalked by a former boyfriend when she was 18, during her freshman year at college. Christy reported that she still had nightmares from time to time in which a current boyfriend (not the batterer) became violent toward her and that she did not have very much energy. She wondered if the nightmares and lethargy would ever go away. Christy's traumatic experience, discussed in chapter 2, demonstrates the value of having a trusting relationship with one's parents, as well as the usefulness of a police report and restraining order in coping with a violent relationship.

Pamela, a 29-year-old devout Catholic and a teacher with two young children, initially attributed the emotional and physical abuse from her husband to the enormous stress associated with his being a medical student. Pamela convinced herself that the abuse would end as soon as her husband completed his residency and had his own medical practice. Chapter 3 describes the ongoing abuse Pamela endured, years after her husband was established as a respected physician, as well as valuable advice Pamela received from her priest.

Intimate partner abuse is one of the most harmful, traumatic, and life-threatening criminal justice and public health problems in American society. Intimate partner abuse continues to be the single greatest health threat to American women between the ages of 15 and 50. More women sustain injuries as a result of intimate partner abuse than from the combined total of muggings and accidents. The following statistics portray the pervasiveness of intimate partner abuse in the United States.

- Every 9 seconds a woman is assaulted and battered.
- Each year, 8.7 million women are victims of intimate partner violence.
- Over 90 percent of the victims of domestic violence are women.
- Every day, four women are murdered by a boyfriend, husband, or former intimate partner.
- Domestic violence is the number one cause of emergency room visits by women.
- The most likely time for a woman to be killed by her abuser is when she is attempting to leave him.
- The number one cause of women's injuries is abuse at home.
- Approximately one in every four women in America has been physically assaulted and/or raped by an intimate partner.

The most accurate statistics on the lifetime prevalence of intimate partner violence come from the National Violence Against Women Survey, conducted by Professors Patricia Tjaden and Nancy Thoennes, with grants from the National Institute of Justice and the Centers for Disease Control and Prevention (CDC). Their study was based on telephone interviews with a nationally representative sample (N = 16,000) of 8,000 men and 8,000 women, and found that 25 percent of the women and 7.6 percent of the men said that they had been physically battered and/or raped by a spouse, cohabiting partner, or date during their lifetime. These national figures document the high prevalence of intimate partner abuse.

In actuality, however, some women are at much greater risk of becoming victims of intimate partner violence than others. Women at the highest risk of encountering violence from dates and boyfriends are high school and college students.

Date abuse, binge drinking, club drugs, and drug-facilitated sexual assault have all been escalating on college campuses, as well as at bars and rave parties frequented by high school students and young adults who are not in school. Female college students, particularly those who are living away from their families during the first year or two of college, are at heightened risk of becoming victims of dating violence because of peer pressure to drink or do drugs combined with a lack of supervision and protection.

The professional literature on domestic violence is replete with citations of the horrendous problems that ensue when women become involved in long-term relationships in which they are assaulted on a frequent basis. The purpose of this book is to educate young women and their families, friends, and therapists or counselors regarding the full spectrum of violent relationships, with the goal of helping them prevent the likely progression from the initial incident of violence to severe beatings later on.

Whenever women begin a new dating relationship, they must exercise caution. Our study of 501 cases identified five distinct categories or levels of violent relationships on this continuum: *Short-term, Intermediate, Intermittent long-term, Chronic with a frequent pattern, and Lethal.*

One of the best ways to fully comprehend what dating and intimate abuse is—and how easily an unsuspecting woman can overlook the initial warning signs of battering and become entangled in a violent relationship—is to read the five case stories in this chapter, and the many case studies that appear throughout the book. As their stories unfold, the struggles and, in many cases, ultimate successes that these women experienced clearly emerge.

We introduce you here to the voices of five different women. Combined, their experiences provide an overview of dating and marital violence on a continuum from short-term to long-term abuse.

The five cases we present at the end of this chapter illustrate several concepts involved in intimate partner abuse: learned helplessness, intermittant reinforcement, traumatic bonding, cultural and religious socialization to gender roles, triggers to violent episodes, as well as risk and protective factors. Also identified are 23 warning signs of men who are at risk of becoming batterers.

The emphasis of this book is to communicate that the first slap or punch that occurs in a dating relationship must be recognized as a neon warning sign of additional, more brutal violence in the future, unless there is an intervention that ends the violence in its earliest stage. During a dating relationship, women may react in two ways to an initial incident of hitting or punching. The first way is for the woman to end the relationship, explaining that she has a zero tolerance for violence. One 20-year-old woman who has benefited from a good therapeutic relationship with a psychologist (following her having been hit by a boyfriend when she was 17) now makes it a practice to tell anyone whom she starts to date that she has a zero tolerance for violence in her dating relationships. She explains that she was slapped around by her first boyfriend and that she will never again allow herself to suffer that type of disrespect and trauma again. Thus far, her boyfriends have been sensitive to her previous victimization, and she has not been abused again. She explains: "I need to set forth these boundaries right up front, on the very first date, to make sure this isn't going to happen to me ever again. And if I ever meet a guy who is put off by my dating ground rules, then good riddance to him!"

The way in which the woman should best communicate her decision to end the dating relationship will depend both on the relationship's duration and the man's personality. If the relationship is casual and the man generally nonviolent (when not drinking), it is more likely that he will calmly accept the woman's decision. (Depending on how the man responds to the end of the dating relationship, the woman may also suggest that he seek counseling so that he can gain control of his anger and not ruin a future relationship.) But if the dating was intimate and had some duration, and if the man is prone to angry outbursts and jealous rages, then the woman should consider having another man (such as her father, uncle, or older brother) accompany her to a meeting at a neutral public location, such as a restaurant or coffee shop, when she breaks off the relationship. If the woman is fearful that the man may explode in a violent rage upon hearing the news, she may want to speak to the police about signing a domestic violence complaint and filing a temporary restraining order. (See chapter 10 for information on the pros and cons of police and court intervention, especially seeking a temporary restraining order, also known as an order of protection in some jurisdictions.)

The second way to end violence in its early stage is for the woman who believes that the dating relationship is worth saving; she will insist that there will never again be any hitting. In these situations, the woman should present the ultimatum that he either agrees to go for couples counseling and/or a series of anger control classes (for the purpose of learning the coping skills to deal with anger in a nonviolent manner) or the dating relationship is over.

The concern about the second approach is that the man may agree to go to counseling and may attend a session or two but not make any significant changes in his abusive behavior. He may then expect that by having attended a session or two of counseling, he will have appeased her concerns. In all likelihood, it will take more than a couple of counseling sessions to bring about fundamental behavior change. Both parties should recognize that, even if he participates in many therapy sessions, there are no guarantees of a successful end to the violence. He may also be in denial, refusing to accept that he has an anger control problem, and will either refuse to attend counseling or use delaying tactics, such as agreeing to have counseling at an unspecified time in the future and then never following through.

The woman should therefore do her best to be steadfast in her zero tolerance for violence position; any additional violence—even if he has been attending counseling sessions—must result in the end of their relationship.

If there is a very serious dating relationship, and a single incident of violence has occurred, the woman is confronted with the dilemma of how to respond. Simply proposing that she should end the very serious relationship may not be realistic. One suggestion is to initiate anger-control counseling and couples counseling prior to either marriage or a decision to live together. The couple should consider waiting for a substantial period of time (to be determined in consultation with the therapist) to have more confidence that the counseling has been effective in helping the man learn how to deal with his anger in a nonviolent manner before they live together. If there is any reoccurrence of violence during the counseling phase, the woman should have the strength to realize that this relationship is too dangerous.

It is also essential that both the man and the woman recognize the role that alcohol (or other drugs) may play as a catalyst to a violent outburst. While there are certainly many men who can drink alcohol without ever becoming violent, there are also men who become violent only when they have been drinking—and others for whom violence erupts irrespective of whether they are drinking. Substance abuse impairs decision-making and reduces inhibitions; this is why heavy drinking or drug use is associated with partner abuse in many of the cases in this book and in most other domestic violence literature. Therefore, if it is determined that substance abuse is involved in the man's violent anger outbursts, it is essential that this problem be addressed simultaneously with the counseling services. Depending on the individual's dependence on the substances that are associated with violent episodes, it may be advisable for him to join Alcoholics Anonymous (AA) or Narcotics Anonymous (NA). These groups have a long history of success with those who genuinely want to be helped.

The situation is extremely difficult for close relatives who know (or strongly suspect) that a woman in their family has been abused by her boyfriend or husband. As much as they may want to, parents cannot dictate whom their adult daughter can and cannot date or live with. The most important action for parents to take is to keep the lines of communication open so that their daughter knows she can come to them for help at any time. While all parents wish that their daughter will never have an abusive boyfriend, they also hope that if violence does occur, their daughter would immediately end the relationship. It is much more difficult for the parents if violence does occur and their daughter continues to stay in that relationship. In such situations, parents should remain outwardly calm and avoid name-calling and threats such as "If you don't leave him right away, I'll never speak to you again." The emphasis should be on the parents' concerns for their daughter's safety, and their desire to be as helpful as possible in ensuring that she gets prompt medical attention; assisting her to locate a counselor to help her make good decisions about the relationship; encouraging her to call and to come to their home whenever she wishes; learning about community resources, such as battered women's shelters; and learning about the assistance the police can provide in the form of arrest and a temporary restraining order, if necessary. (For further information on the important role of the police, courts and victim advocates, see chapter 10.)

In most cases, long-term victimization, which can escalate to life-threatening consequences, begins in the form of a single slap or punch during a dating relationship, before the couple decide to live together or get married. Our research shows that if the dating relationship continues after the initial sign of violence, then the violence often accelerates in severity over time.

Sometimes adolescent girls and young adult women (often women who are very kind and trusting) are willing to overlook sporadic dating violence, for several reasons:

1. A woman may be so madly in love that she is willing to overlook and minimize all of the man's faults, including being slapped or punched occasionally when he is drunk or upset about what is happening at school or his job.

2. A woman may be so overly kindhearted that, even though immediately after the violence she determines to never see him again, she relents when the boyfriend makes profuse apologies, promises that it will never happen again, and brings her flowers and expensive gifts.

3. A woman may feel guilty, believing that she did something to provoke the boyfriend's anger and that he was therefore justified in lashing out

violently. All couples disagree and even argue from time to time. But sometimes a woman has the faulty thinking that if she behaves "perfectly" and does not make the boyfriend upset, then he will never hit her again, and, conversely, that if he does become violent, then she is at fault for causing him to become so angry.

4. A woman may have been raised in a home in which violence was commonplace, and may have witnessed her father or stepfather beating her mother. In addition, during her childhood, some women were abused physically or sexually by parents, stepparents, siblings, or other relatives. For such a woman, being victimized by a boyfriend or partner may become part of the pattern of violence that shaped her childhood. Such women can benefit greatly from therapy provided by a psychologist or social worker with expertise in this type of problem.

The following case stories illustrate some typical ways violence can occur early in a dating relationship.

■ Case 1: Cathy

Cathy was a 24-year-old college graduate whose childhood and adolescence had been quite normal. She grew up in a two-parent home, the oldest of three children. Upon entering high school, she had feelings of inadequacy that are not uncommon for adolescent girls. During her junior and senior years in high school, she had a couple of boyfriends, but the relationships were not serious. During her freshman year in college, when she was living in the dormitory, she met Bryan, a college junior, at a fraternity party, and there was an immediate mutual attraction. Bryan was one of the most popular guys in the fraternity, and, initially, Cathy felt lucky that he was attracted to her. In the spring, when they had been dating for several months, Cathy told Bryan she wanted to work for the summer at a beach resort that was located approximately 85 miles away from the college. Bryan needed to take summer school classes and continue his part-time job near the campus, and he did not want Cathy to be so far away. Their disagreement over this issue turned into a raging argument that ended when Bryan grabbed Cathy's shoulders, shook her very hard, and punched her in the face.

■ Case 2: Keri and Erica

Keri and Erica were both 17 years old, honor roll students at their high school, and best friends since childhood. They obtained fake IDs so that they could drink at a popular bar in the next town. Keri was living in a two-parent family; although Erica's parents were divorced, their relationship was amicable, and they shared custody of Erica and her younger brother. Since their parents would never have allowed them to go drinking, Keri and Erica concocted a phony story about going to a mutual friend's birthday party. Keri's parents gave her permission to drive their car to the party, and the girls promised to be home by midnight.

Keri and Erica were both quite attractive, and when they put on their party dresses and high heels, they could easily pass for 21-year-olds. The girls' fake IDs gained them entrance to the bar, where they quickly met two handsome men in their early twenties who said they were medical students from the nearby university. After only a couple of drinks, Keri and Erica started to feel very woozy and were unable to drive, so the men offered to drive them home. Instead of taking the girls to their own homes, the men brought Keri and Erica to a motel and sexually assaulted them.

When Keri and Erica awoke on Sunday morning, the men were gone. The girls had no idea where they were and they were not certain what had happened the night before, but since they were both naked and their clothing was piled on a chair, they quickly realized that they had probably been raped. Since Keri's parents' car had been left at the bar, and they had no other mode of transportation, they decided they had to call their parents and tell them what had happened. The parents were understandably frantic with worry because the girls had not returned home Saturday night. As a result of the parents' late-night phone calls to the girls' other friends, they already knew that their daughters had made up the story about a birthday party and they were panic-stricken about their disappearance.

Both sets of parents arrived at the motel quickly and were relieved that their daughters were safe. As Keri and Erica told their parents the truth, it became obvious to the adults that the girls had probably been the victims of a date rape drug that the two men had casually poured into their drinks at the bar. There had been opportunities for the two men to tamper with their drinks, as the girls had gone together to the bathroom after a second round of drinks had been ordered.

(For further information on date rape drugs and drug-facilitated rapes, see chapter 11.)

■ **Case 3: Jackie**

Jackie was a single woman in her mid-twenties who came from a close-knit, Catholic family. After starting college at Syracuse University, she transferred to a New Jersey state college to complete her bachelor's degree and then earned a master's degree in guidance and counseling. At the time of the interview, she was working as a high school guidance counselor and living at her parents' home in an upper-middle-class suburb in northern New Jersey in order to save enough money for a down payment on a condo in the area.

Approximately a month after arriving at Syracuse University as a freshman, Jackie began dating Don, a popular junior who was on the football team. She considered herself very fortunate, as an 18-year-old freshman, to be dating Don. Jackie was naive and did not realize (until much later) that many of the male college athletes preyed upon the incoming freshmen and took advantage of their inexperience and excitement at being noticed by the upperclassmen. For the first six weeks that they were dating, everything was going well, from Jackie's point of view, but she was a virgin, and they had not slept together. Jackie described the night that Don raped her:

> We went to a bar with a big group of people and we were all drinking. I went back to Don's apartment with him. I don't remember much about what happened, but that is when he raped me. We started kissing and then he tried more. I resisted, but he wouldn't listen. I tried to push him off of me, but he was so much bigger. I was making a lot of noise, and I know that his two roommates, who were also football players, must have heard me. He slapped my face and bit my neck to keep me quiet. When my friends saw the mark on my neck the next day, they thought it was a hickey. When it was over, I got up to leave and I remember him saying to me: "Don't ever say anything. Don't be foolish."

Jackie did not say anything about the rape to her parents or her friends, keeping her anger and distress to herself. A few days later, Jackie called a male friend from high school, Jeremy, to ask his opinion of the date rape, but she did not want him to know that she was the victim. So she said that her friend had just been raped by a football player at the university, and she asked Jeremy for his suggestion on what her "friend" should do.

> Jeremy asked if my friend had been drinking, and I said that she had, but that she wasn't drunk. Jeremy said that she must have been drunk and she probably woke up the next morning with regret about sleep-

ing with him. He said she had probably wanted it to happen and she must have sent the guy mixed signals. Jeremy said my friend should not do anything.

When Don phoned Jackie a few days after the rape, he acted as though nothing had happened, and he said he wanted to take her out drinking on Friday night. Jackie told him she did not want to see him anymore because of what he had done to her. Don tried to convince her that it was not a big deal and that she was overreacting, but Jackie was insistent that she did not want to date him ever again.

A couple of weeks later, the stalking began. It started as periodic crank phone calls which then accelerated to at least twice a day. Other stalking incidents took place, including delivery of flowers with all of the petals cut off. During the next few months, the stalking incidents increased in frequency and severity. Jackie became very frightened because the stalker was watching her so closely. When she and her girlfriends went to a bar and Jackie danced with a guy, the stalker called her later that evening and asked her pointed questions about the man with whom she had been dancing earlier in the evening. Any male friends with whom she spent time received threatening letters saying that they should stay away from Jackie. The breaking point occurred when Jackie returned to the campus following spring break to find that the door to her dorm had been vandalized with a large spray-painted X. This was immediately followed by a death threat on her answering machine.

Jackie was so distraught that she finally confided in her parents everything that had occurred. She was having nightmares and was not able to concentrate on her school work, and her parents urged her to leave Syracuse and come back to live with them. Jackie was in such a fragile emotional state that she agreed to leave school only part way through the spring semester; she was relieved to return to the safety of home and the comfortable neighborhood that she had known since childhood. Once she returned to New Jersey, the stalking ceased. Her parents arranged for her to see a psychologist, and after a few weeks, she got a part-time job at the mall. The following September, Jackie had recovered sufficiently from her ordeal to enroll in a state college that was within commuting distance of her parents' home. For the rest of her time in college, Jackie continued to live with her parents.

■ Case 4: Sonia

Sonia was a 20-year-old white female who graduated from high school and worked for a year at a department store before going to college. Sonia grew up in a two-parent family in a middle-class neighborhood. There was no violence in Sonia's home. Following her graduation from high school, Sonia continued to live at home.

Sonia met Brad the summer after she graduated from high school. They had been dating for six months before the first violent incident occurred. Brad was majoring in mechanical engineering at the local state university, and he worked part-time. Brad was the first boyfriend she had who took her to expensive restaurants and fraternity parties. He seemed to be a perfect gentlemen and was very polite to her parents and younger sister. Sonia believed that she was very much in love with him, and he professed his love for her as well, but Sonia was upset by his extreme jealousy and possessiveness. Brad said that he was so much in love with Sonia that it drove him crazy to think that she would look at another guy, or that some other guy was looking at her.

On Brad's birthday they had sexual intercourse for the first time. Sonia said that Brad was very romantic, and the wine she drank that night put her in the mood. A week later, Brad's first violent outburst occurred at a party held in an apartment of one of Brad's college friends. Almost everyone had been drinking, but Sonia was not drunk. She had had a few beers, and Brad had been drinking hard liquor, but Sonia did not think he was very drunk. During the evening, Brad thought that Sonia was looking at his friend and became so jealous that he smacked her across the face with the back of his hand. The next day, Brad apologized and blamed the incident on the liquor and his love for her.

During the next couple of months, Brad slapped Sonia one additional time, after drinking a few beers while watching a basketball game; he was apologetic afterward and brought her an expensive gift from Victoria's Secret. Sonia told herself that she really loved Brad and she rationalized that it was just a slap on two separate occasions, and that there had not been any noticeable bruises.

Sonia was completely unprepared for the escalation of violence that occurred at a party a few months later. Brad became insanely jealous because another guy sat next to Sonia for a couple of minutes while Brad was getting a drink. The severe incident occurred the night of a twenty-first birthday party for one of Brad's friends. A large group went to a bar, and all of the friends had a lot to drink; Sonia had only a couple of beers because she was the designated driver.

Sonia described what happened after she and Brad left the bar: "Brad started screaming and cursing at me because I was talking to this other guy who sat next to me at the bar. Brad kept punching my face. My lips were cracked and bleeding and the inside of my gums were torn up."

Since Sonia lived at home with her parents, she could not hide her bruised face and bleeding mouth from them. As soon as Sonia walked into the house, bruised and crying, she saw her mother, who became extremely upset about her daughter's injuries and furious at Brad for what he had done. After checking to see that none of Sonia's teeth had been loosened by the blows and providing ice packs to reduce the swelling, her mother urged her to go to the police immediately. Sonia's parents handled the situation in a straightforward way, without lecturing Sonia on her poor choice in boyfriends. They explained that the most important thing at that moment was to make sure that Brad never did this again, and to do that, Sonia needed to file a police report. Sonia had always had a good relationship with her parents, and shortly before midnight, she went to the police station accompanied by both parents.

The police were quite helpful, photographing her bruised face and asking her to write down what had happened and sign the report. The police then went to Brad's house and served him with a temporary restraining order, prohibiting him from having any contact with Sonia or harassing her in any way. Shortly after the restraining order was delivered, Brad contacted Sonia by e-mail; he apologized profusely, told Sonia how much he loved her, and promised that he would never hit her again. Sonia responded by e-mail and told Brad that she never wanted him to contact her again—their relationship was over. Her e-mail concluded by saying that if he ever contacted her again by e-mail or any other method, she would report him to the police for violating the restraining order. Sonia was interviewed a year after this violent episode, and she was relieved that she had not heard from Brad again. At the time of the interview, she was enrolled at a local college, studying to be an elementary school teacher.

■ Case 5: Roberta

Roberta, a 28-year-old woman with a bachelor's degree from the University of Pennsylvania, had always had a problem with her weight. She was not obese, but at a size 14, she was always trying to lose weight. She had tried one diet after another, and although she usually lost weight, within a few months all of the lost pounds returned, and sometimes, to her dismay, she ended up putting on additional pounds. Her weight was a constant source of bickering between Roberta and her mother. Roberta felt her mom had forced her to be an overachiever, always criticizing her for any imperfections, including her weight problem. She was a very hard-working student, and usually got As in school, but her mom reacted harshly whenever her grades were less than As.

Roberta had met her husband, Jim, during the spring semester of her senior year at college when she was 21 years old. Jim was several years older. He had an MBA and was already established in a midlevel marketing position for a Fortune 500 company. At 29, Jim said he was ready to settle down, and he did not seem to mind that Roberta was overweight. As a struggling college student, Roberta was always trying to save money; she was not accustomed to dining in fine restaurants and having orchestra seats at the theater. Jim pursued Roberta in a glorious (but brief) whirlwind courtship, and was eager to shower her with extravagances.

Shortly after her graduation, Roberta and Jim were married in a lovely church wedding, and they had an unforgettable honeymoon in Hawaii. She was hired by a large market research firm, and she felt like she now had her dream job. She enjoyed her work, and she was married to a wonderful, successful man, and living in a renovated townhouse in a fashionable center city location in Philadelphia.

A few months after their wedding, Roberta accidentally became pregnant. They had been to a friend's wedding, came home drunk from alcohol and the exhilaration of the wedding festivities, and made passionate love without Roberta taking the time to insert her diaphragm. Roberta had not been planning to have a baby quite so soon, but abortion was out of the question because of their religious beliefs.

After such a fairy-tale courtship, the young married couple was completely unprepared for the birth of their baby boy with serious birth defects. Jim was particularly upset with the baby's condition, and he started to drink much more frequently than he had in the past.

The first time Jim hit Roberta, she was 23 years old. She stayed with her husband for five years before leaving him permanently. At the time of the interview, she was living at a shelter for battered women, and she talked about the first time her husband hit her:

> It was when our first child was born with a lot of birth defects, and my husband blamed me for it. He hit me when I was holding the baby in my arms. No one had ever hit me before that. My parents didn't even hit me. He hit me in the face so hard that I was bruised.

There were numerous incidents following the first act of violence, usually after Jim had been drinking. The more he drank, the more frequently he hit her. During the next few years, the violence increased in severity, but it happened very gradually. After each incident, Jim was apologetic, and there were weeks at a time when he did not hit her at all. After each violent episode, the man with whom Roberta had fallen in love reemerged. Jim apologized profusely, brought her expensive jewelry and flowers, and begged for her forgiveness. Roberta never told her mother or any of her friends about the battering incidents. She stopped working when her son was born because his disabilities required frequent visits to doctors, and it was difficult to locate a day care agency that would provide the attention his medical condition warranted. Jim was earning such a good income that Roberta did not need to return to her former job. For a few days after each battering episode, Roberta stayed close to home to let the injuries heal. If Roberta had to go out in public (for example, to a doctor's appointment for her son), she would apply heavy amounts of makeup on her bruised face and wear long sleeved blouses. During those periods, Roberta convinced herself that Jim would keep his promise to never hit her again, and that the violence had ended, permanently. But that was not the case. Roberta described what she called the "final straw," the extremely serious incident that finally made her decide to leave Jim:

> The final straw was back in June at the time of his birthday. We had big plans so my mother took the kids for the weekend. I had to work for a couple of hours and when I got home, he wasn't there, so I took a shower and waited for him. He finally called, very drunk. He had ditched me for his friends, so I hung up on him. An hour later when he came home, I was in the bathroom and he slapped me down to the ground. Then I went upstairs to go to bed in my son's room, and he literally dragged me into our room and sexually assaulted me. Then he did it again two more times. The whole horrible episode lasted about nine or ten hours. I call it the "night of terror."

■ Their Stories and the Scientific and Professional Concepts That Help Explain Them

☐ About the Study

The women just described participated in our research study of 501 women who experienced violence in their dating and marital relationships. The purpose of the research was to locate and interview women whose experience of violence in their dating relationship ended relatively quickly and compare them to women who were battered for many years. A large amount of data was collected and analyzed over a seven-year period. Following an initial quantitative and qualitative analysis of the data, it became apparent that a typology of abuse was emerging from the data that could be displayed on a continuum of duration from short-term to long-term patterns.

☐   Socioeconomic Factors Associated with Ending the Abuse

Research studies have shown that, typically, when the batterer comes from a middle class background, is currently either in school or productively employed, and has a stake in preserving his status in the community as a law-abiding citizen, the issuing of a temporary restraining order by the police generally ends the violence. This is particularly true when the couple is not living together, as in the early stages of a dating relationship. Sonia's case illustrates that date abuse can be ended quickly and permanently when the victim is assertive and seeks assistance from her support system—in this case, her parents—as well as from the police. In sharp contrast, a restraining order may not be a deterrent for men who come from a lower socioeconomic class background, are unemployed, or already have an arrest record for other offenses. In some cases, police intervention results in even greater violence toward the woman because the batterer becomes infuriated that charges have been filed against him.

☐   Triggers to Violent Episodes: Substance Use and Loss of Self-Esteem Due to Shame

In most cases, the first battering incident is mild or moderate in severity, but the violence escalates in severity if the woman stays in the relationship. In general, the batterer apologizes profusely after his violent rampage, and he often (particularly in the early years of the abusive relationship) showers his partner with lavish gifts in an attempt to persuade her not to leave the relationship. The case of Roberta and Jim illustrates several key points. First, although domestic violence occurs in all socioeconomic levels, it is more likely to be hidden when it occurs in middle- or upper-class relationships. Second, abuse of alcohol and other substances is often associated with violent incidents. Third, a loss that threatens self-esteem, such as the birth of a child with defects, can result in anger that later explodes as violence directed at the one who is blamed for the loss or shame.

☐   Resiliency: Protective Factors

Our study showed that there are five distinct types of abused women, based on the length of time they remain in the violent relationship, and the severity of abuse they endure. One of the most significant findings of the study was that women with certain characteristics—self-reported psychological strengths, personality traits, protective factors—were able to leave the batterer after one to three abusive incidents, while other groups of women stayed in the relationship for many years as the violence became chronic. For professionals, the ability to identify whether the woman is assertive and has high self-esteem, along with family support, is critical to predicting how quickly the battering relationship will end.

☐ Socialization, Culture, and Religious Influences

Some women permanently break off a dating, cohabitating, or marital relationship after one to three acts of physical battering. These articulate and self-reliant young women have been socialized by their families *not* to tolerate even one instance of physical abuse. Other women have been socialized by their culture, their religion, or their families to stay in the relationship. They do it out of perceived love, a sense of duty related to commitment and marriage vows, the need for financial support, or because they perceive that staying is in the best interest of the children. Women like these who endure moderate emotional and physical abuse typically remain in the marriage until a severely abusive incident—a broken jaw, a concussion, or a life-threatening act such as being strangled—serves as the last straw. Such an episode acts as a catalyst, triggering the decision to leave. Another decision trigger is often when the batterer starts to physically abuse one or more of the children. The women then decide to obtain a restraining order and legal separation.

☐ Why Do Women Stay in Violent Relationships?

While many women leave violent relationships, too many stay even as the violence escalates in severity and chronicity over many years. To understand these chronic victims, some concepts may be useful. *Traumatic bonding* is a strong emotional attachment that can develop, combined with fear of abandonment and intermittent abuse. *Intermittent reinforcement* occurs when the abusive partner is periodically kind, loving, and apologetic for past violent episodes, promising that the violence will never happen again, but then resorts to degrading insults and abuse. The term *learned helplessness* refers to a victim who learns from repeated, unpleasant, and painful experiences that she is unable to control the aversive environment or escape; as a result, she gradually loses the motivation to change the abusive situation. *Minimization* describes a victim's distorted cognitive beliefs when she grossly underestimates both the frequency and severity of the battering incidents she has endured. These patterns of distorted thinking keep some women trapped in harmful and dangerous relationships for years. Typically and tragically, these extremely violent marriages do not end until the woman's injuries are so severe that she requires extensive hospitalization to heal the injuries, the batterer is incarcerated or placed in a long-term residential program for substance abusers, or one of the partners is found dead.

☐ Warning Signs of Male Batterers

Not all male adolescents and young men are batterers, but some are. It is natural for a woman to want a new relationship to work out, and it is easy to overlook the warning signs of possible danger. Women who are college freshmen and living away from home are particularly vulnerable. On the basis of our research, we identified warning signs of those volatile males who are at risk of becoming batterers. When three or more of these warning signs are present in a boyfriend or partner, then it is considerably more likely that sooner or later he will batter his partner. (It is possible, however, that a man may have only one of these characteristics and still hit his partner. There are no 100 percent guarantees when it comes to predicting potential for violence in dating relationships, but there are warning signs.) These 23 warning signs or red flags are intended to help young women proceed with caution when embarking upon a new dating relationship. In addition, a woman who breaks up with a boyfriend or partner who exhibits three or more of these warning signs should do it cautiously in case the act of leaving triggers violence.

The Warning Signs

- The man is extremely jealous and overly possessive of his date. As a result, he expresses intense fears of being cheated on or abandoned.

- He intimidates and instills fear in his date or partner by raising a fist or kicking or mutilating a pet, or he has a history of having harmed pets.

- He exhibits poor impulse control or explosive anger.

- He gives indications of limited capacity for delayed gratification—most of his desires need immediate response.

- He repeatedly violates his girlfriend's or spouse's personal boundaries through behavior such as standing just a few inches from her face when talking to her in an angry and hostile manner.

- He tries to dominate his partner by telling her what to wear and when to speak, or making punitive rules, such as "I will return the sterling silver necklace to the store if you don't polish all of my shoes tonight."

- He uses extreme and coercive control tactics such as disabling the partner's car, taking the phone receiver when he leaves the house, monitoring the mileage on the car when she goes grocery shopping alone, or never allowing her to shop alone.

- He attacks the self-confidence of his partner with habitual name-calling, putdowns, and disparaging, derogatory statements (e.g., "You are the worst housekeeper in the world"; "You look as fat as an elephant in those jeans"; "You look like a slut and a whore in that blue dress").

- He is emotionally dependent and wants his girlfriend to spend time exclusively with him, isolating her from all of her family and friends.

- He becomes hostile and goes into a rage after binge drinking and/or other substance abuse. At these times, he may become furious over small, inconsequential matters.

- He never takes responsibility for the role he played in the problem when things go wrong; he refuses to recognize that his actions contributed to the upsettting outcome. According to him, it is always someone else's fault; this is known as victim blaming.

- He cannot control his anger. There is evidence of this inability, such as holes in the wall of his apartment or broken objects that he threw against the wall in a fit of anger.

- In a fit of anger, sparked by jealousy or a disagreement with his date, he threatens to hit, slap, or punch her.

- He has poor communication skills and an irrational belief system. For example, he believes that his wife is having an affair with another man because she forgot to bring home a six-pack of beer.

- He has a generational history of interpersonal violence among father or other familial male role models in which he was beaten as a child or he observed his father or stepfather beating his mother.

- He has a history of having abused a previous girlfriend. (He may be likely to deny having hit a previous girlfriend, even if there was violence; if he admits, however, to having been abusive in a previous relationship, that is a serious warning sign of future violence.)

- He is on a college or high school sports team in which violence is emphasized, such as football, or he is a weightlifter who takes steroids or diet pills on a regular basis.

- He is demanding, overly aggressive, frequently rough, and/or sometimes sadistic in sexual activities.

- He escalates intimidating and potentially assaultive behavioral patterns when his partner is pregnant. Pregnancy can mark the first violent incident.

- He exerts coercive control by threatening and then attempting homicide and/or suicide when the woman attempts to leave the relationship.

- He exhibits a narcissistic personality disorder. His behavior is characterized by passive-aggressiveness, overconfidence, egocentricism, grandiosity, arrogance, self-absorption, deceitfulness, hypervigilance, manipulation, and explosiveness.*

- He exhibits an avoidant/depressive personality disorder; he is repeatedly withdrawn, anxious, dissatisfied, and depressed. He exhibits feelings of low self-esteem and suicidal ideation.*

- He exhibits a borderline personality disorder and is highly impulsive, self-punitive, sexually abusive, moody, resentful, and tense. He frequently goes into rages and is unable to express either empathy for others or remorse.*

Of all the warning signs of severe woman battering, the strongest predictors are (1) excessive jealousy and (2) a prior domestic assault history in the current relationship or a previous relationship, combined with any of the other warning signs.

The next chapter focuses on the beginning, middle, and turning points of five different women in short-term abusive relationships. These case studies illustrate the ways these young women responded to the abusive incidents at the hands of their dating or intimate partners, and how their lives were forever changed.

*These warning signs and diagnostic indicators have been documented by the following researchers:

Donald G. Dutton (1998). *The Abusive Personality*. (New York: Guilford Press); Fred Buttell (2002). "Group Intervention Models with Domestic Violence Offenders." In A. R. Roberts (editor). *Social Workers' Desk Reference*. New York: Oxford University Press, pp. 714–716; Edward W. Gondolf (2002). *Batterer Invention Systems*. Thousand Oaks, CA: Sage Publications, Inc.

2

Short-Term Abuse and Getting Out Quickly

We were particularly interested in the group of women who were able to leave abusive relationships quickly. What, we asked, set these women apart? The 94 women in this category reported experiencing from one to three mild to moderate abusive incidents by their boyfriend or partner. Most were young, between the ages of 16 and 27. The overwhelming majority (88 percent) were high school, college, or graduate students in steady dating relationships, and most were not living with the abuser.

In sharp contrast to other women in the study, these women ended the relationship permanently soon after the abusive acts began. What we found were women who had career goals requiring higher education or vocational training, exhibited good verbal communication skills, possessed high self-esteem, and had a strong support system of family and friends. Most important, the overwhelming majority of the abused women in this category ended the abusive dating relationship with assistance of parents, other close relatives, or friends.

Most of the women who were involved in short-term abusive relationships did not live with their boyfriends, and the physical abuse they experienced was primarily limited to pushing, slapping, and punching—violent acts that can be classified in a mild-to-moderate range of severity. Unlike the women who became involved in chronically abusive situations, the women in this category were usually able to put an end to the abusive relationships with the assistance of a parent or older sibling, and for some, with police assistance.

The following five women are representative of those who were able to break off an abusive relationship quickly. We will call them Christy, Erin, Keesha, Nadine, and Amanda.

■   **Background**

Christy had been born in Florida and moved north when she was in middle school. Although she was only 24 at the time of the interview, she had been the assistant manager of a rather large restaurant for the past few years. Christy had lived in a dorm for all four years of college, while working part-time at the restaurant. Her parents were divorced, and her father had remarried; she had a good relationship with both of her parents and with her stepmother as well. Christy also had a younger sister with whom she was very close. She said that she had a relatively uneventful childhood, but that as soon as she became involved with her boyfriend, who was a few years older than she, her life had turned sour and she felt trapped, unable to complain about him because he was a well-known college football player.

Erin, at the time of the interview, was a 19-year-old who would be a college freshman that September. She spent a lot of her spare time working out at the local fitness center and was physically fit. Erin lived with her mother, stepfather, and younger sister. Her eyes were animated when she talked and she smiled quite often, surprisingly, despite the abusive relationship that she was describing. Erin's ability to smile came from the knowledge that the abusive relationship was over permanently. She met her boyfriend as a senior in high school, and the relationship carried over into what was supposed to be her freshman year of college. Her reasons for leaving college after only two weeks had everything to do with her manipulative boyfriend, who managed to damage her confidence and sense of self.

Keesha, 25 at the time of the interview, was born in Washington, D.C. She had lived with a female friend in Philadelphia since leaving her abusive boyfriend. Although they dated for several years, he beat her just once. It was so terrible, she said, that she got out right away. Keesha wears stunning earrings that hang about a half-inch below her lobes, and when complimented on them, she says they are antique and were given to her by her grandmother, who also gave her the matching necklace she is wearing. Her tall, thin figure is reminiscent of that of a super-model; Keesha carried herself with confidence and spoke frankly of her childhood, and of the injuries she had sustained from her boyfriend.

Nadine, 19 years old at the time of the interview, was a high school graduate with the hope of going to community college before transferring to a four-year college. She had been working at a video store since graduation to save money for college, and lived at home with her mother. Nadine had a maturity and a quiet composure that are not typical of a 19-year-old. She did not hesitate to share the details of her life, including the death of her father and the abusive dating relationship in which she became involved when she was only 16 years old.

Born and raised in southern New Jersey, *Amanda* was, at the time of the interview, 19 years old and working as a waitress at an upscale restaurant while living at home with her parents. She had received her high school diploma approximately one year earlier. Amanda was Catholic, and said she still went to church with her parents regularly. She smiled occasionally during the interview, particularly when she related her relief that the abusive relationship was over. She (like many of the women included in this chapter) spoke of the intense jealousy her boyfriend displayed on a regular basis, making it nearly impossible to establish a normal relationship with him because he did not trust her, no matter how hard she tried to please him.

■ Educational and Vocational Experiences

Upon a closer look at the educational experiences of the women in the short-term abuse category, it becomes apparent that the ability to escape quickly from the abusive dating relationship stems not only from the support of family and friends but also from a previous sense of accomplishment and the motivation to pursue career goals.

As mentioned in their individual descriptions, all of these women had completed high school, but their individual plans following graduation differed.

Christy, 24, had been at the same job for several years. She had earned a bachelor's degree and said that she liked her managerial job at the restaurant because of the level of responsibility and the good income:

> I have my degree in art history and world literature, so I'd actually love to get a master's and maybe even a doctorate and teach, eventually. But for now, the restaurant I have been working at for a long time is great because I am personally responsible for a staff of 12 workers, and I help supervise a full staff of over 100 people. I really enjoy being in charge, and I worked long and hard, even through college, to get to the managerial position, so it's comfortable and I know mostly everybody. For now it's great because it's a schedule I can handle and the money is actually really good.

Erin had also learned a great deal of responsibility living at home with her mother, stepfather, and younger sister while all of her friends went off to college:

I was totally lost when I was dating John [her abusive ex-boyfriend]. He made me feel like I couldn't handle anything without him. I probably just wasn't ready to go to school yet, but I was torn between what my family wanted and what he wanted. I didn't even know what I wanted anymore. I got into the first college of my choice, but when it was time to go, I only stayed for two weeks. John came and picked me up. I didn't even tell my mom or my sister that I had dropped out and was coming home. For some reason, I felt safe around him. But that all changed pretty soon after that, and I have been living at home for a year working as an aide at a nursing home. I have demonstrated that I am a responsible person now, and won the trust back from my family and found my self-respect. It's like I found myself again and I'm going away to school this September to study speech therapy, which is what I've wanted to do for a long time.

Keesha was currently living with a very close female friend in Philadelphia. She had an associate's degree in accounting and was an accounting assistant. She said:

I know it sounds crazy, but I really like number crunching. My job consists of processing invoices for the city and working with other accountants, so I'm actually learning a whole lot. I've been doing it for a while now, and I hope to get a promotion soon, because frankly, it's getting a little boring, but the money's good, so . . . I have been thinking about going back to get my bachelor's or even my master's, because I am eligible for tuition reimbursement, and that's something I want to take advantage of while I still have the energy.

Nadine worked at a video store full time, which kept her very busy. She was still living at home with her parents until she felt comfortable enough to be on her own:

It's not the greatest job in the world . . . but I really do like doing it for now. I'm responsible for closing the store, and on Saturdays I am responsible for opening and I run the store for a few hours by myself until one of the managers comes in, as well as another one of my coworkers. I've been there for two years, and I think I'm up for a manager's position soon, or else I'm going to start looking for something else. Not that I want to quit—I just kind of want some more money so I can save up for school. I'd really like to go into social work after all of the stuff that I've been through.

Amanda was working as a waitress but would be attending beautician school soon:

> When I was little, I always liked doing my sister's hair, which I think is pretty normal for a little girl, but I decided recently that I think I'd like to try to actually get paid for it! I have a friend who works in a spa, and she said that if I get halfway certified I might be able to work there while I finish school. It kind of drives me crazy because I want to do something I actually like to do. I realized that a regular job just for money just won't cut it. You have to really like what you do in order to make a career.

These women all displayed a drive to be their own person. They had goals that they admitted were taking a while to reach; nevertheless, they were sticking with what was working for a time being in order to make progress.

■ Critical Incidents during Childhood and Adolescence

Turning back the clock, a closer look at these women's individual childhood experiences provides a better sense of their personalities as they were growing and developing emotionally. Although most of their childhood experiences were positive, there were some occasional, brief incidents of abuse.

As an adolescent, *Christy* experienced the death of her grandfather, which she also associated with the beginning of her relationship with the boyfriend who sexually assaulted her. She sighed, and then began:

> Well, it was not the best timing in the world. Right after my Grandpa died, I think it might have even been a few weeks later, my boyfriend, who was several years older than me, took it upon himself to "comfort" me. We were in his car, his brand-new present for getting a football scholarship, and he just went too far. I wasn't up to fooling around, but he wanted to anyway, and apparently the fact that I didn't want to didn't make a difference. He made me . . . satisfy him . . . telling me that he was stressed out over the beginning of the season and that he needed some "release" and that if I wouldn't, then he could get any of the cheerleaders to "help him out." What a jerk. And that was just the beginning.

Christy quickly added that she had had some great times during childhood, like spending summer vacations at the Jersey shore, as well as winning academic awards throughout school.

Erin said it had been difficult moving to different parts of the country, especially after her parents' divorce:

> We always moved around a lot. I was born in Denver, and then we
> moved to Cleveland, Ohio, for a while, and then, when I was in second
> grade, we moved to New Jersey. Pretty soon after we got here, my par-
> ents separated, which was rough, and [my dad] moved away. I have
> never been very close to my dad because I was so young when he left.
> And my mom and my younger sister and I didn't have too much money
> for a while, and even though we were moving around in the same town,
> I changed schools a lot because of the different boundaries—I was al-
> ways in public school. And then when my mom got remarried . . . it
> ended up being a really good thing, but at first I was really upset. Then
> we moved a couple of towns over, to where my stepdad lives, and I had
> to start all over again. But, that ended up being really good too because I
> finally made some new best friends. They're the friends I still have
> now—I hope to have them for a long time! And I love sports. I was on
> the varsity soccer and tennis teams for most of high school.

Erin added, though, that the death of her grandmother and grandfather had both been hard blows:

> My Grandpa (my dad's dad) died when I was in third grade. He was
> sick for a long time, but my grandma still talks about him, so it's a
> constant reminder. And another one of my grandmas died when I was
> a little older, maybe like around eighth grade, I guess. It was my mom's
> mom, so she was really sad, and it was hard for me to see her so upset.
> It was really sudden, so the whole family kind of suffered for a while.

Keesha also experienced death in her family, but on a much different level, as she explained:

> When I was 11, I found my aunt dead. She was on the kitchen floor . . .
> and I was so scared. She died of natural causes, but as a kid it was
> something I really didn't know how to handle. I had dreams for years
> after that about seeing her there, on the kitchen floor, just . . . dead.
> Yeah, that took me a while to get over.

Keesha also spoke about the positive things she remembered from growing up:

> I can remember when we got our first VCR. It was so great! We taped
> some of the 1984 Olympics, because I actually figured out how to use
> the timer before my dad could. I think I watched that Mary Lou
> Retton routine like a million times before my mom told me the tape

would wear out! And I remember when I got a brand new bike, and my dad taught me how to ride it without the training wheels. We had really uneven sidewalks, I remember, so it was tricky, but I distinctly remember my dad taking care of me when I fell and scraped my knee. [She smiled and revealed a tiny scar on her left knee.]

Nadine had different recollections of childhood, as her father made life at home very stressful for everybody in the family:

I guess when I first noticed I was seven. My dad would go out drinking and get abusive. Not physically abusive, but mentally abusive. My parents talked about divorce a lot. When they (my parents) would get into fights, they wouldn't talk. I would try to be extra nice to my father so that he would be nice to me.

She then recalled the abusive boyfriend she had when she experienced the tragic death of her father:

I was 16 when my dad died. It was like it wasn't just enough to have to deal with that. He had been sick for a long time (he had cancer), so, in a way I guess, it was sort of a weight off of our shoulders. I don't mean I was relieved, but . . . he was just so sick for so long. Anyway, I had an abusive boyfriend at the same time. He had mood swings. He would yell at me, push and shove me, stuff like that. He would just start yelling at me for no reason. If he had a bad day, he would just take it out on me.

But when asked to recall some positive things from her adolescence, she said:

I guess when I lost a lot of weight from when I was fat, between sixth and seventh grade. And I won the spelling bee when I was in sixth grade. We also went on a vacation to Florida the summer after that—I think it was the best time I had with my dad.

Amanda described her recollections of abuse from a neighbor:

When I was about five years old, our neighbor got a little . . . friendly . . . with his hands. He was my friend's dad, so I was always really afraid to say anything, but . . . he made me spread my legs. And it happened three different times, I remember distinctly . . . how could I forget, I guess. That was it, though. I had a pretty happy childhood.

Amanda continued: "Nothing else happened like that. I guess the biggest problems I would consider myself ever having were just growing up and facing the real world." When asked specifically for some fond memories, she smiled as she said:

> I remember my dad teaching me how to ride a bike. He actually demonstrated by riding off down the sidewalk on my brand-new pink bicycle! And becoming a teenager was fun . . . my mom and I got really close.

Since the women in this short-term category are typically young, much of what they recall as memories of adolescence actually involves their abusive boyfriends. In many of these cases, their relationships with these boys (or men, depending on the age difference) happened while they were still adolescents.

Most of the women in this category had relatively positive and normal childhoods with typical stresses such as a grandparent dying, divorce of parents, or moving to a new neighborhood and having difficulty making friends. In sharp contrast to the chronic battering victims, those in the short-term category rarely have had any experience of being sexually molested during childhood. They did, however, report occasional traumatic or abusive childhood incidents.

■ The First Incident and Its Impact

Christy described the first time her boyfriend Pete became physically abusive, when she was 17 years old:

> Well, Pete was stressed out because of the upcoming Bowl game he was going to be playing in. [He was a starter on his college football team.] He caught me flirting with someone else at a frat party, where everyone was drinking a lot. I caught his glance from across the room. I stopped talking to whoever I was talking to, and my boyfriend took me into the bathroom and shoved me against the wall and told me that because I was such a slut, we had to leave the party.

After this initial abusive incident at the fraternity party, Christy's boyfriend continued to be unpredictable, jealous, and quick to become angry at her:

> He really blamed me for distracting him from football. It was his life, and I guess all of his insecurities got the best of him and it was a lot easier to blame me for his nerves and fears. He displayed jealousy all the time. I was constantly checking myself to make sure that I wasn't doing anything to make him upset. I know now that none of that was in my control, and none of it was my fault. But then, it was really hard to see that because he made me feel so guilty. He shoved me a couple of times, too, when he thought I wasn't listening to him. But there was nothing I could do to be a "better" girlfriend.

The first time *Erin* realized her boyfriend's jealousy was a problem was when he falsely accused her of cheating on him while she was on a two-week vacation:

> I had gone to London with my aunt and my mother and my sister, and I even called him while I was there a few times. And when I called, his ex-girlfriend answered the phone, but I trusted him, so it wasn't really an issue for me. But when I got back, all he did was accuse me of making out with some guy (believe me, there was no guy). It was constant interrogation for days. He didn't believe me, and he didn't listen to me when I tried to talk to him about it. Then he shoved me away once when I was pleading with him to just listen to me.

Erin's boyfriend was also using cocaine. As she explained, the mixture of cocaine and his irrational jealousy created a serious danger for their relationship:

> If John was doing coke, he was really manic. Even though he was really jealous a lot of the time anyway, it got a lot worse when he was using, which was a lot. He went to rehab once, but even though I went to visit him all the time, I would always leave crying because he made me feel so guilty about everything. He said everything was my fault, and at the time, I just wished that I could control everything so there would be no reason for him to be mad at me.

Erin also recalled the horrific threats her boyfriend made when he became really desperate:

> I started doing coke too, because he really wanted me to try it with him, so I did. I never did it by myself or anything, just when he wanted to. I know that doesn't give me an excuse, but it really made things a lot worse for both of us. John would threaten me. He used to say, "If you leave me, I'll kill myself," or "I'll tell your family you're using," or "I'll kill you." He threatened to kill my family, my mom, my sister. The worst time was when he held a 12-inch blade to my neck, and he said that if I walked out the door, he would slash my throat and then his own.

Unlike many of the women in the short-term category who became involved with an abusive boyfriend, for *Keesha*, the first incident was also the last. She explained the unpredictability of her boyfriend's behavior, as well as her intolerance of it:

> My boyfriend only got violent with me once, and that was the incident that just passed. He wanted to have sex and I wanted to go out. He was

> drunk and got violent. He bruised my back, my neck, and my arm. He fractured my nose and I had to have x-rays of my jaw. There was only one incident of violence, and that was it. It was the worst because I left, and there won't be any more.

> He was drinking every day, and he was drunk when he got violent with me that one time. I never was concerned about it before then, but as soon as that happened, I knew it could and would happen again, if I stuck around long enough to wait for it. And that's exactly why I left.

Keesha's immediate decision to end the relationship with her boyfriend following one severe battering episode speaks to her high level of confidence and self-esteem, and to her recognition that if she had stayed in that relationship, the violence would only have reoccurred.

Nadine's first incident of abuse by her boyfriend happened when she was 16 years old:

> It had to be when I was 16, because I met him when I was 15. He got really frustrated and slapped me. It was something about me not paying attention to him. We were out somewhere, I remember that much. We were going to the movies, or we were at the mall by the movies. I can't remember that exactly, but I do remember that there were a lot of people around, and I know I didn't ignore him on purpose, but it was like something snapped inside of him, and he got really upset all of a sudden. Right there, in the middle of the mall, he slapped me across the face. I started to cry and he apologized, and we left.

Nadine described her boyfriend's mood swings, which began to haunt their relationship:

> I guess on some days, everything was fine, but there was often some type of abuse. If it wasn't mental abuse, it was something physical like a single slap to my face. It would usually start with yelling, then he would start something. He had mood swings. If he had a bad day, he would take it out on me. But there were periods of peace, you know what I mean? Then he would slap me, then he would be sorry, and the next week it would start all over again.

Amanda recalled her boyfriend's first violent outburst:

> We were at the diner the day before Thanksgiving, just before we had to go home to our families for the next few days to celebrate. I was going to my cousin's the next day, so I wanted to have a little bit of time with my boyfriend before so we could exchange presents and all

> that . . . I don't know . . . you know how it is, when you're 18 you want
> to see your boyfriend all the time. So some of his friends came in, and
> he thought I was looking at one of them, and I got a hard slap under
> the chin. And I don't think anyone saw, but . . . I was embarrassed.

Notably, with the exception of Keesha's situation, these women seemed to be
more embarrassed, shocked, and upset by the initial incidents of dating violence than they were seriously physically hurt. However, the initial incident of
being slapped, shoved, or punched was soon followed by additional violence.
In four of the five cases discussed in this chapter, the dating relationships developed further, and the worst incidents—the turning points—were still to
come.

■ The Turning Point

Christy's worst incident with Pete, her football-player boyfriend, occurred
when his extreme jealousy escalated into a severe battering episode:

> It occurred during August, and Pete was at college with football prac-
> tice every day. I was home and went to visit him. After a whole lot of
> heavy questioning, I finally admitted that I had been out on a date
> with another guy. He started yelling at me, saying he could not con-
> centrate on football with me at home "whoring around." He started
> throwing objects around his apartment. I couldn't help but egg him on
> a little, because he was acting so ridiculous. Then Pete got really angry
> and slammed me up against the wall. Then he started hitting me sev-
> eral times with an open hand in my face. Afterwards, I had swollen
> lips, cuts on my face from where his ring hit me, and some bruises.
> And I was just sore all over from all of the shoving . . . yeah . . . that
> was the last time he hit me.

Christy refused to continue dating Pete, but he called her repeatedly on
her cell phone and sent her threatening e-mails. Initially, the calls and e-mails
were to beg for her forgiveness, trying to convince her to continue their relationship. Then their tone changed:

> When I told Pete that our relationship was finished, his phone calls
> and e-mails became harassing and he was threatening to break my
> arms and stuff like that. Finally, I got a different cell phone number,
> but I was so upset that I asked my dad to call Pete with the warning
> that if he did not immediately stop all contact with me, I would go to
> the police and request a restraining order against him for harassment.

We had the evidence of harassment from his e-mails, which I gave to my father. My father explained to Pete that a restraining order would be detrimental to his football career and might result in his being suspended from the team. After that phone conversation, Pete never contacted me again.

Erin's worst and final traumatic incident resulted from a combination of all of the factors of which she was already aware: her boyfriend's cocaine problem (which had worsened), his jealousy, his mood swings, and his irrational accusations. An additional factor was that Erin had become pregnant, she wanted to have an abortion, and her boyfriend was living temporarily with a friend in upstate New York, while she still lived in New Jersey. She went to visit him:

When I got there, and every single night we went out, he would look for drugs, and he would use me as an excuse. It was like it was my fault that I had gotten pregnant. Then he denied that it was his. He said that I didn't appreciate anything, and that because he borrowed the money from his cousin that I was selfish and ungrateful. Neither one of us had the $450 for the procedure. He didn't even do me the favor of taking me or anything. He even talked me into having sex the day after.

He brought me back to New Jersey, and instead of going home, we went to Newark to buy some coke. It was his connection, but as usual, it was my money. We pulled over to the side of the road, and he started to say things like "Listen, you and I made something together, and it was beautiful." Then he asked me if I was okay to drive, and he ran off without me even responding. He took off, so I started screaming. He came back and screamed at me to "shut the fuck up." I was really, really panicked, and tried to get out of the moving car, twice. He assured me, after all this stuff happened, that everything would be okay, and he told me to stop by the next morning.

The next day, I had to go into work unexpectedly, so I called him later in the morning from work to apologize for not stopping by in the morning. He said, "Why couldn't you have just done the simplest thing and come by to say good bye to me?" So I went there on my lunch break; his parents' house was about 15 minutes from where I worked.

When I got there, no one else was at home. He started hitting me and punching me, and every time I tried to get up to leave, he pushed me down, so I started kicking him because it's all I could do to get out of the house. Then, when I tried to get to my car, he ran outside ahead of me and slashed my back left tire to keep me there. But I quickly drove to the closest gas station—even though the rear tire was slashed, there was still some air in it. I was frantic and called my mom to come and pick me up. I told my mom everything. I spent a week in the psych ward at the hospital. My mom and stepdad took care of me from there. I told them I wanted my phone line removed so he couldn't call me. It was really, really bad.

Although *Nadine's* worst incident also caught her by surprise, it was the last time she allowed herself to be subjected to her boyfriend's abuse:

He didn't always have to be triggered. We were sitting outside in my backyard on a swing. He got mad because he said I wasn't paying attention to him, so he said he was going to walk home. I went after him, and I put my hand on his shoulder. He grabbed my hand and twisted it. Then he pushed me into the pavement and hit me. It lasted for about five minutes. I was badly bruised and he sprained my wrist. It was so scary. I asked him why he did it. He said, "You shouldn't have followed me," or something like that.

Amanda told of the worst incident with her boyfriend, which also involved his jealousy and uncontrollable anger. What occurred during those few minutes was so traumatic that Amanda knew she never wanted to see him again:

A friend from work was driving my car, and, as a joke, he wrote his initials on the steering wheel with marker. I have no idea why he did it, but really, he was just a friend. And it was my car anyway! My boyfriend saw it, and he freaked out. He started punching me and I fell to the ground. That's when he started kicking me in the face. I had a black eye, a broken nose, and a swollen and bloody face. It happened in the parking lot by his house.

All of these horrendous events served as turning points when these women made the decision to stop dating their batterers. While the women were eventually fully healed from their physical injuries, they also suffered a significant emotional impact.

■ Sleep Disturbances and Anxiety

These women successfully escaped from their traumatic relationships, and they are no longer in danger of being beaten by their former boyfriends. Yet even after these women were able to leave their abusive boyfriends, they still had to deal with lasting emotional pain.

Christy said that she still has nightmares from time to time:

> I have nightmares where my boyfriends since my attacker become violent. I also have bad dreams where he shows up in places where he just doesn't belong, like my current job location or my parent's home.

Christy also added that for several months after the relationship ended, she experienced a lack of self-esteem, fatigue, and a constant desire to eat, but those problems went away with help from counseling that she obtained through a battered women's shelter. She also found it helpful to talk to her mother about her anxieties.

Erin has made good progress, but she said she used to have nightmares that kept her awake at night:

> I still have dreams of him, but in those dreams he's actually terrified of me, so it doesn't keep me up the way it used to. I was seriously scared of sleeping for a long time, though, because I was afraid he was going to break into my house and hurt me while I was sleeping.

While benefiting from extensive psychological counseling, Erin has also become much closer to her mother and stepfather, and she is trying to serve as a good role model for her younger sister, in an effort to prevent her sister from experiencing the same type of trauma. Although Erin and her mother and stepfather had previously had a fairly good relationship, during her rebellious adolescent period, she had not wanted to confide in them. They have been so supportive of her situation that Erin has opened up to them more than ever before and truly values their strengthened relationship.

Keesha said that she deals with the memories of the violent relationship daily because it had ended so recently:

> I've had a loss of appetite, and I have been nervous all the time. I worry about what my ex-boyfriend will do because of the restraining order I put on him. I had to press charges, and I don't regret it, but I think about it all the time.

Nadine said that, of all the injuries, dealing with her emotions is the most difficult, because "Mentally, it never leaves you." She added:

> I've had flashbacks, like when I'm with another person, something will trigger my memory and it's like I'm back in the same relationship. You forget where you are for a minute. I've had nightmares about my dad. Mostly about him in the hospital and I get there too late to say goodbye. Once in a while I have dreams that I'm back with my

boyfriend. He yells at me, but before anything physical happens, I wake up.

Amanda was reluctant to discuss her current level of anxiety, but she did briefly say:

If I'm by myself, I think about what's happened. I like keeping myself busy to avoid feeling depressed. Since that whole thing started and ended, I've lost about 20 pounds and I don't sleep too much.

■ Police Intervention

Most of the women in this group did not seek police assistance to end their abusive relationships. In the majority of these cases, the women had the ability on their own (sometimes combined with the support from a parent, older sibling, other relative, or close friend) to end the abusive relationship without police intervention. A likely reason for the absence of police intervention is that most of the women in this survey who fit into this category were living at home with their parents; the mere presence of a parental figure is often a deterrent to a boyfriend persisting in a dating relationship when the woman has ended it.

In close to 20 percent of the 94 short-term cases studied, however, the woman did need to seek police assistance. There are very important issues and concerns related to contacting the police for a restraining order on a batterer, and there are benefits and costs of such actions. See chapter 10 for detailed information on seeking help from the police for an abusive relationship.

■ Hopes for the Future

Having overcome the hurdle of abuse, each of these women cherished a vision of a future that buoyed her up and carried her away from the abusive past. When asked what she hoped to be doing in a few years, each woman had realistic hopes and plans for a bright future.

Christy said:

I really want to go to grad school. I know it's going to be hard working full-time at the same time, but I think that in the end, it will be worth it. Eventually I hope to teach or work in a museum but I haven't decided yet. Keeping my options open, I guess! And as for ten years down the road, I picture myself married with children. I would love to have my own family and career. I'm getting there.

Erin was eager to start college for the second time:

> Well, I'm about to go off to school for the second time, but this time I truly can't wait. It was all my decision, and I'm going to be studying to be a speech therapist. So in a few years, I'll hopefully be doing internships for all of that, and living a normal, productive life. I am mostly looking forward to showing my mom and the rest of my family that I can take care of myself and that I am a responsible, caring person— it's like I've rediscovered myself.

Keesha also said that she would like to return to school and become totally independent:

> I want to go back to school, and I also want to relocate to another state. But I would keep doing accounting for a while. I'm comfortable with it. In a few years, though, I really hope I will have made it to the west coast of Florida. I'd love to run a small store or boutique—to not have to work for anybody else but myself.

Nadine discussed her future plans:

> For now, I'd like to have a job where I have more responsibility, and I'd like to make some more money. I have recently thought about going to school for social work, because I think I'd be really interested in helping people who are in similar situations that I have been through. I think it would help me, too, to learn about the reasons behind all of that craziness. So, we'll see, I guess. I don't want to stress too much. I think I have plenty of time to work things out.

Amanda also had plans:

> I'm looking forward to beauty school and working at my friend's spa . . . I think it's going to be a really good experience to really get my life rolling. So, pretty soon, I'll be working somewhere, even if just at a hair and nails salon. Hopefully, eventually I'll own my own business. It would be great to be my own boss! In the end I just hope I can be successful, and I would love to be married and have a family. But first things first, I guess.

Overall, these women each presented different versions of a success story. Although life was extremely painful for each of them while in the abusive dating relationship, ultimately they had the strength to end the relationship and triumph over significant adversity. These women, subjected to the horror of short-term abuse, have demonstrated that with the right tools, escape from an abusive dating relationship and dreams of a bright future are entirely possible.

Readers of this book who are parents may be wondering: "These five women said that they came from close-knit families, yet those good family ties did not protect the young women from a horribly abusive dating relationship." While it is true that close family connections cannot prevent an abusive relationship from forming, most of the women in this group relied on their parents for comfort when the abuse escalated from a single slap to more severe violence, and many women wanted to return to their parents when the abusive dating relationship ended. Sadly, there are other scenarios in which women who have been abused and are financially dependent live with or marry a batterer because they lack a strong relationship with their parents and feel that they cannot turn to their parents for emotional or financial support.

■ Guidelines for Abused Women on the College Campus

College students are vulnerable to abusive relationships and situations because of the nature of the college environment and the fact that many students are removed from the support of their families. College Freshman are at high risk for physical and emotional abuse from their boyfriends and, in particular, for date rape. As a whole, college administrations have been slow to recognize this reality; many colleges, however, do offer additional protection and services to protect women from abusive relationships and situations. Many campus police departments, residential life offices, student services administrative offices, and student organizations have taken on the issue by designing prevention programs and campus policies to protect students' safety.

In addition, many colleges work closely with victim assistance programs located within the local community to ensure that victims have advocacy and support. The following services are commonly offered by colleges and universities.

- Many campus police departments or departments of public safety have domestic violence and date rape information available in their office or on their website. Most will inform students as to the laws of that specific state and college policies related to these issues. Some campus police departments offer students personal safety alarms with geo-positioning systems that can track the student's immediate location. Most campuses have emergency phones.

- Some campus police departments have full police powers and can make an arrest when a crime has been committed on campus. For offenses that occur off-campus, victims should notify the local police agency. See chapter 10 on what to expect when the police are called.

- Campus officials conduct presentations in the dormitories and/or in specific classrooms regarding the prevention of abuse, recognizing abuse, and what to do if you are being physically abused by a boyfriend. Many officials conduct specific presentations regarding date rape and provide information to students regarding date rape drugs.

- Campus officials also conduct training for dormitory staff, that is, resident assistants (RAs), resident managers (RMs), and/or resident directors (RDs) regarding domestic abuse issues. Dormitory staff should be familiar with campus policies and know where victims can go for assistance. Students should feel comfortable asking dormitory staff for assistance.

- Colleges have an administrative structure to deal with student issues. In addition to the specific staff posted in the dormitories, administrative staff in offices such as the Dean of Students, Student Affairs, Residential Life, or Student Services should be able to assist students or make referrals to the appropriate support services.

- Most resident campuses offer a counseling center. The counseling staff is likely to be very knowledgeable about domestic violence issues and be familiar with services available to students on campus or in the local community. Many centers offer support groups for victims.

- Some colleges offer free legal services to students through a legal aid office. Attorneys are available to assist students with a variety of legal issues and can be a helpful resource in the case of intimate partner abuse.

- Campus authorities can generally provide students with basic safety protections such as allowing a student to change rooms, class schedules, e-mail addresses, phone numbers, and so on.

- Most colleges have a code of conduct for student behavior and a process for dealing with students who violate the code. Often referred to as judicial conduct panels or boards, they generally function to examine student behavior and have the authority to recommend removal of a student from the college community. Judicial conduct boards are generally made up of faculty and staff with student representation and operate like a quasi court. Victims of abuse can access the judicial conduct boards for assistance, whether or not the police have been involved in a particular situation. A student and her family should explore the pros and cons of using either a campus judicial system or the criminal justice system, or both, when making a decision about adjudication. The policies, procedures, and rules of evidence and testimony, as well as outcomes, are different when one chooses campus adjudication rather than adjudication through the criminal justice system.

- Victims can also talk with a faculty member or advisor to inquire about campus policies and available services.

- If a particular college campus appears to be lacking in support services, victims should be able to access services in the local community through a battered woman's shelter or victim assistance program.

For the Step-by-Step Safety Plan and Survival Kit go to pages 114–118 of this book.

3

After the Honeymoon Period

The women in this chapter come from families and socioeconomic backgrounds very similar to those of the women discussed in the previous chapter. The main differences are age and the duration of the relationship. The average age of the women here is about five to eight years older than the women who experienced short-term abuse. These women are more often married or in a long-term relationship, in contrast to the short-term cases, in which women were dating the man who abused them and did not live with them.

■ Background

Mary Beth was a 35-year-old supervisor at a day care center with a college degree. She reported having had a very happy childhood until her father died when she was 10. She endured sexual molestation by her stepfather, which ended when she was 14, when, after a first episode of sexual intercourse, her mother noticed blood on the sheets. Mary Beth was a friendly woman, and her short, brown, curly hair complemented her smile. She stayed with her abusive boyfriend less than two years before finding asylum in a shelter in New Jersey, where she was staying at the time of the interview.

Pamela was a few years younger than Mary Beth at the time of the interview; she was 29 and was well dressed, with an outward appearance of confidence. She had earned a master's degree in education and was supporting her two children. She said that she had had a pleasant family life growing up, and could look to her close-knit family for support. Raised a Catholic, and committed to the teachings of the Catholic Church, she reported that she was able to leave her abusive husband only after her priest said it was acceptable. At the time of the interview, Pamela was a teacher, and was looking forward to finalizing the divorce from her violent husband, a physician.

Jill, the youngest of the interviewees chosen to represent this category, was a 22-year-old college senior who was active in her sorority. She had much to look forward to, especially after terminating an abusive relationship with her fiancé after a year and a half. Jill's impeccable appearance exuded a normal level of self-esteem and contentment. Nevertheless, she too shared experiences and incidents when she was abused so badly that she thought of dying just to make the physical pain end. Jill escaped with the help of friends, and although she was still having nightmares, she was able to look back on the relationship from a safe distance.

Barbara was physically abused during childhood, primarily by her mother. However, she maintained that any physical contact her mother had with her was disciplinary in nature. At 41, she looked older than her years. Barbara wore a small cross with her birthstone at the top, representing her connection both with Presbyterianism and with her mother, who gave her the necklace when she was in her late teens. Her recent employment had been limited to low-paying jobs such as babysitting. Barbara was concerned with how she would support herself and her son after having left her abusive husband. Barbara said she had a wonderful childhood, despite the physical blows she sometimes received. She had been married to an abusive husband for six years. Barbara indicated that the marital abuse began with yelling and then became increasingly terrifying as it progressed to horrendous physical abuse.

■ Critical Incidents in Childhood and Adolescence

Although abuse during childhood was a less frequent occurrence for these women than for the women in the chronic abuse group, this group of women did experience some traumatizing childhood events that had life-changing consequences for them.

Mary Beth's father died when she was 10 years old. Her mother was devastated, and Mary Beth's aunt came to live with them for a while until Mary Beth and her mother could resume normal roles and responsibilities. Her mother later remarried. Mary Beth recalled how she initially felt about her stepfather, Leo:

> Things were better for a while. But then Leo started making me feel uncomfortable. He would stare at me all the time and buy me lots of dresses

and things. At first I was glad to receive all the presents and to be told how "beautiful" I was. Plus, I didn't want to make any trouble for my mom and him. But Leo became more and more physical. He would start to come into my room at night and touch me. He said we had a special relationship and this is what two people who care a lot about each other do. He would always make me promise not to tell my mother. He said she wouldn't understand, and that he would have to leave. He kept talking about the period right after my dad died and how crazy my mom became. He said if he left, Mom's craziness would happen all over again.

But the day after her stepfather had intercourse with Mary Beth, her mother noticed the blood on the sheets:

I didn't know what to say to her. I just started to cry. My mom was confused at first and then she began crying too. I wonder if I ever would have told her what happened if she didn't see the blood. Anyway, Leo left, and Mom didn't go as crazy as she did when Dad died; she just became dependent on me. Not only did I have lots of household responsibilities, but my mom treated me like an older sister. I felt like an old lady at 16. I didn't feel I could do anything people my age were doing. I felt guilty if I went out with my friends, and most of them didn't want to come over to my house because she was always hovering close by.

In contrast, *Pamela* said she had had a perfectly normal childhood and adolescence in which she could rely on her close-knit family. When asked about any serious problems during adolescence she said, "Just the usual heartbreak of teen dating. I had a great childhood, terrific friends, supportive family, great family trips—I remember feeling terrible failing a test." Although she sometimes argued with her parents during her teen years, Pamela described her overall relationship with her parents as great:

We fought about the way I wore my hair, but it was nothing serious. My parents were great and I had a good childhood. I hope that I am as good a parent as mine were—sometimes I get nervous that I am not being a good enough parent with the divorce and everything. My son is really confused. I try to distract him the best I can from what's happening between "Mommy and Daddy," but divorce is unfortunately part of life and I will help him to deal with it as best I can.

Jill also described a happy life growing up:

My childhood and family life during every stage of my life was happy. My parents are very supportive and caring. I suppose the most negative incident was my grandfather's death when I was 12 years old. It was also terrible when one of my closest friends was killed in a car accident. Then probably just the awkward stage of being a teenager, and the insecurities involved in growing up.

Barbara recalled an episode of corporal punishment when she was younger that made her very upset at the time. In retrospect, however, she viewed the event as a necessary disciplinary action:

> My mother cracked me on the butt with a whip from the weeping willow tree because I did something I wasn't supposed to do. She left a welt, too. I was angry with her for a while. I remember not talking to her. I was most insulted because she did it in front of the neighbors. I was embarrassed and it hurt. But really, I look back and I see that sometimes you have to hit your children—sometimes there is no other way to raise them. Especially when they don't listen . . . a good crack on the butt now and then is harmless. But then I wasn't knowledgeable. I held a grudge for about a week, and then we just never talked about it again.

Each of these women would later in life find themselves involved in abusive relationships for a time—some for as short as a year, and some for several years of a marriage.

■ First Incident and Its Impact

Since the women in this group were living with the batterer, after the violence had begun, they did not have the moments of respite that the women in the short-term group had. (The women in the short-term group were usually living apart from their boyfriends, which allowed them an extra measure of peace and security that the women in the other groups did not have.)

Mary Beth indicated that Chuck had been different from the type of man she usually dated:

> Chuck was a tough type of guy. My friends hated him and had no idea what I saw in him. He wasn't the type of person I dated in college. He never went to college and worked mostly in factory and construction types of jobs. I guess I just liked how totally different he was and how tough. He seemed to want to take control, and I wanted someone who felt strong and, foolishly, who I thought could take care of me. We dated about three months and then he asked me to move in with him. I was thrilled, and we moved my stuff in the next weekend.

Soon after Mary Beth moved in with Chuck, he assaulted her for the first time. Notably, Chuck had consumed a lot of alcohol earlier that evening:

> About two weeks after I moved in with Chuck, we went out with some friends of his from work. We were at a bar, and Chuck was drinking a lot. I was drinking too and trying to be sociable with his friends. I really didn't feel like I fit in, but I tried to be friendly and make conversation as much as I could. When it was time to go home, Chuck was really loaded, but he insisted on driving and I let him. We got home, and I got ready for bed. I think Chuck was having another beer in the kitchen. He came into the bedroom and accused me of trying to make it with one of his friends. He was yelling and cursing about how I was doing it right in front of his face. I was shocked at his reaction. Then he hit me, first across my face, then my chest and arms. I just cried. The next day, Chuck was very affectionate and acted like nothing had happened.

Pamela initially thought the beatings were the result of all of the pressure her husband was dealing with at medical school and a grueling residency. Pamela convinced herself that as soon as he had completed the residency and had his own medical practice, he would be calm and never hit her again.

> When we first got married, I could understand the pressure he was under, so I took the physical and mental abuse because I believed he would change when he got what he wanted [his own medical practice and financial security]. Then he became financially successful, but the abuse got worse instead of better.

Pamela described one of the horrific incidents perpetrated by her now ex-husband:

> I asked him to leave me alone, and I threw the keys at him. Then he got on top of me and started smacking me and hitting me in the stomach. He wouldn't get up, and he just kept smacking me over and over again. I couldn't get him off of me, and he seemed to enjoy hitting me. I cried and yelled, but he continued to hit me. When I tried to get away, he resorted to dragging me across the floor and choking me.

Pamela talked about the events that served as a turning point in her decision to leave her violent husband:

> He would punch big holes in the wall and throw things at me while the kids were in the same room. The verbal abuse would go on day and night. As soon as he would walk into the house, he always said I owed him because he made a lot of money. He had become a well-respected

physician, and he threatened that if I left him he would say that I was crazy and take the kids away. At that point, I was so afraid that he could, so I kept putting off leaving him out of fear.

Then, the night before I left, he told me he was throwing out my birth control pills. I remember saying to myself, "Oh, dear God, I'll have baby number three, he'll keep me barefoot and pregnant. I won't have a job or career. I'll never be able to leave him."

Divorce is not allowed in my religion, but I spoke to my priest about what my husband was doing to me and showed him some of the injuries. My priest gave me permission to take the children and leave.

Jill, the college student, was living with Victor, her fiancé. Their engagement lasted for approximately a year and a half. She explained that his physical and verbal abuse did not begin until they decided to get engaged and started living together. The first abusive incident was precipitated by an argument they had about her going out with her friends:

Victor asked me what I was doing for the night, and I told him I was going to hang out with my girlfriends. When he asked me if I was going to wear what I had on (a short skirt and a blouse), I said yes and asked him what his problem was. Then he grabbed me by the back of my shirt and held me there while he made me promise to change my clothes. I didn't even end up going out that night.

Jill indicated that her ex-fiancé's jealousy was usually at the root of his violent behavior:

Since the time my ex-fiancé and I decided to get engaged, he repeatedly victimized me physically and verbally. He was terribly jealous, and anytime I went somewhere without him or without his permission, he would slap me, kick me, throw me across the room, call me a whore and a bitch.

Despite using birth control, Jill became pregnant. She knew that she and her fiancé were not ready to become parents, and she was planning to have an abortion. When she informed Victor that she was pregnant, he "punched and kicked me in the stomach so hard that I lost the baby anyway." Jill wanted to break up with him, but when she talked about ending the engagement and moving out, he threatened her with a large butcher knife.

Barbara described her ex-husband's unpredictability:

My ex-husband had a real short fuse. Anything seemed to trigger him. Throughout our marriage, he was very possessive, but, in the beginning, I was flattered by that. Then it got to the point where I could do nothing on my own without reporting to him.

Contrary to other women's reports of abuse beginning during dating, Barbara's recollections did not include any physical abuse while they were dating or during the first few years of their marriage. Barbara's husband became physically abusive when they argued about the effect his possessive behavior was having on their marriage:

> Finally, we had a big fight about it, and I tried to walk out, but he grabbed me by the hair and started choking me. And when he saw that I wasn't able to breathe and my face started turning blue, he let go and shoved me to the ground and spit on me several times. Then he left the house and didn't come back until an hour later with flowers and he begged me to forgive him. Deep down inside, I knew it was over, but I decided to give him another chance—after all, he was my husband and the father of my child.

Barbara said that her husband never used drugs, but around the time that the violence began, he was becoming intoxicated every weekend and sometimes during the week. She believed the beatings were connected to his loss of control due to his excessive drinking:

> Well, the time he choked me, you know the first time, I remember smelling alcohol on his breath, and he does drink a lot, basically every weekend and some weeknights. He always gets violent when he drinks too much.

In spite of the abuse recounted here, these women continued to live with the batterer. While the women may have been so distraught from the repeated abuse that they considered leaving, they did not do so until an event occurred that each woman viewed as so horrific that it was the final straw—the turning point. In some cases, the woman stayed in the relationship because she truly loved her partner or husband and wanted to believe that she would never be hit again. In other cases, the woman was so afraid of her abusive partner's rages that she became paralyzed by the fear of being permanently injured if she tried to leave him.

■ The Turning Point

Mary Beth described the severe assault that made her decide to leave her partner:

I went out after work with a friend of mine. Things with Chuck and me were pretty bad. I was scared of him and scared to leave. I had a few drinks after work with my friend. I made sure I was home before seven o'clock. When I got in, Chuck was in the kitchen. He asked me where I was, and I told him. Then he started yelling, "Mary Beth, tell me the truth! Where were you?" Then he said, "You were out fucking another guy, weren't you?" I said, "No," and tried to leave the room. He threw something at me and it smashed. Next thing I knew, he was grabbing me and shaking me and screaming, "You want to fuck around, okay, if that's what you want." He pushed me in the face and threw me on the kitchen floor. Then he ripped off my clothes and forced me to have sex with him. I didn't try to fight him off. I was scared to death that he might kill me. Afterward, he seemed happy and calm.

Pamela viewed the worst incident as one that was traumatic both physically and emotionally because the violence occurred in the presence of their children and her husband's parents. The argument was about the appropriate parental response to their young daughter's misbehavior:

The worst was when he flattened me at his parents' house and no one helped me. To me, this was the worst emotionally, not necessarily physically. I had reprimanded my daughter and he wasn't in agreement with why. So he starts, "What the hell is the matter with you?" He knocks me to the floor and then starts to pull at my hair. Then he jumps on top of me and smacks my face. He keeps me down and pulls my hair as he's sitting on top of me. I started to scream that I was going to call the cops, and he finally let me go. *But this was done in front of his parents and the kids.* They watched him do this to me. Then his parents did not say a word but quickly took the kids out of the room. His parents did nothing to help me, and that's what bothered me the most. His parents felt I should take it. They kept saying, "You've got a beautiful family." The mentality of the family was, "So what's the matter with getting smacked?" My kids would wake up with night terrors about their daddy hitting or smacking me.

Jill's most horrendous victimization by her fiancé nearly left her paralyzed:

I was home alone with him, and he was screaming about something, probably something ridiculous like what I was wearing or if I wanted to go out with my friends, the usual, and he pushed me to the ground. When I tried to get up and leave, he hit me in the back with a golf club until my spine was cracked, my back was bleeding, and I passed out before I could dial 911.

Luckily, Jill survived this incident, and with the aid of excellent medical care, she had a full recovery. Jill was treated for a fractured bone in her spine and bruises all over her body.

Barbara explained that the worst incident with her husband began with the typical verbal abuse but then quickly escalated into horrendous physical violence. Her husband's anger was so out of control that Barbara feared that he would have killed her if a neighbor had not called the police:

> I had a friend over for dinner when he wasn't home. He called me a lot of names and demanded answers to his ridiculous questions: What time did he leave? How long was he there? Did you sleep with him? You know, the whole nine yards. He was calling me a slut and a whore, and he was throwing things at me. He threw our lamp, a couple of hardcover encyclopedias. I saw that he was acting crazy and I knew I couldn't talk to him. He came after me with that crazy look in his eyes. It really looked as though he was possessed.
>
> I tried to leave the house, and he grabbed my arm and started twisting it around my back, and then he threw me to the floor and jumped on top of me and started hitting me over and over again, and I remember being so scared, but I don't remember exactly what he did. I thought he was going to do away with me. I kept screaming, and thank God the neighbors heard me and called the police. I think the police coming so quickly saved my life.

■ Separation from the Batterer

Following her horrible sexual assault, *Mary Beth* went to a shelter for battered women:

> I think my decision to leave Chuck was a lot less complicated than it is for other abused women because there weren't any children and we were not married. I need to work on being completely financially self-sufficient so I won't need to go back to Chuck or any other man just for financial security. My best friend was so worried about my relationship with Chuck that she had checked on the locations for the battered women's shelters in a three-county area. She gave me the names and phone numbers in case I ever needed to go to a shelter, and I always kept it in my wallet.

> While I'm living at the shelter, I'll save the money for the security
> deposit and rent on a decent apartment. I may need to get a second
> job for a while because rent is so expensive. But I'm getting my life
> back, and that is the most important thing.

Initially, *Pamela* attempted to cope with the repeated incidents of physical and emotional abuse by praying and going to church. As the situation at home worsened, she confided in both her priest and her mother. It was Pamela's priest who urged her to take her children and leave her husband. Pamela also took her mother's advice and joined a support group at the local battered women's shelter. Shortly thereafter, with the additional courage and strength she gained from this group, Pamela was able to leave her husband, moving back to her parents' home with her children. Pamela never contacted the police and did not file for a restraining order. With assistance from her family, she packed up her essential items and left with her children while her husband was at work. Although Pamela's husband had repeatedly threatened that he would kill her if she ever left him, once she did so, he did not harm her any more, not wanting to damage his status in the community as a highly respected physician. She was also careful to never again be alone with him. In handling the divorce, Pamela made very few economic demands; she just wanted the divorce to be finalized as quickly as possible.

Jill described the help she received during her breakup with her fiancé. After being released from the hospital, she moved into her sorority house, and she confided in her sorority sisters about the numerous assaults she had suffered. Opening up to her closest friends about the repeated beatings was particularly difficult for Jill to do. She said, "I knew I had people to count on, but I was too afraid to ask for help and have to admit that I was ever a victim of anything. It's not my personality to allow myself to become a victim." When Jill decided to break off the engagement with Victor, she sought help from her closest girlfriend:

> I didn't want to face Victor alone. I had been staying at the sorority
> house for a few days, and I first told him that was because I needed
> nursing care so the injuries would heal faster. When I gathered all my
> courage, I went with my girlfriend to the police station to file a
> restraining order against Victor. The police were great. I got a police
> escort to accompany me back to the apartment we had shared. We got
> there when he was at work, and I packed up all of my things and
> brought them back to the sorority house. Then I sent him an e-mail
> telling him it was over and about the restraining order, and if he ever
> tried to contact me or see me, I would have him arrested.

A couple of weeks later, when Victor was drunk, he came to the sorority house in a rage. He attempted to kick in the front door, yelling that he was going to drag Jill back to his place. Jill was terrified, even though she was safe in an upstairs bedroom:

> One of my sorority sisters called 911 right away, and the police arrived very quickly. Victor was arrested and charged with criminal mischief, terroristic threats, and violating the restraining order. Subsequently, the judge required him to pay $200 in restitution for the property damage to our front door. The judge gave Victor a harsh lecture and said if this ever happens again, he will be put in the county jail. Victor got the message and left me alone after that. I think he was really scared about going to jail.

Barbara described her positive experience with the police after her neighbor called 911. They arrested her husband and helped her and her son relocate to a shelter for battered women:

> When he was beating me and I was screaming, the neighbors called the police. I worry he would have beaten me to death if the police didn't arrive. When the police came to the door, he jumped off me to answer it. They saw that I was all bruised and bloody, and the police took Polaroid pictures of my bruises. The police called the local first aid squad to come to the house and fix up my injuries.
>
> My husband was taken into police custody, and they took my son and me to the police station in a separate car. The police did all the domestic violence paperwork, and I obtained a temporary restraining order. While my husband was still with the police, an officer drove me and my son back to the house, and I packed our most important things. Then the police drove us to a shelter for battered women.

■ Adjustment to Living Apart from the Abuser

Mary Beth was fortunate to have had wonderful support, not only from the staff and other residents at the shelter but also from her childhood friend who had stood by her throughout her whole relationship with Chuck. Mary Beth recalled what her best friend used to tell her:

> My girlfriend who I've known forever was skeptical. We've seen each other date some losers [she laughed], but she was so worried about me, with good reason, when I was dating Chuck. We even went to

college together. She gave me the connection to the day care center I worked at before becoming the supervisor at the place where I hope to go back to.

I've always been lucky in friends and family. I think I'm very fortunate to have been able to finish school, too, because it makes me remember that I have my own life to live. I love my job.

Pamela, who had her master's degree in education, also illustrated the importance of having a life outside of her husband's. She had completed her degree while working as a teacher, with one child at home and another on the way. Her roles as mother and teacher helped her prioritize the important things in life. Pamela, a devout Catholic, was also troubled about the abuse in her marriage, and resorted to asking her priest for advice:

When I went to see my priest, it was because I couldn't take it anymore. I was so confused about what to do, because I thought maybe this was what I was supposed to deal with, or that it was okay for my husband to treat me like that. But then I would look at my kid, and I worried for her.

Pamela found work brought her comfort as well:

I also found comfort when I went to work, because first of all, I was out of the house . . . and was doing what I have worked so hard for, and for a long time. Going to school at the same time as working was a challenge, but I finished, and so when I was able to excel at work, I remembered a little piece of who I used to be when my husband wasn't terrifying me.

Jill also illustrated the importance of independence as she talked about the desire to complete her education:

Really, what matters the most is that I make sure I follow the goals that I have set for myself. If I let what Victor [her ex-fiancé] did to me get in the way of what I wanted to accomplish, then I would be a failure, and of course at the time I really didn't think of it that way. It was really hard to deal with that. It still is really hard to deal with that, but it's better now. I mean, it was never anything I talked about, but his jealousy was turning me into a robot, I guess. I lost myself.

That sensation of not wanting to "lose" herself perhaps kept her afloat despite the emotional and physical abuse from her fiancé. She said, "I will still get my B.A. at 21, which makes me remember that I can do it. My friends helped me a lot, especially in their support after Victor and I broke up, which was a really difficult time for me because it's when I had to be my strongest."

Vocational training provided a sense of security and enjoyment for Barbara: "I do people's hair and nails, and baby-sit. They are only side jobs." These side jobs, however, provide the self-esteem and enjoyment that sustained her. "I love what I do because it's fun and I'm good at it."

By taking a look at these women's lives as *they* see them, the differences between the categories of women on the continuum truly becomes apparent. Women who are chronically abused for many years tend to suffer a lifetime of victimization; the cycle is tougher to break because the circumstances of their lives have taught them that they have learned that their efforts to escape and build a better life are to no avail. Because the women in this chapter had healthy childhoods and family lives, as well as fulfilling professional lives, they were able not only to overcome the incidents of severe abuse but also to move forward to create a better life for themselves and for their children. Recovery and permanent separation from their abusive partners became part of survival, and, fortunately, the women discussed in this chapter were bolstered by a strong support network and a career.

■ Sleep Disturbances and Anxiety

Battered women commonly experience sleep disturbances during and after the abuse by their partners.

Pamela told of the lasting effects of living in constant fear:

> Nightmares—I had many about my husband after I left him. I would have awful nightmares about him coming after me. I would dream that he would be at the door or at the window, just looking for me or he would be coming up the stairs after me. He would not be hitting me, but just the thoughts and nightmares would be so scary for me to see him that I would get up right out of a deep sleep. The nightmares would make me feel so awful that I often went into the kids' beds because I was so shaken up.

She continued: "I couldn't eat. I would have such knots in my stomach. He would be screaming, just grab something quick to eat and keep moving, 'cause the house had to be perfect, the kids well behaved."

Jill also spoke about the difficulties she was having in getting rid of thoughts of her ex-fiancé:

> Right after I broke up with my ex-fiancé, I was having terrible nightmares and suffering from insomnia. I went from eating healthy to hardly eating at all and lost weight. My symptoms [flashbacks,

headaches, nausea] caused me to be nervous, frequently leading to vomiting and migraines.

Also now away from her husband, *Barbara* reported:

I've been on edge lately because I never could tell when he'll blow up. I guess in my mind I'm afraid to sleep. But I haven't had any night-mares—the problem is that I just can't sleep. I do have fears (I guess you could call them intrusive thoughts) that he will hurt my son. I know he is a good father and he loves my son, but he also loved me and he hit me. I think that is what is making me leave the house, once and for all. I divorced him because of the violence.

■ Hopes for the Future

Most of the women discussed in this chapter had pleasant memories of child-hood, and most were able to terminate the relationship in which they were battered before they became so financially dependent on their husbands or partners that they felt that they could not leave them.

What seems to differentiate most of the women in this group from those in the chronic abuse category is their post–high school education coupled with work experience, allowing them to be more financially independent, even though losing the batterer's income was a concern for all of the women. This parallels the statistical findings of the study as a whole: women who were able to leave an abusive partner after a limited amount of time were better equipped to support themselves without relying on financial support from the abuser.

Having nearly successfully divorced their husbands or terminated the re-lationship with the abusive partner, they began to generate plans for the fu-ture.

Mary Beth was looking forward to meeting a man with whom she could have a normal and balanced relationship. She said, "I just want to go back to work. Maybe someday soon I'll go for another degree, but for now being back at the day care center where I used to work would be great."

Pamela's ability to come to terms with her abusive spouse was the result of her priest's approval:

My other problem was that I was Catholic and I was afraid that the church would never let me get the divorce. But my priest said, "Get out of the house," and supported my beliefs that I should leave. That really finalized my decision to leave.

With her master's degree in education and her previous years of teaching experience, Pamela was probably one of the more financially secure women in this group.

Through her participation in a domestic violence victims' support group run by a professional counselor, *Jill* managed to reduce the fear and shame she felt about her abusive relationship. She said, "Sometimes, in a different and new relationship with someone, it takes me some time to warm up to them, to trust them. But I know exactly what I am looking for and what I want in the future." At the time of the interview, Jill was a college senior and would be graduating on time, a huge accomplishment considering all that she had been through.

Barbara threw her hands in the air when asked about her future. She really did not have any definite plans, but the look on her face and the tone of her voice when she said, "God only knows . . . getting my son settled," signaled relief and a feeling that she, like the other women, was learning to begin again and believe in the future.

While these women still remembered some of their worst experiences in graphic detail, they could move on and begin a new life. They were able to protect themselves and recover by removing themselves permanently from their abusive partners. Most were able to escape from their abusive relationships by staying at a friend's or relative's house or at a battered women's shelter, and most have worthwhile plans for the future.

For the Step-by-Step Safety Plan and Survival Kit go to pages 114–118 of this book.

4

Women Caught in the Grip of Circumstances

Living with Sporadic Long-Term Abuse

Women who experience intermittent, long-term abuse become involved in a world in which there are long periods of calm but then, without warning, a severe assault occurs, which sometimes lands the victim in the hospital. The severe battering episode may be followed by perhaps six or nine months of calm, a loving relationship resumes, and the woman once again begins to believe her husband's promise that he will never hit her again. She clings to the hope that he has changed. Many of the women in this group remain married for several years before leaving the abuser; sometimes it is the abuser who leaves them. Generally, the women remain in these abusive marriages for three reasons: (1) they want to believe that, since the battering is so infrequent, it will not reoccur; (2) they want their children to grow up in an intact family; and (3) they are dependent on their husband's income, and they want their children to be able to maintain their current lifestyle, including remaining in the same school district with their current friends.

Many of the women discussed in this chapter were either physically abused as children by one or both parents, or observed their mother being intermittently battered by their father. Some of these women reported having very unhappy childhoods during which they were not able to build confidence or self-esteem until late adolescence or beyond; many spoke of college as the way out of the house. In their own marriages, they rationalized that their spouse's brutal outbursts were a result of the enormous stress from his job, and, sadly, they minimized the severity of the abuse they endured. As the assaults happened so sporadically, and the man's apologies and promises seemed so sincere, the women's fear would dissipate enough for them to believe that the most recent assault was, in fact, the final one.

When the women in the intermittent, long-term abuse category land in the hospital or a doctor's office after a severe beating, they typically tell the doctor a cover story such as having tripped while wearing high-heeled shoes or falling down the stairs. The characteristics of this group are illustrated through the personal stories of *Anita, Heidi, Marlene,* and *Danielle.*

■ Background

Married for 18 years, with the exception of a temporary separation, *Anita* was representative of a hidden group of extremely wealthy women who are in long-term relationships that expose them to intermittent battering. Anita was socioeconomically different from the other three cases depicted in this chapter. The combination of her Trust fund and her husband's income was more than $1 million annually. Her husband was a partner at a Connecticut law firm, and she had, among other holdings, a trust fund. At the time of the interview, she lived with her husband and two teenaged children on an estate in Greenwich, Connecticut. She was very attractive and well dressed, almost in a formal sense; every detail, down to her perfume, was flawless and upscale. The diamond wedding ring she wore was an eye-catcher and was so heavy that it rotated seemingly by its own will around her slim fingers. Her childhood was not so bad, she said, but included sexual abuse by her uncle when she was sent to stay at his house while her parents went away. She was still very close to her cousin, who actually bore the brunt of the abuse, as the abuser was her cousin's father, and she lived in the house where his alcohol-induced episodes had resulted in not just sexual abuse but also verbal and physical "punishments." Anita's husband had battered her so severely that she had been in the hospital twice, for several days each time. She hoped that when the children were in college, she could find the strength to leave her husband. She believed herself to be aware enough of his behavior patterns that she could anticipate and cope with the situation until the day arrived when she felt able to file for a divorce. Although her unearned income was sizeable, Anita knew she could never afford her current lifestyle and that of her two children relying solely on her annual trust fund allowance. Anita also knew that her attorney husband would pull every conceivable maneuver to hurt her if she tried to divorce him, including claiming that she was an unfit mother to obtain legal custody of the children.

Thirty-three years old at the time of the interview, *Heidi* had an associate's degree and worked as a dental hygienist. Heidi was the second daughter of two, and had two younger brothers as well. Born to Polish parents, Heidi described her childhood as emotionless and confining. Her father was a high school graduate who worked as a menial laborer in the local factory. Her mother was a housewife who never graduated from high school. During her childhood, the six family members lived in a small house. Heidi recalled being occasionally physically and verbally abused by both parents. Heidi had one child, a three-year-old boy.

Petite, slim, and soft-spoken, *Marlene* at 28 looked much younger. She chose her words carefully. Marlene's stepfather adopted her soon after she was born, and she grew up in a middle-class neighborhood with her mother, stepfather, and younger half-sister. During her childhood, Marlene was subjected to much verbal and physical abuse from her mother. At the time of the interview, Marlene was an elementary school teacher, and she enjoyed teaching young children. Her intermittently abusive marriage had lasted seven years. She had recently become engaged to a man who had helped her restore some of the self-worth and confidence that was eroded during her abusive marriage. Marlene had also recently gotten a second, part-time job for additional income and to ensure that she had savings independent of those of her new fiancé.

Danielle, the oldest of three children from an upper-middle-class Catholic family, was 39 years old. She was well-dressed and used modest makeup. A mother to two children, she had made a firm decision not to allow her children's lives to have any similarity to her own. She said that her childhood, while not completely miserable, did not contain many happy memories. Constant guilt was instilled in all of the children by both parents, whom she said were occasionally verbally abusive. Her father, who worked as an engineer, hit her "only a few times" during her whole childhood; these times, however, were the most instrumental in her loss of sense of self. She worked at the time in the human resources department of a large corporation, and she hoped to go back to school for a master's degree when her two children were older. Newly divorced, Danielle was content with her job, which would provide a stable financial future for her and her two children, without any economic dependence on her ex-husband.

■ Critical Incidents during Childhood

All four of these women had stories of abuse from their childhoods. Some scenarios were more outwardly violent, while some displayed the subtleties of emotional abuse. Regardless of the nature of the childhood abuse, the impact was apparent in each woman's explanation of why she had remained in her marriage.

Anita did not immediately speak of the sexual abuse she experienced from her uncle; first, she explained why she and her brother never wanted to go to their cousin's house for the weekend:

> We would go to my cousin's house a lot when I was little. My parents would sometimes leave my brother and me there for whole weekends while they went away somewhere. We hated it there. We would try to find hiding places and create a different place for us to be. My cousin would come with us as well.
>
> There was a lot of tension there. I mean, much more so than at our house. My uncle drank quite a bit and would lose control often. He would then come to look for us to play, but we would be hiding already and that would make him so angry that he could not find us. Once he called the police to report us missing, but he was so drunk the police knew to ignore him. He was well known in that town.
>
> People tolerated him, even my aunt, I guess.

Anita took a breath and continued, detailing her uncle's habit of sexual abuse with all three of the children:

> It started happening when I was four at my cousin's. My uncle abused all of us, including my brother, but only a little while with him. It started out with baths. He would take baths with us. He would force my cousin to have oral sex with him while he fondled me. A lot of this I don't remember. Things like this weren't discussed. Family scandals were to be avoided at all times. It continued until I was 11 for me, but for my cousin it lasted a lot longer, because she lived with him.

As for her own household, Anita said that she felt most of the tension came from her father because he would maintain control over her through finances. She maintained that she was happy, though, and only mentioned one other tragedy growing up:

> My first love, I was 18 and he was 20, was killed in a car accident. It was a long time before I was able to come to terms with that. We had been dating for almost two years, and it happened shortly before my high-school graduation and debutante ball. I remember that I had just gotten home from the last dress fitting when I got the call. I still think about him all the time.

Unlike Anita, *Heidi* revealed a most stressful childhood in her immediate household; she spoke of her parents in a tense and angry tone. Growing up, the children in her household, she said, were often told "to be seen and not heard." Affection had been limited; despite her remarks that her parents were stifling, it was hardly a quiet household. Heidi spoke about the strict behavior her father exhibited:

> My parents were very strict and unaffectionate. My father used corporal punishment and he periodically hit us for little things like lying or not going right to sleep. As far as I know, my father never hit my mother. My mother was very subservient. It was always "Yes, dear," or "No, dear."

Emotional abuse also took place in Heidi's household. She said that throughout adolescence, she had considered herself to be ugly and stupid. She believed that her self-esteem was never properly nurtured:

> My father always claimed that I was a disappointment because I wasn't a boy. My mother said there was no need for me to be smart because I would only get married and my husband would take care of me. What a joke: she still thinks my place is with my husband. Anyhow, I was ugly when I was kid. That kind of stuff follows you into adulthood. It's always easier to believe the bad instead of the good.

Aside from the constant oppression she felt from her parents, two specific critical incidents stuck out in her memories. Heidi had skipped classes from time to time in middle school, and she described how she was punished by her parents:

> When my parents punished me, my father would hit us with his belt. Then he would make us stay in our bedrooms and only come out to go to the bathroom or maybe to eat. I don't know how often, but sometimes he would forget to call us. We were never forgiven, and years later he would bring up past incidents and laugh at us. When I was grounded for skipping school, I felt like a caged animal. I begged for forgiveness from my father, but he wouldn't let up. I climbed out of my bedroom window and went to my boyfriend's house; he was much older. My best friend helped my parents track me down, and they actually seemed sincere when they apologized, and they said I would no longer be confined to the house. That only lasted a few days, though.

At this stage in her adolescence the second critical incident occurred. She was almost 18 years old when her father found birth control pills in her dresser drawer:

> I was in the shower getting ready to go out. I had no clothes on and shampoo in my hair and my father was calling me a prostitute and he was hitting me. I mean really hitting, slapping, and punching. He was merciless and crazed. The worst part was that I was naked. It was hu-

miliating. I guess the beating went on for about a half hour until my baby brother started crying. What hurt the most was that my mother was in the kitchen the whole time ignoring my yells and screams.

This horrible incident amplified and perpetuated Heidi's acting-out phase:

My father threw away my birth control pills, but that didn't stop me from having sex. I went out and did it that night, just to get back at him, kind of like doing one for old glory. I did that a few times and ended up getting pregnant. It was a shock; I never thought it would happen. I had an abortion, and prefer not to talk about that.

Marlene also shared her recollections of physical abuse from her childhood. It was Marlene's mother, rather than her stepfather, who inflicted most of the physical abuse:

My mom is a lunatic. She would be hysterical, screaming and yelling, beating me, and then she would be telling me she loved me and would never do it again. Over and over and over and over. She is manipulating, controlling, jealous, and she brainwashes. The brainwashing was the worst part. My stepdad was nonexistent. He was a workaholic and was never around. He hit me sometimes, but it was more like I would lie to him, and then get hit. He was very disciplinarian-like, very blue collar.

Marlene remembered the physical abuse starting when she was approximately six years old; her mother seemed as if in a trance when the first incident occurred:

My mother became very angry at me. I can't remember why. She hit me all over my arms. The bruises were so bad that I had to march in the Memorial Day parade that day with my brownie troop in a long-sleeved orange turtleneck.

As this abusive incident initiated a long-endured trend in Marlene's life, she began experiencing emotions that were probably unfamiliar to her peers. In addition to feeling the shame and pain of physical abuse, Marlene also suffered from a learning disability, both of which served to alienate her from the rest of her classmates at a very early age:

I didn't get along with any of the other kids. They were too babyish. Their lives were different from mine. On my way home from school every day I threw up. I hated school. I was dyslexic, so nothing came easy to me.

As if school were not bad enough, Marlene would have to go home to a mother she knew she could not trust. Marlene described the torturous abusive cycle that her mother inflicted on her during childhood:

> It was like living with an alcoholic. When I came in I could feel if the room was a certain temperature. I knew when the beating was going to come. I had to be on my guard watching her. It's like you're at the whim of their emotional behavior. Sometimes I knew that something was going to come flying at me and sometimes I knew she was going to be ranting and other times she could give me a hug. But mostly I could tell. I got really good at knowing because my survival depended on it. When I was 12, she made me stand in the closet and repeat over and over again that I was worthless. She ignored me for long periods of time. At the end, my mom would buy me clothes, shoes, whatever I wanted. I would get lots of clothes and shoes then.

The turning point for Marlene was her strong relationship with her grandmother:

> I called my grandmother and asked if I could live with her for a while. And grandma convinced my mom that it was the right thing to do. Moving in with grandma was great. She helped me with my homework and made me believe that I wasn't stupid.

When Marlene started college, she moved back into her parents' home. Her mother was still abusive, but it was primarily emotional abuse. As Marlene was spending so much time out of the house with her college classes and a part-time job, she was able to mostly stay away from her mother. As a reward for getting good grades in college during her first three years, Marlene was permitted to live on campus for her senior year. This made Marlene very happy, but this happiness was short-lived because she shortly fell in love with a man who would batter her:

> I thought I was closing a door. I was finally free and could move on. I had a new life. I was confident I had escaped the abuse. Now, I had it all: a normal life with a job, apartment, and best friends. I was going out, socializing with people my own age. It was like freedom. Mom's abuse had disappeared. I had a car, not a great one, but it was mine. I even had savings. I found out I could really be happy. That was who I was. My self-esteem was way up. I met Zach two months later. A mutual friend introduced us because we both liked kids and we were both Jewish. My friend knew Zach made a lot of money, and knew I would like that, but no one really knew him.

Danielle described the very strict lifestyle she remembered from her childhood. She spent most of her early life embarrassed and timid; she spoke about excelling in school as an escape:

When I was little, I would feel so much better at school. I had really good grades, because I knew what would happen if I didn't get As. Even a B every once in a while, not even on my report card but on a report or something was clearly not good enough. My dad sent me to bed without dinner and told me that Bs would never be good enough, that I might never be good enough. He made me feel like a failure most of the time. I liked the attention I got at school from my teachers, who started to expect more of me. I always felt under so much pressure—school was definitely better than home, but eventually it got to be too much.

Danielle never really rebelled against the harsh conditions at home. She kept her angry feelings tucked away deep inside. Danielle remembered what happened when she stayed out later than her curfew one night when she was 15:

I was out at a movie with my friends, and it was the middle of the summer. The movie ended, and we wanted to go out for ice cream, and then we went back to one of our friends' houses, and I really just lost track of time. I got dropped off, and tried to be quiet walking in the back door, but my mom and dad were waiting for me. My dad said nothing and hit me right across the face. It took me by surprise, and I just fell right to the kitchen floor. I remember looking up and seeing my mom just standing there with her arms folded, and she said nothing. "Go to bed," my dad said, and then they both left to go upstairs. I was left on the kitchen floor, and I fell into tears when I heard them shut the door to their room. I don't even know how long I was sitting there.

Fearing her father's sudden bursts of anger for the slightest wrong step, Danielle said that she walked a fairly straight line with her father and tried not to do anything that would make him angry. As a responsible young adult, Danielle got birth control pills when she became sexually active. In an episode similar to Heidi's experience, Danielle's parents discovered them. The scenario that ensued was a dreadful memory for Danielle, who was 17 at the time:

I came home from school, and my mom was very quiet. By the time my dad got home, I knew something was up. They talked in their room, and then my dad called me from my room. He was standing there, in the middle of my room, holding my diary. I immediately became afraid of what was going to come next. He called me a whore and told me to give him my birth control pills. He grabbed my hair and pulled on it so hard I started to cry. I knew my mom could hear us and I wanted her protection, but she never even spoke about it afterwards. He wouldn't let go of my hair until I got my pills out of my drawer. He threw my head, and I fell against the side of my bed and hit the floor, sobbing. He threw my pills at the wall and took my diary. I felt so violated. I could never be good enough. We never talked about that again, and they changed my curfew so I could practically never go out and have fun for the rest of that school year.

Danielle was required to live at home through her sophomore year of college. Although she was allowed to move to campus for her junior year, her parents kept her under their control by stipulating that she could move into an apartment with friends *only* if she could pay the entire cost associated with living away from home—rent, food, and utilities—in addition to continuing to pay for her car payments, car insurance, and all of her own clothing and entertainment. From her part-time job on campus, Danielle scraped together the money to live away from home for her senior year of college.

In addition to the varying degrees of abuse experienced during childhood, three of the four women discussed in this chapter have one other thing in common—they fell in love with their future husbands quickly, and at a relatively young age; it was an escape from the problems at home and, in part, a means to financial independence.

■ First Incident

Before delving into the initial incidents of abuse for each woman, it is important to understand the overwhelming love that they felt for the men they married. In two cases, love was instant as well as intense. The engagements were relatively short, and the abuse began shortly before or shortly after the wedding.

Anita's future husband was from a very wealthy family, which was important both to Anita and her parents:

> It wasn't like an arranged marriage or anything, but eyes were on us to meet at one of the annual balls at our club. At first sight, he was gorgeous and the sweetest guy I had talked to in a long time. He was funny, and I loved that he could make me laugh. We danced a lot that night, and started dating. I fell in love with him so fast. He was so successful, too, which was something that was really important to my parents.

Heidi remembered the terrific way she was treated, initially, by her new boyfriend:

> When we were dating, Larry treated me like gold. He always called me honey or sweetheart and always told me how beautiful I was. He said we never had to win the lottery; we were the lottery. One day it was raining, and there was this big puddle of water. He threw down his coat so I wouldn't have to get my feet wet. Those were the good days. I miss them. Now he treats other women like that.

Marlene shared her memory of first meeting Zach, who fell for her immediately:

> Zach was nervous, timid, overwhelmed, and insecure when I met him. He had no self-esteem. He was very enamored with me. It seemed like we had so much in common. I didn't know the things he told me were lies. I was just out of college—energetic, free. I was very worldly to him. When we met, my old boyfriend had just broken up with me. I was okay with being alone finally. I didn't really want to date him. But Zach did all the right things. He had access to money, and money was something I never had. He gave me anything I wanted. I only had to say I liked it. I know the day, the moment, he hooked me in. I told him the whole story of my past abuse, and basically told him to take it or leave it. He literally cried. He said he wanted to take care of me.

Sweet-talking also won over *Danielle*; the new feeling of being doted on filled her with joy:

> I was just out of school, still living at home and hating it. I didn't have a job lined up, but really wanted to work, so I temped. I was working in this big office building just answering phones all day. It was really boring, but it gave me time to get my resumes out to places where I really wanted to have a career. In walked Jason—all of a sudden I found a reason to put my resume on hold! We actually had lunch together that day. He was temping too, and we had a lot to talk about since he was looking for other work too. He was impressed that I had finished college, because he had dropped out a year before. For the next three weeks while I still worked there, he took me to lunch, and we officially started dating. He brought me flowers on Mondays, and really swept me off my feet.

All of these situations changed for the worse, but because of the romantic and idyllic beginning to their relationship, each woman clung to her original expectation of what her married life would be like despite the warning signs.

Anita's husband first abused her on their honeymoon:

We were out at a posh restaurant in Paris. Charles had been drinking a lot. A waiter came to the table when we had finished and asked if we would like anything else. Charles and I spoke simultaneously. I said, "No, thank you. Check please." Charles said, "Double martini, straight up, please." I reasoned that it was getting late and he didn't want to drink so much that the rest of the evening would be lost. Charles smiled and said, "Of course, sweetheart, if that's what you think is best." His voice was a little funny, but I thought everything was fine. We walked back to the hotel. He didn't say anything. I asked him if everything was all right. He nodded. When we got back to the room, he closed the door and took off his dinner jacket. He helped me off with my coat, then he slammed me up against the wall holding me with his entire body. One hand was tightly grasping my hand, and the other was clenched around my face. Then he told me I was never to contradict him in public. Then he ordered me to get ready for bed.

Heidi's torment started two weeks before the wedding, when Larry lost his temper in a department store:

He backhanded me, and I slid into the cosmetics counter face first. All I did was start to cry, I think because I was in shock. He never acted that way before. I didn't fight back—I was just so passive. On the way home, he subjected me to all kinds of raunchy verbal abuse. He started calling me a whore and a slut, and I wasn't. This was the first time he used foul language. I told him I wasn't a virgin when we started dating, and it didn't seem like it was a big issue at all, but all of a sudden he got all crazed and mad. From there on in, every time we would fight, he would call me a slut and a whore. The next day I had bruises on my face, and I was completely humiliated, although I felt a little better when I received the flowers he had sent. He could be so loving. I thought it was the wedding day stress that was eating him up and everything would be fine once the wedding was over.

Heidi continued:

We had our honeymoon at Disney World, a welcome relief after that horrible wedding. Because of that church we belonged to, there was no music or alcohol. And Larry got so mad when his nephew and his nephew's girlfriend went to the bar downstairs and had drinks. All through the wedding he was fuming about the way they ruined the spirit of the wedding by drinking, and it didn't help that his nephew's girlfriend was my good friend. He kept telling me that they were an unfortunate influence and that after we returned things were going to change. They were a disgrace to the family, and he didn't want them, especially her, around me. He kept calling Darlene [the nephew's girl-friend] a whore and his nephew a loser. The nightmare of my honey-moon began when Larry told me that we had to have sex every day because that is what honeymooners did. I wasn't feeling well, and I was worried about him saying things were going to change, that I was going to have all new friends, ones that were powerful and successful. All I can say is that when I refused to have sex with him every day, he raped me. Can you believe he raped me at Disney World? He was so sweet and loving the next day that I could almost forget it happened, and to tell you the truth, I did forgive him. It was months before our next real fight. He even said he would try to tolerate Darlene and his nephew if they were so important to me.

Marlene described the first signs of trouble in her relationship with Zach:

I found out that he was in debt a couple of months before the wedding when I was doing something with the invitations. I was looking in the kitchen cabinets for something and I found a wallet with credit cards, like 30 of them. He only carried a few in his wallet when we went out, but there were so many in this one I couldn't believe it. He explained it away. His manipulation and control was so subtle. It wasn't until after we were married that I found out that he had a ton of debt and was just keeping the creditors at bay. If money could buy it, we could have it with a credit card. When I moved in, he was getting dozens of magazines sent to the apartment each month. Even though he was in debt, I didn't want to give up on the relationship, so I accepted it.

Marlene proceeded with the wedding plans, which led to Zach's first abusive actions:

He was angry about something with the wedding—it seemed to come out of nowhere. He took a crystal clock and threw it at me, at my head. I ducked and it didn't hit me. He shoved and pushed me a little, but he threw the clock hard. He also ripped up a book that he made for me. I really didn't think twice about the whole thing. I just assumed it had to do with all of the stress of the wedding and family. We were both under a lot of stress with all of the planning.

Danielle's new husband, Jason, waited until after the wedding ceremony was over to start abusing her. His anger first appeared on their honeymoon when they were seated late at an expensive restaurant:

I consider myself to be a pretty patient person, but Jason is not, which is what I found out our first night on our honeymoon. We had made reservations weeks before, but they couldn't give us our table for close to an hour, which really didn't bother me too much, but it really pissed him off. So, it was that whole thing and then the waiter screwed up his order. Mine was cold, but I didn't dare say anything. He yelled at the waiter, and then stormed out of the restaurant and left me there, but I followed him to the elevator. When the doors closed, I tried to talk to him, but before I could get a sentence out, he screamed at me and then slapped me really hard. I was amazed that I didn't have a bruise, but it hurt for days. He made it up to me the rest of our honeymoon. He was as sweet as when we had first met. I was hoping that that was the one and only time I'd have to worry about stuff like that.

For all these women, these incidents were the first in a long line of intermittent abuse, followed by long periods of calm and rational behavior after each violent outburst.

◼ Escalation, Isolation

What is most intriguing about this stage in each of these relationships is the power of isolation. A few of the women had experienced social isolation while living with their parents, but none expected it to happen when they were grown up and married.

Anita described her husband's irrational jealousy, which triggered the abuse. He was even outraged by the time she spent in the stables and out riding—so much so that he threatened to kill her horse. Early in their marriage, most of the physical abuse he inflicted upon Anita was in their bedroom, and his demeanor was calm—until it was time to go to sleep:

> On any given night there could have been something wrong with the house, the grounds, whatever. It was my job to oversee the estate and all its functions, so if there was anything amiss, even if I wasn't directly responsible, I was held accountable. In the beginning I never knew he was upset until we got to the bedroom. We would continue with our evening, and I never knew. We would tuck the children in and then go back downstairs for a while, and then it was time to get ready for bed. It would start as soon as the door closed. Charles would sit on the bed and make me kneel at his feet, and he would interrogate me as to what the problem was at the time. He would reduce me to tears and when

that would happen, he would say, "Crying? You want something to cry about? I'll give you something to cry about." Then he would start slapping me in the face and throw me down. When it wasn't going to be bad, it would end after about 10 or 15 minutes. If it was going to be bad, he would take out that saddle strap, and it could last on and off for hours. He was careful never to hit me with a closed fist in my face or welt me there because then he would have to explain.

Charles would even go so far as to send the help out for the evening, so that they would not be able to overhear the attack:

The children were away at school, and Charles sent all of the domestics off duty for the night. There is always someone in the house, but Charles will often send them off duty if he feels a mood coming on.

Heidi's husband, Larry, was very insulting and manipulative, as well as very violent from time to time. Body image was important to her and her husband, and both were regulars at the gym. The steroids Larry was using may have contributed to his violent outbursts. Heidi described one episode that occurred after a lengthy period when Larry had been nonviolent:

I really wanted to believe that all of that hitting stuff was in the past. I just put my head in the sand. Anyhow, we went to the ice cream parlor like we usually did. Inside there was a young couple, and the woman was hardly wearing any clothes. She had workout clothes on, not like the stuff I work out in, but a thong and a spandex sports bra. The guy was all pumped up and looked so gorgeous. Larry started saying that I should wear little clothes like that and that I should lose weight because I was so fat. At the time I weighed 105 pounds. We got into such a fight. He was screaming and throwing ice cream, and he dragged me to the car and drove home real fast and started ripping up my clothes and telling me that I could only wear what he picked out for me, and that I had to start acting sexy. I mean, what was I supposed to do, wear a thong and bra to Shop Rite? I can remember for a fact that this was the night I figured out that if I had sex with him, he wouldn't hit me. It was horrible. I think the steroids he was taking affected his sex drive, so it would take such a long time. It was awful, but I got through it.

Heidi continued:

He had never let go of the whole wedding thing, even though I kept telling him to forget about it. His nephew was going to come back, and I knew there were going to be problems. He was tense all the time and slapped me for the littlest things for the two weeks before Andrew [the nephew] was going to come over. When he finally showed up, there was yelling and screaming and maybe some hitting. Andrew left but told me that if I ever needed help to call him and that Larry was a piece of shit. I never did make that call. Larry told me that I could never speak to either one of them again, and if I did he would put me in the hospital. The next day I made the hardest phone call of my life. I went to the payphone and told Darlene that I couldn't speak to her anymore if I wanted my marriage to work. At this point I thought it could be saved. Darlene and I did not talk for a long time.

Marlene's husband was very controlling and emotionally abusive. He would make use of all of the things she had told him about her mother's abusive behavior. Marlene described Zach's behavior as being primarily emotionally and verbally abusive rather than physically harmful:

Zach fed on the information he knew about my past. He knew exactly what buttons to press. My mom ignored me for months at a time, and he did the same thing. My stepdad criticized my driving and so did Zach. I never drove when we were together. He knew just how to hurt me emotionally. He threw everything from my past back in my face. After a while I could tell. I knew whether he was going to ignore me or if something was going to go flying. It was exactly the same as with my mom, to a T. He never gave me directions to go somewhere on my own, we had to go together. I didn't know where the bills were. He kept them somewhere, and I never really looked for them. He had a system to do it. He thought I would mess it up, because I didn't handle money well. Each time we were planning to go out together to meet my friends, he would pick a fight so that we were unable to go out with them. Friends didn't stay around—they got sick of hearing about it. He bought 90 percent of my clothes, and if I wore something he didn't like, he would ignore me or hit me. He got angrier and angrier at me for causing him to get so mad. He would say I caused him to love me less. I guess I believed him.

Finally, she explained how she was really affected by the way Zach treated her:

I was slowly degraded into nothingness. He degraded me to the lowest emotional point in my life. When he was blaming me for him being angry and making him hurt me, he would stop doing nice things for me. I always knew when everything was okay again because he would suddenly make my lunch for me the next day. It could go on for weeks at a time. Everyone thought we had such a great marriage. People had no idea.

The last time Zach ignored Marlene, she chose to handle the situation in a different way:

> I didn't threaten to leave this time, I didn't yell. I stayed at school a lot and spent almost no time at home. I was always in my classroom or with my friends from work. My friend taught me how to balance a checkbook and work out a budget. This time, he could see he wasn't upsetting me. I didn't react at all. I was just numb. I pretended it didn't bother me that he was ignoring me. He cried and cried. He begged me not to leave, that was the only time. He swore to me that it would never happen again. I didn't believe him at all, but I didn't tell him. I wasn't ready to leave yet. Six weeks later, he was ignoring me again. I told him it was obvious that things were not going to work out between us. He seemed completely calm. We agreed it was over. I wanted to handle it all maturely, and I thought he was okay with it.

Marlene was wrong in her assessment of Zach's state of mind, and what appeared to be a plan for an amicable separation from Zach was actually the calm before the storm.

Danielle explained that, initially, the abuse was more verbal than physical, with Jason wanting to keep her to himself:

> We really never fought that much—he didn't even hit me that many times. But when he would have an outburst in public, it was so memorable because of how embarrassing it was for me. Sometimes he would call me names—once we were getting cotton candy at a carnival and there were kids around when he called me "loose" and "cheap." I wanted to sink into the ground. He made me feel guilty about spending time with my friends, even when he wasn't around. It was like he wanted me all to himself and couldn't handle me having my own life outside of our little apartment. He sent my best friend home once; we were having coffee in the kitchen, and he told her harshly that she had to go because he had to get up early the next morning. It was uncomfortable for me and my friend both. I felt like it was totally out of my hands, and I didn't want to make him upset, since he had to go to work the next day.

■ Worst Incident

These are some of the women's worst memories; in essence, their troubled marriages were reaching a rock bottom.

Anita's worst beating came after her husband believed that she had embarrassed him at their dinner party. In addition to maintaining the home and grounds in perfect condition, she was also expected to throw the perfect party:

> We had Charles's partners, associates, and a few clients over for dinner one weekend. This was a very important dinner to him. He let me know well in advance so that the proper preparations were made. All of the instructions were given to Consuela (she manages all of the domestics), except one. I told Consuela that I would pick up the liquor at Charles's favorite liquor store. That store and every other specialty liquor store was out of this expensive brand of bourbon. So I substituted. I thought maybe he wouldn't be able to tell the difference. I lied to him about it in front of our guests. One of them remarked on the type of bourbon it was and Charles said no, you are mistaken, it is so and so, and then he went into the kitchen and looked for himself. He came out and apologized to our guest and complimented him on his keen sense of taste. I could see it in his eyes that he was going to explode. A little while before our guests left Charles let most of the staff go; he said they could clean up in the morning. I knew then I was going to be in trouble. I called my cousin but she wasn't home. I was trying to figure out what to do. Where was I to go? I was trying to figure that part out and he came bursting into my dressing room. I now had three major mistakes: I wasn't at the door to wish good night to our guests; I lied to him when he asked me about the bourbon in front of people; and I continued to let him think it was something else until it was commented on and let him embarrass himself, not to mention the fact that I came home with the wrong brand of bourbon when he gave me plenty of time to find it. Something that difficult to find you should not leave until the day of the party. I know better than that. I've been entertaining for years. So, you see, he had a perfect right to be furious with me (self-blame). He came in and called me some very bad names, and then he pushed me into the bathroom. He accused me of having an affair and that is why I was too busy to entertain properly, because I was getting f'd all day. He ripped my dress off and told me I was a dirty whore, and then he threw me into the shower and told me to cleanse myself. I hit my lip on the shower faucet and it started to bleed. I was crying and begging him to stop. He grabbed me by the neck and pulled me out of the shower. He was screaming I don't remember what . . . there was so much blood. He was beating me with a long leather belt. He kept ranting you are screwing our neighbor and the gardener. He left me alone for a few

minutes maybe longer, and went downstairs. I tried to get up to call my cousin but couldn't move. I heard him coming back. Next thing I knew, I woke up in the hospital.

Heidi's worst experience happened in the car on the way home from a vacation shortly after Heidi learned that she was pregnant:

> I was so happy, I thought since we were coming back from the beach and it was a two-and-a-half-hour ride we would have fun picking out baby names from a book I had bought. I thought he wanted to have a baby, and I didn't know he had changed his mind. Larry snapped, and we were on the highway going 80 miles an hour. He would slow down and then speed up, but I swear we never went below 60. Yelling, screaming obscenities about how he wanted my uterus to fall out. It lasted for about two hours, the whole ride home. He was kicking me with his free leg and slapping me. I could already see the bruises from him hitting me. He didn't threaten to use a weapon, but he was smashing my head on the windshield by yanking my hair back. I didn't go to the hospital, but I had a really bad headache for days afterwards. I think back now and I must have had a concussion. The next day he apologized over and over again, and he bought the usual gifts: chocolate and flowers. This was the fight he bought me the stereo system I wanted. Then we talked, and he told me he didn't want my figure ruined and he was worried that a baby would change our lifestyle too much. Our earning potential would go way down.

Marlene, who had decided to divorce Zach, was in for a terrible shock:

> Zach turned on the TV in the living room, and I stayed in the kitchen, cleaning. He began ranting and raving from the living room, yelling stuff. All of a sudden, he was in the kitchen. He became abusive in the kitchen, shoving and punching me. Then he threatened me with a knife. I ran to the bedroom and locked the door. He took the doorknob off the door. He sprayed me in the face with Lysol, and then he closed the door to the bedroom. Then I tried to get out of the bedroom—he didn't know he locked me in there when he took the knob apart—but once he figured it out, he left me in there. He walked away. He told me he would open it in the morning. But I started to panic and worry that he might not let me out the next morning to go to school, and told him if he didn't let me out, I would call the police. He yelled that when I went to sleep, he was going to take the knife and slit my throat. That is when I called the police. The police officers asked me why I didn't just call 911 right away. If he says he's going to do

something in the bedroom, then as a victim, you lock the door. The police said, "You don't think out the whole process, you just think about what you can do to not get hurt." I was in a first-floor bedroom with two windows, and it never occurred to me that I could get out of that room.

In *Danielle*'s case, she was already pregnant with her second child. On this night, she made the mistake of mentioning that she was tired before bed:

I was actually in a really good mood. We had just discovered I was pregnant about a week before. I said that I was happy to get to bed because I was so tired, and Jason was testy, as he had been since he started to think about the fact that we were going to have a second child. Our son was asleep across the hall. Jason walked out of the bathroom and yanked the alarm clock off the night table and ripped the cord right out of the wall and started screaming and yelling about how I had no reason to be tired, that he was working hard to support our family, and that it was my fault that we were having another baby. I lay on the bed, not moving, for fear of what was going to happen next. He took stuff from the night table and threw it at me, like magazines and books, kind of taunting me and telling me to clean up the mess, that he would give me something to be tired from. I sat up, hoping that my son would not be awakened—that's when he threatened to strangle me with the cord to the alarm clock. He told me that he was sick of my complaining and that I was spoiled, while he wrapped the cord around his hands like he was actually going to kill me. I started to cry, and he beat me over and over again with the dangling clock radio and then I curled up on the bed, protecting my head. I was sobbing. I don't think it lasted very long at all, but I was terrified. The next day, things shifted back to the normal way it had been, and he went to work as usual.

■ Sleep Disturbance and Anxiety

Heidi, Marlene, and Danielle left their abusive husbands, but at the time of the interview Anita was still married to the batterer. All of the women suffered emotionally, even the three women for whom the abuse had ended.

Anita, still married and believing herself to be trapped in her abusive marriage, said that she experienced sleep disturbances as well as appetite disruptions:

I've been plagued with insomnia and nightmares for as long as I can remember. I can sometimes lie in bed for more than four or five hours before I get to sleep, and often when I get to sleep, I have this one nightmare: it is always a large dark figure laughing while I try to run away. I will run for days it seems, and it is never far enough. The figure never moves, but it reaches out for me and is just about to grab me when I wake in a cold sweat, sometimes screaming.

And I know I don't eat well. I have always used food for comfort. So if I was having a particularly bad day, I might eat a lot more than I normally would, and so for the next couple of days, I might not eat at all. Charles despises fat people. I wouldn't call it a change in diet, per se. I suppose I get depressed. Don't we all?

Heidi explained that her way of coping with the anxiety from her marriage to Larry was to eat:

When we would go to have sex, all he would do is point out my fat, which only made me eat more. I didn't care that I was gaining weight, and I didn't care that it made him madder. It was something I could control, I guess, but after a while, that became out of control too, and I was so unhappy with myself. That was it—it was officially a disaster, because by then he was regularly abusing me on a intermittent basis, and I felt like there was nothing to do to stop it. I was completely overwhelmed by everything.

Marlene said that she had exactly the opposite problem—she couldn't eat anything:

I didn't really have any appetite. I also had a lot of trouble sleeping and sometimes I would sleep too much. I had nightmares. I couldn't wake up. Pictures of my past would flash through my mind. I had these nightmares every few months, and I still have them now. I would get really hyperactive, and obsessive/compulsive about cleaning and work.

Danielle said that when her husband, Jason, was away—usually out with other women—she would get her three-year-old son and have him sleep in bed with her:

I was so lonely and exhausted, and I could never sleep. Just thinking about what he was doing out with whoever he was out with made me feel sick. I desperately wanted to leave. I had just had my second baby, and was devastated that he would leave me. I would try to sleep, but would sometimes go across the hall and get my older son to invite him to sleep with me in my bed. Even though he was so little, it was comforting to have him in bed with me because I knew he was mine. There was still something I could save and protect. It was nice to have him there if I had a nightmare, which I did quite often when I could actually get to sleep. I was miserable even when my husband wasn't there; it was like he didn't even need to be there for me to be hurt.

■ Moving Forward

Anita, not yet able to leave her abusive husband, said she was waiting for her children to get older:

> I go to therapy, and I have the kids go also, but Charles won't because he says he's much too busy with work. Maybe within a couple of years, I will have gotten him to get some counseling. But in ten years or so, the kids will be grown, and maybe I will be strong by then and will be able to find some peace. If I was ever so strong as to successfully get out of this marriage, I don't think I would ever allow another man into my life again.

Heidi was finding it difficult to sever all ties with her ex-husband. Larry still maintained contact with her and wanted to see their son more often:

> I recently got my degree as a dental hygienist, and I actually am in a really good relationship, but the whole custody thing is so hard. I have to see Larry all the time, and it's for the benefit of our son, but Larry actually uses our son to try to get closer to me again. I don't know what to make of that; I want our son to have two normal parents, but I don't feel as though I can have a normal relationship with him [Larry]. I guess we'll see how things turn out. I'm trying, though, and I have a lot of support from my new boyfriend.

Marlene, although she was engaged to be married again to a supportive and loving man, was still going to court to settle things with her ex-husband. She had individual therapy, and told of her progress:

> For quite a while, I was afraid that everyone I met who was male would end up abusing me and that I would not be able to stop the pattern. I would keep being attracted to the same type. I couldn't figure out why. My current therapist understands the symptoms and behaviors of both the victim and the batterer, and the others did not. This is her specialty. She understands the thought patterns of the victims and, therefore, she has been a huge help to me.

Danielle had successfully ended the abusive marriage. Jason's job had required him to move to the Midwest, so there was very little contact between them. Danielle worked every day, and was lucky to be in a community in which she could rely on a good friend to take care of her two young children when she was working:

> It's really hard, but I love what I am doing, especially because I get to go home to my sons. I hope that they will understand when they get older that their dad isn't around for a very good reason, and I will do my best to keep them as far away as possible from all of that stuff that I had to go through for so long. I would like to go back to school for my master's degree, but that's a ways off. Things are just fine like they are now. I have enough to worry about!

5

The Hitting Habit

The women included in the chronic abuse category have all endured many years of abuse from a husband or live-in partner—they have been financially dependent, insecure, lacking in job skills, and afraid that the batterer would ultimately kill them.

The women in both the intermediate category (chapter 3) and the chronic long-term group suffered extremely severe beatings. What differentiates the women in the intermediate group from the chronic long-term group is that the women in the former group had the emotional strength to leave the relationship after a few years of victimization, while those in the chronic abuse group have suffered a lifetime of violence.

The six women discussed in this chapter spoke about situations that were strikingly similar. Although the specific details of their experiences varied, these themes emerged from a review of their life stories: the women were abused during their childhood or adolescence (by a parent or other relative); the husband/partner's frequent acts of violence over many years were intertwined with his alcohol or drug abuse; and the women lacked the confidence that they could be successful if they were on their own.

■ Background

Luanne, like many other women in the chronic abuse category, experienced an extraordinary level of violence from a very young age. The abuse began with her father and continued when she married a police officer who would beat her with his nightstick or another nearby object. Luanne was in her late forties and devoutly religious. Her eyes were focused as she discussed various instances of torment from her childhood and marriage. She had few positive recollections from her childhood. Luanne had remained in her abusive marriage for close to 10 years, and had been apart from the batterer for the past 16 years, during which time she had created a new and successful life. Luanne credited a shelter for battered women with helping her to turn her life around. The shelter staff helped her realize that living with domestic violence was not normal and that she had the strength to survive on her own.

Maria had lived in her native country of Colombia for her entire life until approximately one year before her interview was conducted. In her early forties, Maria said that when she finally left Colombia, she was not able to bring her son; her ex-husband would not allow it. On her own, raising two daughters in New Jersey, she was able to gain some distance from a past that consisted of severe physical, sexual, and emotional abuse that began in her adolescence and continued through a marriage to which she swore she would never return.

Theresa, age 30, identified herself as a born-again Christian. She was a high school graduate and, when interviewed, was working in a clerical position for a Fortune 500 company and raising her two children on her own, grateful to be recently divorced from her abusive husband. Theresa's face looked older than her 30 years, possibly from being out in the sun too much, or possibly from the anguish brought on by so many years of abuse. At the time, Theresa's children had no contact with their father. Theresa was concerned about her children's financial security, and she was conscientious about handling her responsibilities at her job.

Raquel experienced a multitude of emotional hardships growing up, and she took on the burden of caring for her younger siblings as a teenager. Although she was in her early thirties when interviewed, she looked 10 years older. She had a scar above her left eyebrow, a constant reminder of a violent episode in which her husband had thrown a glass at her face. For the first few years of her marriage, Raquel kept her hair long, but after a horrendous incident in which her husband dragged her into the bedroom by her hair, she had it cut short. Raquel was interviewed shortly after leaving a shelter for battered women that had helped her turn her life around. One aspect of Raquel's background differed from the histories of most of the other women in the chronic abuse category, and would probably make it easier for her to restart her life: she had a college degree, and she was excited to start the new job the shelter staff had found for her.

Raquel said that she had been overweight all her life, a characteristic that her mother would use to emotionally abuse her. Raquel spoke about being constantly scrutinized and degraded by her mother for one thing or another; usually her mother's criticism revolved around school or her weight. In addition, when Raquel was 16 or 17 years old, her father admitted that he was gay—but only after a lifetime of depression that had put an enormous amount of strain on the entire family.

Justine, like some of the other women in this group, did not graduate from high school. When she smiled, a small scar around the bridge of her nose became noticeable, the permanent reminder of one of her worst incidents with her now ex-husband. While unable to recall anything specifically positive from her childhood, Justine, not surprisingly, could provide vivid accounts of her negative experiences. During adolescence, she was sexually abused by her uncle.

Su-Li, the oldest woman who was interviewed in this category, was also, sadly, the only one who remained in an abusive relationship. She was a 51-year-old woman who had come to the United States from Korea with her husband many years ago. She spoke English with a heavy Korean accent. She said she had been beaten by her husband for close to 30 years, but she would not leave him.

We try to capture some of the harrowing childhood and adult traumas these women endured in an effort to educate other women who may fall into the same tragic circumstances.

■ Critical Incidents in Childhood and Adolescence

For these women, a cycle of abuse began in childhood or adolescence, years before they fell prey to chronic partner abuse. What was both chilling and unusual about many of the women in this group was that when they were asked to recall positive experiences from their childhood, some women were not able to remember any; for others, the rare positive recollections involved other relatives or friends but not their own parents.

Luanne described her alcoholic father and the violence she experienced on a regular basis as a young child, both as a victim of her father's anger and as a witness to her father's assaults against her mother and brother:

> My father was very abusive. He had no patience when I was a little kid. He hit me and my brother and mother. My brother usually got it the worst—since he was the boy, he needed the most discipline. The worst case was when my brother left home. My father was furious and he took it out on me.
>
> My father beat us for no reason. He didn't need anything specific

to motivate him. If we were too noisy, or he didn't like his dinner, or even if he just had a bad day at work, he would beat us.

I remember my father beating my mother regularly until he died in 1981.

During her childhood, Luanne had frequent nightmares: "I would always dream my father was chasing after me. I would wake up terrified but I could not yell for my mother 'cause that would make my father mad, and then he really would have come after me." Luanne said that her father's abuse of her continued until she was 18 and she left the house.

Maria also had childhood memories of nightmarish proportions:

> My father used to beat me with anything he could get his hands on. He was a disciplinarian. He really believed that hitting was the way to go, but it wasn't just hitting. I totally passed out after one of his beatings. He hit me with his fists, and I guess he meant to hit some part of my body, but he hit my face, and all I remember was seeing stars. When I woke up, I was in the hospital because my mom said she tried to wake me up, but I just wouldn't come to, so she took me to the hospital and told the doctors that I fell. I had a concussion. Ever since then, I have had headaches. My mom said I used to cry myself to sleep. That happened when I was seven. You'd think after that my dad would stop; the only thing that changed was that he hit me below the head from then on. After that, I had bruises on my legs, arms, my back. He'd grab the whip you use with horses. He used to beat me with that.

Maria's childhood victimization continued outside of her home with a friend of her older brother when she was 16 years old. When asked about her most horrific incident as a child, instead of telling the story of her father, this was what she had to say:

> He started kissing me and grabbing my breasts, but grabbing them really tight. Then he just busted my dress open and started sucking on my breasts really hard. I think even blood came out. I couldn't scream because he had his fist in my mouth. I thought he was going to rape me, but you know what the bastard did? He put his penis in my mouth and was just shoving it down my throat. I felt like I was going to throw up because he pushed it in very hard and deep. This happened for at least 15 minutes. I was exhausted and had no energy to fight so all I was trying to do was survive this ordeal. After he was finished, he just grabbed my face and threatened me. Then he threw mud on my face and started laughing and calling me a slut and a whore.

In contrast to the other women in this category who recalled being abused by a father or other male figure, *Theresa* had harsh childhood memories of her mother's repeated acts of physical and emotional abuse, culminating, when she was 16, in being removed from her home by her mother. Throughout the many years of her mother's abuse, her father did nothing to help Theresa:

> My mother was physically abusive to me. It happened many times. I can even recall a time—I was 11 years old—when she threw me down the stairs, and my father did nothing. I really believe my mother was having a nervous breakdown and could have benefited from some psychiatric treatment. She physically and verbally abused me repeatedly.
>
> When I was 16, my mother initiated a JINS [Juvenile in Need of Supervision] petition to have me removed from my home. My girlfriend's parents were appointed my guardians. I stayed with them, and I didn't have any further contact with my parents.

Raquel's parents had a rocky marriage, with two short-term separations during her childhood and a final separation when she was 12 years old; they divorced two years later. Raquel believed that her parents had never been happy together and should not have married. She recalled emotional abuse in her home, but no physical abuse. There was a lot of tension in the home and she felt as though she was always "walking on eggshells" because her father was depressed and ignored his children:

> My father would lock himself in his room when he got depressed. He would just totally cut the whole family off. It felt like you were always walking on eggshells, and I was the oldest, so I felt like I had to keep my brothers and sisters calm. My father's actions angered me because he should have taken control, and to this day I don't deal well with people when they are depressed. My mother was always irritable. It was taken out on us through emotional abuse, nothing physical.

After Raquel's father left their home, her mother focused all of her energy on her children. Raquel said that, as she was the oldest, she got the worst of her mother's emotional abuse, which was usually focused on her weight and her school achievements:

> My adolescence was also disturbing because of the emotional abuse from my mother. I have been overweight all my life, and my mother used to harp on that. Also, all my life she pushed me to be an overachiever, and if I ever got a C she would throw it in my face for weeks.

The most positive memories from Raquel's childhood were connected to her relationship with her grandmother, whom Raquel described as very supportive and a good listener when Raquel wanted to talk about her home life. She also recalled enjoying the summer vacations when she was able to visit three aunts who lived in different parts of the country. She had fond memories of those visits, which allowed her to spend the entire summer away from home.

When Raquel was 16 or 17, her father admitted that he was gay. She felt almost relieved when she learned about her father's homosexuality because she believed that it explained why her parent's marriage was such a failure:

> Eventually, my dad moved in with his lover, but this didn't make me feel uncomfortable because I had grown used to the fact that he was gay. Also it was a relief knowing that he had one person who cared about him.

Justine said that she was not abused by her parents. She remembered the worst incident in her childhood that occurred when she was 10 years old, when her uncle initiated what would become a pattern of sexual abuse:

> When I was 10 years old, my uncle asked for my help at his store. He would have me sit on his lap and would put his fingers down my pants (inside of me) while customers walked around on the other side of the counter.

Su-Li did not remember any details about her childhood, saying that she was too old to remember her youth. Her primary recollection was that she was a good child who never caused any trouble for her parents. During her adolescence, Su-Li's father died, and she was very sad and lonely because she missed him so much. She said, "I wanted someone to replace the empty space from his death. But my husband is nothing like my father."

■ The First Incident

Luanne drew a direct comparison between her husband and her father. She explained that her husband was initially very calm and loving, and as he was a police officer, she had expected that he would never hit her. His violent streak surprised her completely, but hurled her back into an all-too-familiar situation:

> My husband was a perfect gentleman until a few months into our marriage. Then he turned into my father. The first time he hit me, he did

so because he was having guests over, and he thought that I didn't fix the house up nice enough, so he slapped me. I started to cry, and he apologized and said that it would never happen again.

Maria, who lived in Colombia for 20 years before leaving her husband behind and coming to the United States, described the first time she was abused by her husband, two days before their wedding:

> [He]came home with red blotches on his neck. I knew he had been with another woman. He didn't deny it, so I told him he was a worthless piece of shit and that I wouldn't marry him. He grabbed my arm and told me that I would never be able to get rid of him. I told him to let go, and that he was scaring me. He said, "I'm glad that I'm scaring you!" Can you imagine that? So I still wanted to leave him. That's when he pushed me on the ground, and I started to scream. He put his fist in my mouth and he kept on pushing it in. I thought he was going to kill me. After he saw me crying, he stopped and promised he would never do it again. I believed him.

Theresa recalled that her husband first assaulted her when they were living together, prior to their marriage:

> He was drinking that night, and we started to argue. He became enraged and punched me in the face and broke my glasses. Then he hugged me immediately and told me he was very sorry.

When *Raquel* was a senior in college, she started dating a man whom she had met while working as a waitress at her part-time job. She had not dated much, and she was quickly infatuated with the man who had taken such an interest in her. Several months later, Raquel became pregnant; she refused to consider an abortion because she was a devout Catholic. When Raquel told her boyfriend about the pregnancy, he immediately said they should get married, and she agreed. There were no signs of violence while they were dating and no violence in their first few months of marriage. The abuse began after their son was born with birth defects:

> My husband blamed me for our baby's birth defects. He started drinking and abusing me physically and emotionally. The first time he hit me, I was holding the baby in my arms, and he hit me in the face.

The first violent incident against *Justine* occurred when her husband was drunk. Justine recalled what took place:

> I came home from work about five minutes before Ron. He was drunk and looking for money. He went into my purse and found a pack of

cigarettes. He screamed at me and called me a fucking loser and punched me in the face. He took all of my money and left home until the next morning.

Su-Li recalled that the abuse began a month after the wedding. Although she did not recall the details of the initial incident because it was so long ago, she believed that she was at fault for causing her husband to be angry at her:

I guess I did something to make him mad at me. He is not a patient and understanding person. I wasn't smart enough to avoid the mess when I was young. I thought all men were like my father, gentle and understanding.

■ The Turning Point

These women remained with their husbands until, after many years of being terrorized on a frequent basis, they reached rock bottom and made the decision to leave the batterer. (The exception was Su-Li, who continued at the time of the interview to live with her violent husband.) In most cases, the abusive men whose wives are discussed here were heavy drinkers or drug abusers, and the most severe violent rages were associated with the men being under the influence of alcohol or other drugs.

Luanne was beaten repeatedly during her close to 10 years of marriage. The violence was all the more shocking because her husband was a police officer:

He beat me with that stick that cops carry. I forgot what it's called. He liked to beat me with what he had handy. He mostly used his feet and fists, but sometimes he would beat me as soon as he got home from work and he would have that club on him so he would use that.

Luanne described a very brutal incident that occurred after they had been married for many years:

My husband had been having problems at work. He came home one night with liquor on his breath and out of the blue he just [started] yelling about how I didn't appreciate him and how I just sat around all day doing nothing while he worked all day. I got mad because I had been cooking and cleaning all day. I yelled back at him. That drove him over the edge. He started punching me. I tried to get away and ended up trapped in the corner while he punched and kicked me. The beating lasted about five minutes. I had a broken nose and two broken ribs and bruises all over my body.

Luanne's husband did not threaten to kill her—until she left him. She recalled her husband warning her, "If you ever leave me, I'll kill you." She did not take him seriously, and once she had decided to leave him, his murderous threat did not cause her to change her mind. She sought refuge at a battered women's shelter in a different county than the one in which she and her husband lived and he was a police officer.

Maria remarked that her husband was always drunk when he beat her and frequently threatened to kill her. She said, "I didn't believe he would ever kill me until the last time when he almost threw me off the balcony. He had hate in his eyes that night. It was different somehow." Maria described that night of horror:

> He had been gone for like two days, on one of his little adventures with whores that took his money. When he got home, he was dirty, stinking of alcohol, with no money. I was so upset that my kids were seeing this that I just started packing my bags. I [had] had it. He was sleeping while all of this was going on, but by the time I was ready to leave, it was too late. As soon as he saw the bags, he knew that I was leaving, so he told the kids to go to bed and not come out of their rooms. I knew right then and there that this was going to be it, either I [would kill] him or he'll kill me. He took me to the bedroom, took all of my clothes off, even my underwear, and just started kissing me and stuff. I felt horrible. Then he wanted me to . . . suck on his genital organ. I almost bit it off, but I was really scared because I'd never seen him like this. So after he was finished he tied me up. My arms with my feet, on my back. It hurt for days after that. He picked me up and tried to throw me off the balcony. I passed out before he even did it. I really saw my life just pass by me, but the Lord is so good because when I passed out, I guess I was too heavy, so he couldn't just throw me off. So he kicked me down the stairs, all tied up and everything. By this time I was unconscious, and he just kept on kicking me, rolling me over like I was a ball until he kicked me out into the street. I couldn't even scream because when he would kick me sometimes he would kick me in the face, and my mouth was bleeding. Everything just hurt. I spent the night out on the street in the rain, naked, bruised up, and all tied up, until a neighbor saw me and brought me into her house and took me to the hospital. I had broken arms and bruises all over. I could have gotten a severe head injury, but the doctor said I was lucky. My ankles were so swollen that I couldn't walk for days. I was in bed for almost two months.

In *Theresa's* home, her husband's alcohol consumption was intertwined with the frequent beatings:

> After work, he would drink until he got drunk. When he arrived home, he would be extremely nasty and start picking fights. The fights almost always ended up in his beating me.

Theresa was very upset when her children witnessed her husband's brutality. She vividly recalled one event in which her young daughter's screams may have saved her life:

> We were in bed. We were arguing and he started choking me. My daughter came in and started crying and screaming. He stopped and told her he would throw me out the window. It never got to the point that I was gasping for breath. My daughter's screaming seemed to be what stopped him.

In addition to the physical abuse, Theresa's husband was frequently emotionally abusive, making her believe that it was her fault that her mother had beaten her as a child:

> He constantly brought up my past, and that I deserved to be beaten by my mother. He had me brainwashed thinking it was always my fault that I was beaten by both my mom and my husband.

Theresa recalled the worst episode, which became even more brutal when her husband became determined to prevent her from calling the police for help:

> We had been arguing, I can't remember what it was about. He was always threatening to kill me. He became violent and ripped the phone wire off because I tried to call the police. He tied me up with the wire and burned me with an iron. Then he ran outside and ripped some kind of plugs from my car so that it wouldn't work. He didn't want me to be able to go out and get help. He eventually left, and I was able to have a girlfriend drive me over to the police station. The police explained my rights to me and helped me file a restraining order.

Theresa said that she never went to the emergency room for her injuries because she was too embarrassed to talk to medical personnel about what had happened to her.

Raquel explained how the violence became more severe as her husband started drinking more heavily:

> Every weekend, he would go on long binges, starting Friday night through Sunday, and when he got home, he would be very violent and

abuse me. He would hit me for the littlest things. One time he hit me because he didn't like what I made him for lunch.

Raquel said that the cultural differences (she was American and her husband Mexican) that she found exciting initially were the source of many arguments, particularly after their son was born:

> When I got married, I became a piece of property, not a partner. He used to say that it was a cultural thing. He's Mexican and he used to say that all American women were sluts. His father used to say that his mother was a slut. All of my in-laws are on a leash, and because he couldn't do that with me, he would get mad. He always did things that would make him seem macho. He would always like to rip my clothes off me because I would be trying to get away. He used to force me to have sex with him almost daily.

Raquel had a vivid recollection of the most severe battering incident:

> He was out drinking with his friends and he didn't come home for dinner. He finally called, very drunk. He ditched me for his friends, so I hung up on him. I really thought I was safe at that point because he was so drunk and was an hour away, so I thought I was safe for the night. I didn't expect him home, and I thought I would deal with it the next day.
>
> But when I hung up on him, that made him mad, and he drove an hour home, very drunk. When he got home, I was in the bathroom, and he slapped me down to the ground. Then I went upstairs to go to bed in my son's room, and he literally dragged me by my hair into our room and sexually assaulted me. Then he did it two other times. The whole episode lasted for many hours. I couldn't sleep the whole night. I call it the Night of Terror.

Over the years, Raquel had numerous injuries from being assaulted so often:

> Usually he would hit me in my head, so my head would be sore, but nothing visible. He hit me in my back. The sexual assault—that in itself was an injury, and it became very frequent towards the end. Because of the sexual assault, I went to the E.R.

Justine was aware of her husband's cocaine habit and his uncontrolled rages when he was using drugs:

> He was especially jealous when he had been using cocaine. He threatened to kill me. He said I was a whore and deserved to die. This is when I really became scared. There were times I really thought I was going to die.

Justine recallsed her worst incident, which occurred during a vacation when her husband was high on cocaine:

> We went to Tampa, Florida. We walked into the hotel bar and I smiled at a man I passed. Ron was really coked up and paranoid. He grabbed me by my hair and bent my arm all the way back to the room. He dragged me out of the elevator and said he was going to kill me. When we got into our hotel room, he started pounding away at my face. I ended up with a broken nose, stitches, a black eye, and my whole face was swollen.

Justine was so seriously injured that she went to the hospital emergency room for treatment, but she told the doctor her injuries were caused by a car accident. She said, "I don't know if he believed me or not, but the E.R. was packed that night, and he didn't ask me any questions about my car accident story."

Su-Li described how her husband's abuse escalated shortly after they came to America from Korea. He blamed Su-Li for urging him to leave his native country:

> As soon as we came to America, and he realized that it wasn't anything like he expected, he was mad. It was all my fault since I made him come to America. He hit me, spit on me, kicked me in the back. The yelling and hitting and bruises were happening almost every day. He also scared me a lot when he used to say he wanted me and the children to die with him. I know he will never kill himself, but it used to scare me.

Su-Li also spoke about her husband's drinking problem and her belief that he used the drinking as an excuse for hitting her:

> He drank almost everyday. At first, I thought it was the liquor that caused him to act that way, but soon I realized it was only an excuse. He didn't act drunk when he drank the same amount with his friends. But when he hit me, he acted as if he were drunk, although the same amount of alcohol was consumed.

Su-Li experienced threats of a murder-suicide, sparked by her husband's depression. Her recollections of her husband's murderous discussions:

> He said: "You and I are so miserable together. Why do we need to go on? You are a whore. I know you tried to make me kill myself by making me miserable, but I won't go alone. I will take you with me." He was cursing a lot when he said these things to me.

Since Su-Li was still living with her violent husband when she was interviewed and was still subject to his violent rages. At the time of the interview, she reported the most violent incident to date:

I was in the shower, and he started beating me with his belt. He was angry because I had not come home as early as he expected. I turned my back to him so the belt wouldn't hit my breasts and my face. I was crying and begging him to stop, but he kept doing it. Then he shoved me really hard and I fell and hit my head on the faucet and was unconscious. All I remember after that was waking up fully clothed in bed with bruises all over my body and a gigantic headache.

Seeking Help

Many women who have the courage to leave a battering husband or partner after many years of victimization are given refuge by a shelter for battered women. Sometimes the women live with friends or family members until they have the financial resources to live on their own. Often the women in this category sought help from the police.

Luanne, however, never reported the beatings to the police. Since her husband was a police officer, she thought that the other officers would try to protect him and would never believe her. On the occasions that Luanne went to the hospital emergency room, the doctors and nurses treated the injuries, but they did not ask for details on how she had been hurt:

They were nice to me. I think that they felt bad for me but they didn't know how to help. It's not like they could have him arrested. He was a police officer. They taped me up, stitched my cuts, and sent me home with my husband.

They did not ask any questions. People who have never been trapped in a violent relationship sometimes wonder why anyone would remain in such a relationship. In Luanne's view, the women are afraid to leave because they do not have any money or job skills. She said that was the reason she endured nearly 10 years of beatings. "He was constantly telling me that I wouldn't be able to survive on my own, and I believed him."

When Luanne was finally ready to leave her abusive husband, she made arrangements to go to a shelter for battered women that was far from her home. She wanted to be certain that her police officer husband would not be able to find her. She had learned about the shelter in a remote location from a caring attorney at a legal aid office. With the assistance of a friend, Luanne packed her personal belongings while her husband was working, and she left him a note saying that their marriage was over and she was going to divorce him.

Maria said that with her sister-in-law's help she was able to leave South America with her two daughters and fly to New Jersey. Maria had never sought help from a state or local domestic violence program because her country had no such programs. Maria indicated that the police in her country were all men and did not believe that there was such a thing as domestic violence.

Theresa credited the police with being very helpful in getting the restraining order and protecting her at her home while she was collecting her things to move out of the apartment. For ongoing support, Theresa relied on a group of close friends. She also sought counseling from her pastor prior to the divorce becoming final.

Raquel had very positive comments about the assistance she received from the police. The morning after the repeated sexual assaults, Raquel was determined to get the help she needed to end the violence. She ran over to a neighbor's house and called the police from there because she did not want to take the chance of calling from her home and having her husband overhear the phone call. Raquel explained that the police arrived very quickly, in "less than five minutes," and they arrested her husband "on the spot." She was also pleased by the kind manner of the two police officers as they called a shelter for battered women and assisted her and her two children to pack their most important belongings and go to the shelter.

Justine was so distraught by the years of beatings that she attempted suicide at one point—a traumatic incident that she wanted to keep at an emotional distance and was unwilling to discuss. She was thankful for the counseling she had received that had helped her regain her own sense of self-worth.

Su-Li had never sought help from the police, a shelter, or other counseling service. Saying that she would never leave her husband, Su-Li explained: "I have learned over the years what makes him angry, and I try as hard as I can to never do anything that will upset him." In recent years, she had been doing volunteer work with immigrant children, and she found that work very fulfilling.

■ Future Plans

Luanne mentioned her job successes in the 16 years since she had the courage to leave her abusive husband:

> When I left my husband I threw myself into work. I started going to college part-time, and I got a full-time job working as a secretary. I spent my time making a future for myself and trying to just forget about him. When I finally got my college degree, it was a huge accom-

plishment. I have been counseling other battered women, and I find that very fulfilling.

Luanne had not remarried, but she was in a long-term relationship with a man she described as "very caring and nonviolent."

Maria reflected on the ending of her marriage:

> I would like to think that my husband loved me, at least when he married me. You should have seen how he was crying when I left him for good. He writes me letters and he sends me things begging me to come home. Well, maybe he loves me, but then I remember how he tied me up and tried to throw me off the balcony. I can't believe that's love.

After having escaped from her brutal husband in Colombia and seeking asylum in Los Angeles with her two daughters, Maria said:

> You know, I never would have thought I would have to clean somebody else's shit, excuse my language, but this bastard pushed me to the limit. So now I have to do whatever it takes for me and my girls to survive. I'll tell you though, cleaning anything is better than putting up with his beatings!

In the short term, *Theresa* was hoping to be promoted by her employer and to continue her education. Her number one priority was to provide a loving and stable home for her two children. Theresa's long-term goal was to have an intimate relationship—a positive relationship—with another man. She offered this advice to all women in abusive relationships and are afraid to leave the batterer:

> There are options for women in abusive relationships. It is not their fault and they shouldn't take the abuse. Call the police and seek protection. Don't just think they'll eventually change. It won't help you to keep quiet about it. When it happens once it is sure to happen again. And one last thing: Not all relationships have to be this way. The hurt does eventually go away. You can live a "normal" life again, if you want to.

Raquel was eager to be successful in her new job and to be a good mother to her children.

Justine had gotten her high school equivalency diploma, and she was hoping to become a nurse. She was interested in working with elderly people.

Su-Li, at 51, continued to hope and pray that her abusive husband would stop drinking or seek help for the depression that had plagued him for so many years. She expected that as he got older, he would have less strength to hit her, and that the habitual beatings would become less frequent.

6

Lethal Domestic Violence

The victims of domestic violence come from all races, ethnic groups, religions, income levels, and types of communities—urban, suburban and rural. It is also a gruesome fact that domestic violence sometimes ends in homicide. An FBI Supplementary Homicide Report says that approximately 1,500 women are murdered by their male intimate partners or former partners each year. Approximately 700 men are killed by their female intimate partners annually.

According to the CDC's *Surveillance Report on Homicides by Intimate Partners in the United States*, the majority of homicides during the eight-year period 1990–98 were committed by men or women who killed a spouse, former spouse, boyfriend, or girlfriend. Approximately 50 percent of the domestic violence victims of both sexes were killed by their spouses, while 33 percent were killed by girlfriends or boyfriends.

Domestic violence homicides occur in all regions of the United States, and in the majority of these murders, the weapon used is a handgun. The national nonprofit Violence Policy Center, located in Washington, D.C., prepared a state-by-state ranking on women who were murdered in the year 2000 and found that, overwhelmingly, the perpetrator was a husband, boyfriend, or other close relative, rather than a stranger. The study found that in the year 2000, 1,689 women (86.7 percent of the total number of homicides of females) throughout the United States were killed by a man they knew, compared with 137 women (13.3 percent) who were killed by a male stranger. The states with the highest per capita number of women who were killed by men in 2000 are (in order of prevalence): Mississippi, Arizona, South Carolina,

Tennessee, Louisiana, North Carolina, Arkansas, New Mexico, Nevada, Oklahoma, Alabama, and Virginia.

Although most perpetrators of domestic violence homicides are males, a considerable number of women, following repeated acts of violence by their partner, lash out and kill their partners, sometimes accidentally or in self-defense. There has been much media coverage of battered women who were murdered by the batterer, with far less attention given to battered women who killed the abuser, were convicted, and are serving time in prison. In conducting the interviews with the 501 women that form the basis for this book, we interviewed a subsample of formerly battered women who had been convicted of killing their husband, partner, or ex-partner. All of the women who had killed the abuser and who were interviewed as part of this research project were incarcerated at a women's prison at the time of the interview. Convicted of murder or manslaughter and other charges, these women were sentenced to an average of 12 years in prison. Some of these women will probably be released on parole before serving their full sentence.

Often a specific death threat was made against their lives by their abusive partners in the 24 hours prior to the homicide, and sometimes the death threat occurred just prior to the homicide. Some batterers were very specific about their threats to kill their female partners, naming the time, lethal method, and location. Some of the deaths of the abusive men seemed to be accidental, or in self-defense, as the man and woman were fighting over a weapon; other deaths were caused by impulsive, violent, retaliatory acts on the part of the women.

Many of the women indicated that they were suffering from posttraumatic stress disorder (PTSD) symptoms, which include nightmares, sleep disturbances, flashbacks, and intrusive thoughts. The overwhelming majority of the battered women in our lethal domestic violence category were more likely than the women in the other categories to have a history of substance abuse and to have engaged in mutual combat in which they fought back physically rather than reacting passively to the man's brutal beatings. These women also were more likely to be high school dropouts and to have erratic work histories in low-paying jobs.

Of the 105 women in the study who killed their abusive husband or partners, this chapter features the experiences of three women—*Alicia*, *Tamika*, and *Lucinda*. They described painful childhoods; abuse of alcohol and other drugs, often by both the woman and her partner; overwhelming anger; and mutual combat among both partners that resulted in lethal violence in which the woman who had been brutally victimized killed the abuser. Their interviews revealed frequent use of hallucinogenic drugs such as methampheta-mine, LSD (acid), cocaine or crack, or PCP (angel dust), and a much higher occurrence of attempted suicide than the women in the other groups. The fi-nal commonality among this group of women was their incarceration at the same prison.

■ Background

Alicia was a 28-year-old Caucasian woman who was surprisingly attractive, considering that she had been incarcerated for six years at the state women's prison. She endured physical and emotional abuse from her mother and brother while growing up. Alicia, like many other abused women, blamed al-cohol and drugs for her husband's violent actions. But Alicia was also a sub-stance abuser; her husband's violent rages, combined with the mutual volatil-ity when both partners were taking drugs, led to the murder. Alicia said that she killed her husband one month after their one-year anniversary, and she admits that she had used a large amount of cocaine the night of the murder. In sharp contrast to the majority of the women in this category, Alicia had gone to college for one year, but then dropped out and got married at age 20. Prior to the murder, she was working as a real-estate agent.

Tamika, a 33-year-old African American woman, was missing a front tooth, the result of having been punched in the mouth by the batterer. She also had a pronounced overbite, as her family had been unable to afford or-thodontia for her when she was a teenager. Tamika's father had been in and out of prison for most of her childhood and adolescence, and her mother was constantly sick. She was one of six children; her two older brothers had mo-lested her on separate occasions, and she had been verbally abused by her grandfather and laughed at by her grandmother.

Lucinda was 36 years old and of Latin descent. When she was a child, her parents were always fighting, and the arguments were so loud and violent that the neighbors regularly called the police. After Lucinda and her husband were married, his problems with alcohol became more apparent. He became an al-coholic, and his violent rages usually occurred whenever he had been drink-ing. At one point, he promised to stop drinking; he even joined Alcoholics Anonymous for a short time, but after a couple of months he stopped going to meetings and resumed his old drinking habits.

■ Critical Incidents during Childhood and Adolescence

As was common for many women in our study, these women typically endured physical, emotional, and sexual abuse as children or adolescents. Family stressors included poor or neglectful parenting, substance abuse, illness, and family violence.

Unlike many of the other women in this group, *Alicia* reported having many fond memories from her childhood, particularly of her father, who taught her to ski, fish, and swim. She also reported positive memories of taking ballet classes and going to the ballet and symphony with her father. But Alicia also had some terrible memories of being abused by her mother and raped by a girlfriend's older brother:

> I was abused by my mother and it was ongoing, physical, mental, and emotional. I don't remember when it started, probably when I was very young. As a teenager, I was raped by my girlfriend's brother. We were at a party together, and I was involved with drugs by then. Lots of bad incidents with drugs. I never told anyone about the rape for a long time.

As an adolescent, Alicia rebelled through experimenting with drugs ranging from downers to speed—"everything except crack." When she drank, she did so excessively, and she often blacked out. Her parents required her go to an addiction treatment program, but after leaving the program, she started using drugs again.

Tamika recounted a very traumatic childhood with repeated incidents of sexual abuse. She removed her glasses to rub her eyes as she tried to remember how old she was when her father went to prison:

> My father went to prison when I was seven. My mother and father used to argue all the time. My father was a thief. He used to rob things. I came across a lot of money one day, thousands of dollars that were hidden. A couple of days later, the police came and took him away. Right after my father was taken away, they put my mother away in a hospital. She had six kids.

Tamika also described the sexual abuse she sustained from her brothers while she was young:

> I was sexually abused by my brothers. First, it was my one brother that was one year older than me. He only did it once. I was seven or eight. I don't think it was sex, but it was something. Him and his friends did stupid things to me like that. Then my oldest brother sexually abused me and beat me for a long time. My grandmother saw him fondling

me when I was 12. Then it stopped. I didn't really know what was
going on. I knew it was wrong. There was no one to tell. For a while, I
couldn't remember—you block it out.

Tamika found that alcohol could numb the pain of her tumultuous and
violent childhood, and she began drinking heavily in junior high school. She
then dropped out of school after she was assaulted by three men:

> I started drinking and having blackouts and not remembering things.
> In high school, I was assaulted by three men. They tried to rape me,
> but I got away. That's why I stopped going to school. I wanted to go to
> night school, so I did after I became pregnant by a boyfriend.

The emotional pain was so overwhelming that during her adolescence,
Tamika tried to commit suicide three times:

> When I was 14, I took pills—sleeping pills, my grandmother's. My
> grandfather punished me because a guy came to the door. My grandfa-
> ther called me a whore and punished me. He sent me to my room. I
> felt paranoid at the time. I told my grandmother I was going to kill
> myself. She said, "Go ahead," and laughed. I took the pills, about 21 of
> them, in my bedroom with a sip of wine. I remember going into the
> kitchen to the refrigerator's bottom shelf to eat a tomato and I fell. My
> brother told me later that he saw me and took me downstairs and
> stuck a toothbrush down my throat so I would throw up. He said he
> was holding me upside-down by my feet, and he was shaking me. I
> threw up. He saw the pills, and then he called the ambulance. When I
> woke up, my grandmother, uncle, and the police were in the hospital.
> They had pumped my stomach and everything.

The second time, Tamika was at a party where everyone was doing a lot
of drinking. When some of the guys tried to force themselves on her, she attempted suicide:

> Another time, I tried to cut my wrists at a party. All of the guys were
> trying to force me to do stuff against my will. I told them I would kill
> myself and I locked myself in the bathroom. They kicked the door
> in to get me out of the bathroom so I wouldn't hurt myself. I was
> about 17.

The third suicide attempt occurred when Tamika was 18 years old, and a former boyfriend, the father of her young daughter, took the little girl away:

> I was 18. My daughter's father took my daughter away from me. We
> were living together, and I cheated on him. I was working and had a

babysitter. He came while the babysitter was there and took my daughter and kept her. I stayed in a room for four months because I was so depressed. During those four months I tried to commit suicide. My grandmother was ill and had cancer. I was taking Percocet and all her medication. I was locked in the bathroom and took a few pills. She was outside the door. I told her I would kill myself if she didn't get my baby back.

■ First Incident

The initial incidents of violence recounted by these women were very comparable to the first signs of abuse reported by the women in the other categories. Nothing in these early recollections foreshadowed the lethal violence that would ultimately take place.

Alicia recalled that the first violent incident had occurred when her boyfriend was drunk:

> It happened before we got married. He was angry about something and threw a lamp against the wall. It didn't hit me, but it was frightening. Once he sobered up, he was very apologetic. Alcohol always triggered his violence.

Tamika described the first time she was threatened; even though the abuse in this incident was verbal, the implications were frightening enough:

> He has a nasty mouth, and one time we were arguing and it got real nasty—it was when I caught him in a lie. He had taken our state income tax check and forged my name on it. I found it in his pocket. I was really mad, and I told him I was thinking of going to Florida, and he said, "If you ever left the state with our daughter, I'll kill you."

Lucinda described one of the first times her husband hit her:

> I was slapped, but why I can't remember. We were outside the 7-11 store. I always thought it was never his fault. He had an alcohol problem, and it happened after he was drinking. He always made me think it was my fault. I did something to make it happen. I'd look at someone, or the dinner burned, or I talked to a guy. I couldn't look at a man while I was talking to him. It would happen over anything.

■ Escalation of the Batterer's Assaults, Including Death Threats

Alicia spoke of her husband's drinking problem as a catalyst for the violent rages that occurred with increasing frequency, even though they were married only a year prior to the murder:

> Alcohol always triggered it. He was an alcoholic. If he didn't use me as a punching bag, he would destroy personal property. I had bruises all over my body, black eyes, and choke marks. Sometimes I would fight back, and it would only make it worse.

Alicia also suffered a miscarriage after she fell down the stairs when her husband was chasing her. Her husband's violence was so extreme that she feared he was going to murder her:

> He tried to kill me. I was late coming home from work, and he called me a liar, this, that, and the other thing. He was drunk and drugged out. I was at a girlfriend's house, having dinner, and he pounded on the door. I came outside to see what he wanted, and he came after me and told me he was going to kill me, and when I saw the knife I ran. He was coming right at me, and he chased me down the street. My friends had already called the cops, and the cops came and he took off. I saw him the next day and he took off. I tried to talk to him and asked him why he tried to kill me. He has a history of calling me from time to time and leaving messages that he's gonna do this to me or that to me.

The injuries Alicia sustained from the beatings were so severe that she needed to go to the emergency room on numerous occasions. Although at least some of the E.R. staff probably suspected that Alicia had been beaten by her husband, she refused to discuss what had actually taken place:

> When I went to the emergency room, they would stitch me up and send me home. I would always make up a lie so they didn't know. My husband took me to the hospital a few times and was worried about me, so it looked good for him. One time a nurse questioned me about possible abuse, and I wouldn't answer any questions, so she stopped asking.

On one occasion, Alicia did get a temporary restraining order against her husband, but he ordered her to drop the restraining order with the threat that if she didn't, "they were going to find my body washed up on the beach." Alicia complied with his demands.

Tamika said that her husband was using drugs, which was the trigger for his violence. She also said that she wanted to leave him because he was so violent, but he did not want her to leave. Sadly, she never had the courage to take her children and flee to a shelter for battered women:

> We used to fight over drugs. Drugs triggered the abuse. I wanted to leave him, and he would always try to stop me from leaving. I was the type of person [who] wouldn't allow a man to hit me. I called the police on a lot of occasions. He was robbing money from me. I had my children. That's another reason why we used to fight. He used to want to have sex in front of the kids. I didn't want to. I thought it was wrong. The kids used to mimic us—it was terrible.

These are *Lucinda's* recollections of how her husband's assaults against her escalated as his problems with alcohol worsened:

> He was drinking more and more, and he was hitting me more often. I had black eyes. He hit or punched me. We were in the bathroom at his mother's at the time. I was pregnant and I ran down the street barefoot and called the police. They came an hour later. He insulted me and called me names—I was stupid or a bad mother. His mother did nothing.

Lucinda described how she actually did leave her husband—for a while. She and her husband had been living in another state, and, after a brutal assault, she asked her mother for the money to come back to live with her:

> One time after he beat me, I called 911 and the police came and I said to arrest him. He told them I was nuts 'cause I was on pills from the doctor. The house was a mess. I had the baby. The police officer believed me and arrested him. One officer asked me if I had anywhere to go, so I said I was from New Jersey. He advised me to go back to New Jersey with the money I had. He said it would happen again. My daughter was just six months old. So I called my mother and told her, and she wired me some money. My girlfriend brought me to get the money, and I bought a ticket and planned to leave the next morning. I had $450 and the ticket was $256. He called me and told me to drop the charges while I was packing to leave. I told him "No." He said, "I love you." He kept calling and finally I stopped answering, and I took my daughter and went back to live with my mother.

Lucinda's husband followed her back to New Jersey from the West Coast, and she allowed him to live with her at her mother's home. He continued to make death threats:

He told me he'd kill me on the evening of our next anniversary. He said, "When we go out to celebrate our next anniversary, you'll be dead if you even look at anyone else." He always got that way—his jealousy got the best of him. But I was really scared, since our anniversary was less than one month away.

■ Worst Incident

Each woman recounted her story of the worst incident with obvious emotion; some broke down.

Alicia recalled her husband's most violent abuse of her:

> We were drinking at a bar. The beating lasted about 25 minutes. He beat me with a barstool. I had bruises from head to toe. He also destroyed the house. We had a .22 caliber, which I took and threw into the bay because I was afraid he would kill me with it.

Immediately after this brutal assault, Alicia stayed with a girlfriend for four days. The friend begged her to not go back to her husband and cautioned her: "Somebody is going to end up dead." But Alicia said she felt she had to return to her abusive husband because "it was kind of an obsession. I wasn't really in love, but I didn't know that at the time." Although Alicia had gotten rid of one gun, there were two other guns in the house—a .357-caliber Magnum and a .44 handgun.

Tamika's tumultuous relationship with her husband was also characterized by some incidents in which she hit him back, as well as occasions on which she started the hitting, and he retaliated with extreme violence. As her husband was much bigger and stronger, she usually suffered injuries that were far more severe than his. Tamika recalled some instances in which she was the aggressor. On one occasion, she was infuriated because he was smoking crack, and she grabbed a knife from the kitchen drawer. "I yelled at him, 'You want to die? I'll do it for you.' I had the knife and he tried to grab it, and I pulled it away and slashed his hands."

Tamika recalled that the worst incident was incited by an argument that started when she became furious that her husband had used their rent money to buy drugs, and ended when they were fighting over his gun, and she shot and killed him:

> It was over drugs, when he took the rent money to buy drugs. I hid the money and he took it. I started hitting him, and then he started beating me. He held me down to keep me from hitting him. When I hit

him, he started hitting me and kicking and slapping me. He beat me bad as I was trying to leave. He was pounding my face like hamburger meat, screaming "F-you bitch." I think he was trying to stop me from going upstairs to call the police. Then he went for his gun and said he was going to kill me, but I got to it first.

As they were fighting for control of the gun, Tamika shot her husband and killed him.

Lucinda described the incident that culminated in her accidentally killing her husband with a knife:

I moved in with my mom. He came back to New Jersey after 10 months. I had another baby during this time. He moved into my mother's house and got a job. I told him to move out 'cause the arguments started again. He was physically abusive when my mom wasn't around. He was still drinking, and we were fighting. I don't remember the exact details of the incident. A guy came over to visit my brother, and my husband called me to the door and said, "Someone is here to see you," and the guy said he was looking for my brother. The guy left, and we started arguing about it. He was drinking that day. I told him to get out and he wouldn't. Somehow or another I picked up a knife, and he kept coming towards me, and I hit him with the knife. I remember doing it once, but the police report said three times. He fell to the floor, and there was blood all over. I tried to stop the bleeding and he was talking to me. So then I grabbed the phone and couldn't dial. I ran to the neighbor. They called the police. He went to the hospital, and I went to the police station, and I gave a statement to try to protect him. I don't know why. They charged me with murder one and a weapons charge.

■ Confined to Prison

Alicia described how, after she realized that she had killed her abusive husband, her despair led to an attempt to kill herself:

I have only vague recollections of what happened after I killed him. I went to my friend's house, and I locked myself in my friend's bathroom and cut myself real bad. I wanted to die. The paramedics came and took me to the hospital. I was in surgery for several hours and had over 70 stitches.

Alicia had fired a single shot at her husband, which killed him. She was charged with first-degree murder, but the private attorney hired by her father negotiated a plea bargain in which Alicia pled guilty to a reduced charge of aggravated manslaughter. She was sentenced to seven years in prison. Alicia's concluding words demonstrated how she had matured during her incarceration:

> The most difficult part about being in prison is the culture shock, mixing of personalities, overcrowding, and the loneliness. The noise level is unbearable. It is degrading and humiliating. The prison environment strips away one's self-esteem. You are given a lot of time to think and reevaluate your life. There is nothing here—unless you're bright enough and lucky enough to look inside yourself and find something good.

Alicia had been clean (no alcohol or drugs) for the six years of her incarceration. She was planning to return to college to pursue a degree in psychology after her release from prison.

The jury found *Tamika* guilty of second-degree murder. The public defender tried to have her acquitted, arguing that it was self-defense. He presented some graphic photos, taken by the hospital emergency room staff, showing the severe domestic violence injuries that Tamika had sustained during the course of their marriage. The prosecuting attorney pointed out that Tamika had aggravated the volatile situation by being physically combative with her husband on numerous occasions and sometimes causing him serious injury, such as the time she cut his hand with a knife. The jury weighed the aggravating factors against the mitigating factors; their verdict was that Tamika's husband was the primary aggressor more often and, on balance, he was responsible for the most serious injuries, including an occasion on which he had broken her jaw. The judge sentenced Tamika to serve 10 to 15 years in the women's prison.

Lucinda was initially charged with first-degree murder and a weapons charge. The prosecutor then reduced the charge to aggravated manslaughter as part of a plea agreement. Lucinda was poor and did not have the benefit of a private attorney, and her public defender urged her to accept a plea bargain of a 20-year flat sentence, to which she agreed. As a result, the earliest time she could be released was after 18 years of incarceration.

The women in this category endured repeated violent assaults from the batterers who were usually alcoholics or drug abusers, or both, and who had repeatedly brutalized their wives and threatened to kill them. Many of these women also had their own history of abusing drugs or alcohol, and many fought back in very violent ways. Some of the women had terrifying nightmares and sleep disturbances, and attempted to commit suicide. The women were traumatized by the emotional and physical violence, and angry at being repeatedly brutalized by the batterer. This seemed to be a volatile combination that spelled disaster for all of the women in this category. Sadly, none of these women sought help from a shelter for battered women. They did not want to allow themselves to be viewed as "victims" of domestic violence who needed help from professionals to end the relationship in a safe manner.

Although many women in short-term and intermediate abusive relationships do get out, there are some who are not able to leave the batterer. A small percentage of these women do become homicide victims.

■ The Exceptions: Two Relatively Short-Term Abuse Cases That Turned Deadly

☐ The Murder of 22-Year-Old Cindy Ann Nannay

This case is an example of a short-term abusive relationship in which the victim was murdered at her college. Even though this case was not part of the study, we include it here as a cautionary note on the unpredictability and volatility of current and former abusive dating relationships. This case is summarized from news stories about a tragedy that occurred in Glassboro, N.J. on August 12, 1996, when Cindy Ann Nannay, a 22-year-old student at Rowan College, was murdered by her former boyfriend, 28-year-old Scott Lonabaugh, who then killed himself. Cindy and Scott had been living together, and there was a history of violence perpetrated by Scott. The police had been summoned to their residence because of domestic violence on at least one occasion; in April 1996, Scott was threatening Cindy with a knife when the police arrived. Following this harrowing incident, Cindy obtained a restraining order against Scott, but subsequently she requested that the restraining order and all charges against him be dropped. The case was dismissed, and they continued their living arrangements. At the end of July 1996, Cindy finally had the strength to end the relationship with Scott, and she moved out of his residence. On August 9, Scott purchased a 12-gauge shotgun from a local sporting goods store. (He filled in all of the required paperwork and was able to obtain the shotgun because he answered some of the questions falsely.) Then, on August 12, Scott made arrangements to see Cindy at the college radio station where she worked part-time, under the pretext of returning some of her personal belongings that she had left at his apartment. Cindy asked the radio station manager to stand outside the radio station building, as protection in case Scott tried to hit her. As Cindy was retrieving her belongings from Scott's car, he pulled out the shotgun from his trunk and murdered her. Scott then used the gun to kill himself.

☐ The Murder of 29-Year-Old Jodi M.

Excerpts follow from an article published in the *Asbury Park Press* on March 12, 1999, describing an accountant, Robert Giordano, age 32, who was arrested for the murder of his girlfriend, Jodi M., age 29, in Monmouth County, New Jersey. The article provides a heart-wrenching depiction of lethal violence in which Giordano brutally murdered his girlfriend just two days after they started living together. At the time of the murder, Giordano had served two years of a five-year probation for terroristic threats and attempted strangulation of a previous girlfriend. But his new girlfriend was unaware of his violent history. According to the Middlesex County Criminal Court records in New Brunswick, Robert Giordano suffered from major depression, and the mandated conditions of his probation were that he be medication-compliant to combat his depression and avoid alcohol.

> Giordano . . . moved in with [Jodi] . . . two days before her body was discovered behind a baseball field. . . . [Jodi], who was 5 feet 6 inches tall and weighed 130 pounds, was beaten to death, according to autopsy reports. Giordano, 6 feet 5 inches and 250 pounds, drove to Neptune police headquarters Tuesday, started a conversation with two policemen and was arrested. [Jodi's] body was discovered about 20 minutes later.

Two years earlier Giordono had been charged with aggravated assault, terroristic threats, and criminal restraint following a violent, life-threatening attack on his previous girlfriend, Lisa. As a result of a plea bargain agreement, however, Giordono pled guilty to making terroristic threats, and the other two charges were dismissed. The specifics of his earlier assault against Lisa were as follows:

> In her complaint to police, [Lisa] said Giordano had tried to strangle her with a scarf, attacked her a second time with his hands and threatened her and family members in days previous to the attack. She and Giordano had been dating but the relationship had ended before the attacks occurred, records show.
>
> [Lisa] said she survived the scarf attack by biting his finger. Subsequently, she told authorities, she waited for what she called a psychiatric episode to pass.

The news article concludes by saying that in 1997 there had been 50 domestic violence murders in New Jersey.

The violence perpetrated against the two women just described was not part of the study of 501 women who were interviewed for this book. These two cases are cited specifically because they are exceptions to the domestic violence continuum that forms the basis for this book, and as such, illustrate an important limitation to the survey results and the continuum. The continuum is based on the responses from 501 women and the general patterns of abuse that were evident from the experiences they reported. There is no predictive certainty when trying to comprehend human behavior and acts of violence.

The study results showed that—among those women who were interviewed—when violence began in a dating relationship, it began with the man slapping or shoving the woman, and over time, it escalated to more severe (but not lethal) violence. Typically, the women who ended the dating relationship at the earliest signs of physical abuse suffered less severe injuries than the women who lived with the abuser, or married him.

In the aforementioned case in which Robert Giordano murdered Jodi, however, they had just started to live together, and even if there had been some previous violence in their relationship (which was not discussed in the newspaper article), one would never have anticipated such a horrendous outcome. There were some extenuating circumstances that led to this tragedy. First, Robert Giordano had a criminal history of violence with a previous girlfriend that was so severe that he had been arrested (and then placed on probation). Second, he had a diagnosed mental health disorder for which he was required to take medication and to abstain from drinking alcoholic beverages. Although the news article did not mention whether he had violated that aspect of his probation, given the severity of his assault on his previous girlfriend, it is reasonable to hypothesize that he may well have violated the terms of his probation either by not taking the prescribed medication or by becoming intoxicated.

There is no "safe" level of violence and no guaranteed way to predict whether a boyfriend, partner, or husband will become violent—even if it is early in a dating relationship, and even if the man has never hit the woman previously. There are, however, many "warning signs" that are often linked to violent behavior, as listed in chapter 1, and they should be a helpful guide for women who are ready to insist on zero tolerance for violence in their relationships. The next chapter applies one of the case-studies to our step-by-step safety plan and survival guide for women in abusive relationships.

7

A Step-by-Step Individualized Safety Plan

Our study and others have documented the elevated risk of severe and life-threatening injuries to women when they begin the process of permanently leaving their abusive partner. As noted in chapter 1, we recommend that women in abusive relationships proceed with caution and be alert to the overt as well as the subtle cues and warning signs of danger and an escalation of violence. This chapter suggests planning ahead and using a strategic safety plan. An illustration follows of how one of the women in our study used a safety plan.

Sally, a 25-year-old administrative assistant with one five-year-old child, had been repeatedly abused by her husband, Carl, during a four-year-period. As a result of the repetitive abuse and her own lack of self-esteem, Sally experienced an inability to concentrate, anxiety, nightmares, and depression. The turning point for Sally occurred when Carl came home drunk from his job as a construction worker, and broke her jaw, during a violent rage. Soon after, he passed out in a drunken stupor; Sally took her daughter and drove to the emergency room for treatment. Sally finally decided that she had to leave her husband, and she began to implement the safety plan she had received from a domestic violence hotline.

Four weeks earlier, following Carl's previous drunken attack, he had promised that he would stop drinking and go to AA meetings. Sally had decided to give Carl one last chance to stay sober, since his violence only erupted when he had been drinking. Sally knew, however, that in the past Carl had told her that the drinking would stop, but within a few weeks, he had once again returned to stopping off at the bar on his way home from work. To protect herself if Carl reneged on his promise, Sally had prepared the following safety plan:

1. Sally left the house, with her purse and her daughter, and drove to the emergency room. While en route to the hospital, she called her best friend, Judy, from her cell phone and asked her to meet them at the hospital. Sally also asked Judy to bring all of the emergency items that Judy had been keeping for her — two small suitcases with clothing, a few toys for her daughter, her marriage license, her daughter's birth certificate, and extra cash. At the emergency room, the social worker took photographs of Sally's injuries, emergency medical treatment was provided, and the hospital contacted the police and a battered women's shelter. Sally also signed release forms so that the police, county prosecutor, and her attorney could obtain medical records relatively quickly.

2. When Sally was medically cleared to leave the E.R., the domestic violence advocate from the battered women's shelter accompanied her and the little girl to the police station to get a copy of a temporary restraining order. After leaving the police station, Sally and her daughter were housed at a shelter for battered women.

For obvious reasons, the locations of most battered women's shelters are highly confidential, and extensive efforts are made to prevent batterers from learning the location.

Some examples of how shelters for battered women generally react to domestic violence crises such as Sally's:

The House of Ruth in Alabama immediately gives the client food and other physical necessities. Upon entering the shelter, she is asked if she would prefer talking about her ordeal or getting some sleep and talking the next day. The complete intake is handled the next day, after the client has had a chance to rest. When the client is ready, the staff explains the options and the consequences of her choices. The staff helps the client to recognize her own feelings, supports her decisions, provides advocacy, and assists her in obtaining her goals.

The Domestic Violence shelter in Oregon offers food, blankets, and a room in which to sleep to women who have been abused and their children. The next day, a staff member sets up a one-on-one meeting to finish the paperwork and let the client debrief. It is important to tell her that she is brave and strong to have left the batterer. The shelter staff listens to her story without judging her and lets her tell her story in her own words as many times as she needs to. If she requests, they give her information on the cycle of violence, tell her that she is not crazy, provide her with information on resources, and offer to help her get through barriers to services.

The Family Crisis Center of Baltimore County, Maryland, conducts a crisis intake in which the staff assesses the nature and intensity of the crisis. They provide shelter for up to 31 days. The shelter provides counseling and makes referrals to appropriate agencies, including legal aid. This shelter utilizes the following techniques in order to empower the client: (1) Take slow steps. (2) Make the client aware of the judicial system. (3) Encourage her to look at all options. (4) Set up regular counseling sessions while at the crisis shelter. (5) Encourage the client to design, with the help of staff members, emergency plans in case she decides to return to the abuser after leaving the shelter. The philosophy is that the shelter staff cannot make anyone do anything that she is not ready to do.

Horizon House Shelter for Women in Pennsylvania also provides for assistance to the children. The staff inquires about possible injuries to the children. They work to reassure the children about being in a strange place by involving them in selecting their bed and toys and showing them the play area and, for school-age children, the classroom where individual and group instruction takes place.

Unity House in upstate New York also transports abused women with mental health problems to the local community mental health clinic, where clinical social workers responsive to survivors of domestic violence provide individual treatment. Unity House helps the woman find an attorney who is knowledgeable about and experienced in domestic violence to explore custody, visitation, and divorce provisions that will protect her and her children. It is extremely important for attorneys to understand the dynamics of domestic violence, how to assess lethality and severity, how to present evidence of domestic violence to the court, and how to advocate for reasonable financial support and custody of the children.

Every individual in an abusive dating, cohabiting, or marital relationship (as well as those who recently ended an abusive relationship) should create a personalized safety plan. It is important to plan ahead so that when the woman makes the decision to leave the abusive partner, she does it as safely and expeditiously as possible. All too often the man's anger and violent outbursts escalate when his wife or girlfriend tries to leave the abusive relationship, file for divorce, or show signs of independence. As the abusive male may then become desperate and more volatile, it is critically important for the woman to develop a safety plan ready for quick mobilization.

Once a violent incident has occurred in the relationship, the battering is highly likely to reoccur. The research study discussed in this book demonstrates that the longer a woman stays in an abusive relationship, the greater the likelihood that she will experience more severe and possibly more frequent physical abuse.

■ **Step-by-Step Safety Plan and Survival Kit**

There are a number of planning strategies and actions that an abused woman can put in place so that she and her children do not have to be battered again. If you are counseling a woman who has been abused, use this list to instruct her in steps she must take.

Contemplation, Planning, and Preparation

- Make a mental image of all escape routes, including front, back, and side exit doors, first-floor windows, garage exits, elevators, stairwells, and fire escapes in case you need to leave your apartment or house quickly.

- Become aware of the precursors and warning signs of an imminent attack such as drug and alcohol abuse; increased verbal abuse; anger, rage, and terroristic threats; recent breakup, separation, or divorce due to domestic violence; major depression or other mental illnesses; abuse of pets; suicidal or homicidal threats; and punching the wall, throwing objects, or destroying furniture.

- Keep your purse and an extra set of car keys ready and accessible for a quick exit, if necessary. Decide ahead of time whether your means of transportation will be a car (in which case you should have car keys, registration, and certificate of title), taxi, bus, or train, and make sure you have credit cards or cash to pay for transportation, food, and housing if necessary. If you are fearful of keeping these emergency items in your regular purse (or in an old purse), then consider hiding them in your house (as long as they are easy to get to in an emergency), outside your house, or with a trusted friend or neighbor.

- Prepare your children by teaching them how to dial 911 in case of another assault.

- Select a safe and secure place to go to such as the home of a trusted and nonjudgmental friend or relative, a motel, or an emergency shelter for battered women. The "safe place" should be one where the abuser will not be able to find you. Therefore, even if you are very friendly with the neighbor next door, that residence is not good as a long-term "safe place" because it is probably the first place the batterer would search for you. (However, the neighbor's home may be helpful in an emergency as a place to wait for a few minutes until the police arrive.)

- Have the phone numbers of the following resources easily accessible in case you need emergency transportation to escape from the batterer: police (911), domestic violence detective division, a victim assistance program, a battered women's shelter, and a crisis intervention hotline.

- Select a code word to use with your children, neighbors, or close relatives when you need them to call the police for you.

- Keep your order of protection (temporary or permanent restraining order) with you at all times. Notify all close friends, neighbors, relatives, coworkers, and clergy of the protective order. Make a duplicate copy of the order of protection and give it to a friend or relative for safekeeping, in the event that the batterer finds and destroys the original.

- Give a copy of the order of protection to the police department nearest to where you work if you work in a different county or city from where you live. In case you escape to another city or county, there usually is a county registry of protection orders through which all police departments can telephone to verify or get a copy of the order of protection.

- Immediately call police dispatch 911 for help if you have an order of protection and you hear or suspect that the batterer is outside your door or window, or if you are away from home and he is lurking in your vicinity.

During a Violent Incident

- If the abusive partner starts to yell at or threaten you, try to get to a room that is near the front or back door (not the bathroom or kitchen because of potential weapons such as razors and knives in these rooms).

- If possible, carry a small cell phone in your pocket at all times (not in a purse). If he is attacking you, and you are able to be out of his sight for a brief time, use the cell phone to call 911 police emergency. Some communities have a program that provides free cellular phones for battered women to use to contact the police. These phones are preprogrammed to "911" and can be used only to call the police. Usually, a woman would not be able to receive this type of cell phone unless she has an active order of protection. For further information on the availability of free cellular phones, contact your local police department or the toll-free National Domestic Violence Hotline at 1-800-799-SAFE (7233) or the National Coalition Against Domestic Violence at (303) 839-1852.

- Whenever you feel you are in imminent danger or after an assault has begun, try to leave as quickly as you can and use your cell phone, or go to a public place to call the police, a 24-hour domestic violence or crisis intervention hotline, or a battered women's shelter for help. An alternative is to go to a friend or relative's house or apartment and call for help from there.

- Use your code word so your children or next-door neighbor can call 911. An alternate method is having a whistle or (ADT) electronic pendant alarm. This type of pendant alarm is available in more than 200 cities across the United States. The woman wears this pendant around her neck, and if she is in danger from the batterer, she activates it by pushing the button on the pendant; it sends a silent alarm to ADT, which in turn notifies the police to respond immediately.

- If you are injured, even if the injuries appear to be relatively minor, go to your physician's office, a clinic, or hospital emergency room. Tell the nurse or doctor what happened and ask them to photograph your injuries for the records. Tell them also that you want to sign a waiver or release form so that the county prosecutor or your private attorney can obtain copies of the medical records relatively quickly when necessary.

- If possible, save evidence, including torn or bloody clothing, photographs of your injuries, and destruction of property. Be sure to get a copy of the police report and investigation and names and addresses of any witnesses (e.g., neighbors).

- Talk to someone about your options. There are always advocates to assist and support you in whatever decisions you make, for example, domestic violence advocates at the local battered women's shelter, victim advocates at the prosecutor's victim/witness assistance program, police-based crisis counselors or peer advocates, hospital emergency room social workers or nurses, and counselors at the local women's center that specialize in providing services to domestic violence and sexual assault victims.

■ Survival Kit

Instruct women in abusive relationships to do the following:

Have copies of the following important documents in a safe place (e.g., a bank safe deposit box—if it is in your own name, not jointly registered) or leave copies with a trusted friend or relative. If you decide to keep these items in a bank safe deposit box, select a secure and accessible place to keep the key. In some relationships, the man is so domineering and controlling that he keeps all of the important household documents locked away where you cannot get to them. If you cannot get access to some of the items listed here, that is okay. But it is essential that you keep track of your personal papers, such as your birth certificate and Social Security card. Find and make copies of the following items.

- Birth certificate
- Social Security card
- Driver's license
- Credit cards and ATM cards
- Children's birth certificate(s)
- Prepaid long-distance calling card
- Picture of your injuries from an earlier abusive incident as identification to serve court papers
- House deed, apartment lease, rental agreement or mortgage bill
- Income tax forms from last year
- Passport or green card
- Children's school records
- Pay stubs or unemployment insurance booklet
- Disability award letter, court support letter, or court statement of unpaid child support
- Insurance papers

- Medical records for all family members
- Separation agreements, divorce papers, custody papers
- Restraining orders
- Documents of joint ownership

If you have the time to activate a plan to leave the abuser, have ready a suitcase that contains essential clothing, medication and prescriptions, a checkbook, and cash. Include toiletries such as deodorant, toothpaste, and toothbrushes. Other important items are valuable jewelry, family pictures and keepsakes, address books, your children's favorite toys, and books. If possible, remove from the home any items that have special meaning for you or your children, including the family pet. Some of these items can be stored with a friend or relative. The reason for removal of items that have special meaning (e.g., a gift from your grandmother) is the possibility that when the batterer learns you have left, he may vent his anger on household objects that he knows were valuable to you. However, if your decision to leave is made hastily—due to a particularly violent attack—the most important action is to protect yourself (and your children) by leaving the abuser as quickly as possible. If you seek assistance from the police or a shelter for battered women, they will help you to retrieve your essential belongings later.

8

About the Study

A Typology on the Duration and Severity of Abuse

The purpose of this chapter is to inform mothers and fathers, daughters, other family members, clinicians, and other informed citizens about patterns of abuse in dating and intimate relationships. Our research-based typology of abused women can be used as a danger assessment tool in helping to prevent the vicious cycle in which (over a period of time) an initial slap or punch escalates into frequent and more severe injuries or death.

■ The Research Study

All of the women described in this typology participated in our study of 501 females in dating, cohabiting, and marital relationships. The first stage of the project involved completing the research proposal, and writing and revising a 38-page interview questionnaire. The revision was based on suggestions from 20 formerly battered women who participated in two focus groups. The research proposal and tentative interview schedule was submitted to the Rutgers University Committee on Research with Human Subjects and received approval at their next meeting. The second phase consisted of training the interviewers and conducting the in-depth interviews.* We obtained a volumi-

---

* The study design was a qualitative, exploratory survey design using a structured, standardized interview format. The nonrandom sample consisted of 501 battered women drawn from four different purposeful populations in New Jersey. Because the design sampled battered women in only one location (New Jersey) the study findings are not generalizable to the population of all battered women. The sample consisted of: Incarcerated battered women in a New Jersey state women's prison who had killed their partners,

nous amount of data during the next four years. After three more years of quantitative and qualitative analysis of the data and report writing the authors became more aware of the fact that violence against women can be viewed on a continuum. We learned that the women who had been abused could be grouped into five distinct types, based on the length of time they remained in the violent relationship and the frequency and severity of abuse.

One of the most significant findings of this study is that women with certain characteristics—self-reported psychological strengths, personality traits, and/or protective factors—did leave the batterer early in the relationship, usually after one to three abusive incidents while they were dating. Sadly, other groups of women remained in a violent relationship for many years, as the violence accelerated from an initial punch or slap to chronic beatings with serious injuries.

Identifying the level of an abusive relationship in the continuum may well provide important clues as to the likelihood that the woman will be able to extricate herself from the relationship more easily.

Some women who have been abused are able to permanently break off the dating, cohabitating, or marital relationship after one to three incidents of physical battering. These self-reliant women are usually in dating relationships in which they are not living with the abuser, and they have been socialized by their mothers to *not* tolerate even one instance of physical abuse. Other women—usually those who are married or living with the abuser—stay in the relationship because of their marriage vows, financial support, or because they think the children will suffer if the marriage ends. These women often endure intermittent physical abuse in which many months elapse with no violence at all but the periodic uncontrollable anger outbursts become increasingly violent over time, until the "last straw"—a severely abusive act (e.g., a broken jaw, a concussion). Sometimes the triggering incident that causes the woman to leave after so many years of violence is the batterer's finding an additional outlet for his rage and starting to physically abuse one or more of their children. These women then decide to obtain a restraining order and legal separation.

Still other abused women stay in the violent relationship for many years as it escalates in severity and chronicity. Many of these chronic victims origi-

---

N = 105; three suburban New Jersey police departments, N = 105; three battered women's shelters in New Jersey, N = 105; and a convenience sample of formerly abused women living in New Jersey, N = 186. Dr. Gloria Bonilla Santiago assisted the authors in gaining access to the first 105 women interviewed. Dr. Michael Camasso wrote the codebook and supervised the statistical analysis on all 501 cases.

nally stayed for a combination of reasons, including religious beliefs, for the sake of the children, the positives in the relationship (e.g., the husband is charming when he is not drinking), blaming themselves, and/or minimization of the intensity and frequency of the battering incidents. Typically and tragically, these extremely violent marriages do not end until the woman's injuries are so severe that she requires extensive hospitalization to heal the injuries; the batterer is incarcerated or placed in a long-term residential program for substance abusers; the batterer dies from cirrhosis of the liver or another terminal illness; or one of the partners is found dead.

■ The Need for a Typology

Despite the evidence that family violence is a frequent occurrence, few qualitative studies on battered women exist. While some researchers have examined woman-battering as a lower-class or pathological phenomenon, ours is the first qualitative study in which a large number of battered women describe critical incidents during childhood and adolescence, how they got into a abusive relationship, what took place, and how they ended it—if they were successful in leaving the batterer.

Common themes in the interviews were extracted. Examination of the self-reports led to the creation of a typology that distinguishes between the characteristics of the women who were hit by a boyfriend one, two, or three times versus women who were beaten repeatedly for many years. Being able to make such a distinction may enhance the clinician's understanding of the variety of ways in which battering relationships occur and endure. The typology ranges from short-term battering to chronic, long-term battering. The severity of the assaults ranges from less severe acts of violence such as a push, slap, or punch to very severe acts such as choking, blows to the head, stabbings, specific death threats, and attempted murder.

This typology may also be useful for women who have been in longer-term violent relationships. Many married women have successfully ended a violent relationship, even when the violence was endured for 20 or more years. However, these women should be forewarned that there are more complications when they are married, with children, and the violence has been ongoing. In these situations, women often rely on help from staff at a local battered women's shelter and an attorney, as well as their parents or friends; sometimes police assistance is also sought. (See chapter 10 and the glossary and for information on restraining orders and other types of contacts with the criminal justice system.)

■ Findings: Conceptualizing the Continuum

In this exploratory and qualitative study, we classify battering on a continuum according to five types: (1) short-term, (2) intermediate, (3) intermittent/long-term, (4) chronic, and (5) lethal. As shown in the table, the duration of battering varies within each category, as does the severity and number of assaults. Correlations between socioeconomic class and the type of battering pattern are also shown.

■ The Continuum

Level 1. Short-term

There were 94 women in the study who reported that after experiencing one to three incidents of violence from a boyfriend or partner in a period of a year of less, they ended the relationship. Most were high school or college students in a steady dating relationship; the overwhelming majority were not living with the abuser. Prior to the last straw, these women may have experienced as many as 5 to 10 instances of emotional abuse, harassment, and low-level abuse such as being slapped, grabbed, pushed by their shoulders or kicked in their leg. In retrospect, these abusive incidents were warning signs. But the "last straw" of clear violence could usually be classified in the moderate to serious range of severity, for example, pushing to the ground, throwing across the room, throwing heavy objects, choking or punches to the face, arms, and upper torso, with no broken bones, concussions, or permanent injuries. Most of these women were between 16 and 27 years old and ended the relationship with the help of a parent, older brother, and/or sometimes the police.

Level 2. Intermediate

The level and duration of battering of women in this category ranged from 3 to 15 incidents over a period ranging from several months to two years. The 104 battered women in this category were usually living with the abuser in either a cohabiting or marital relationship. None of the women in this level had children. Following a very severe battering incident, the women ended the relationship with the help of the police, a family member, or a friend. Many of the women had sustained terroristic death threats and/or severe injuries such as a broken jaw, stitches, broken ribs, and/or a concussion. These women often obtained a restraining order against the batterer and moved out to a safer residence.

Table 1. Continuum of Types of Woman-Battering Situations

	Short-Term (N = 94)	Intermediate (N = 104)	Intermittent Long-Term (N = 38)	Chronic and Predictable (N = 160)	Lethal (N = 105)
Duration	Less than 1 year	Several months to 2 years	5–40 years	5–35 years	8+ years
Type of Relationship	Dating	Cohabiting or married	Married with children	Married with children	Cohabiting or married
Severity	Mild to moderate, e.g., push, shove, sometimes severe beating	Moderate to severe, e.g., punch, kick, chokehold, or severe beating	Severe and intense violent episode without warning; long periods without violence, then another violent episode	Severe repetitive incidents; frequent, predictable pattern; violence often precipitated by alcohol or polydrug abuse	Violence escalates to homicide, precipitated by explicit death threats and life-threatening injuries
Number of Incidents	1–3 incidents	3–15 incidents	4–30 incidents	Usually several hundred violent acts per woman	Numerous violent and severe acts per woman
Socioeconomic	Usually middle class and steady dating relationship	Usually middle class and recently married or living together	Usually upper-middle or upper class, staying together for children or status/prestige of wealthy husband	Usually lower socioeconomic or middle class, often devout Catholic with school-age children at home; husband is blue-collar, skilled, or semiskilled.	Usually lower socioeconomic class; high long-term unemployment; limited education (majority of battered women usually suffers from PTSD and BWS)
	Woman leaves after first or second physically abusive act	Woman leaves due to bruises or injury	Woman stays until children grow up and leave home	Abuse continues until husband is arrested, is hospitalized, or dies	
	Caring support system, e.g., parents or police	Caring support system, e.g., new boyfriend or parents	No alternative support system		

Source: Roberts, A. R. (2002). Duration and Severity of Woman Battering: A Conceptual Model/Continuum. In A. R. Roberts (ed.). *Handbook of Domestic Violence Intervention Strategies* New York, N.Y.: Oxford University Press, pp. 64–79.

Level 3. Intermittent/Long-Term

The assaults are usually serious, and the duration of battering was 5–40 years. There may be periods of several months when the husband is nonviolent, but then, because of stress (e.g., his job, problems with the children), the husband vents his anger and frustration at his wife by beating her. Almost all of the 38 women in this category had children and were economically and socially dependent upon their husbands. In addition, many of the women were religious and would not divorce for that reason. They were nurturing and caring mothers and wanted to keep the family together for the sake of the children. These women did not want to go to the hospital for treatment of their injuries. When they went to their family physician for treatment, they were embarrassed or afraid to discuss what actually happened, and they made up a story such as having had a car accident or falling down the stairs.

Level 4. Chronic and Severe with a Regular Pattern

The duration of battering in this category was 5 to 35 years, with the severity of the violence increasing over the years. The 160 battered women who composed this category reported a discernable pattern of abuse during the recent past (e.g., every weekend, every other weekend, every Friday night, etc.). Many of the batterers (68 percent) had serious drinking problems, including blackouts. However, about three-fourths of them also assaulted their partners when they were sober. After many years, especially when the children are grown and out of the house, the battering has become more extreme and more predictable, and includes the use of weapons, forced sex, and generalized death threats. The injuries for these victims have been extensive and include sprains, fractures, broken bones, head injuries, and so on that require treatment in the hospital emergency room.

Level 4.5. Subset of Chronic with a Discernable Pattern—Mutual Combat

Twenty-four of the 160 level 4 cases fit the mutual combat subcategory. This category sometimes involves dual arrests, and sometimes the police arresting the partner who appears to have the lesser injuries. The level of violence is usually severe. The study identified two types of mutual combat. In the first type, the man initiated a violent act, such as punching the woman, and she retaliated (e.g., slapping or punching him back). He then retaliated even more violently by beating her severely. In the second type, typically the man and woman are having a heated verbal argument, and the woman becomes the aggressor by hitting the man or throwing an object at him. He then retaliates very violently, with the women sustaining a severe injury. Of the women in this category, there were cases in which both the female and the abusive male had a drug problem. A smaller number of women had a history of violent aggressive acts during adolescence, for example, using a knife against a peer or an adult. Generally, in level 4.5 there are severe injuries to one or both parties.

Level 5. Lethal Domestic Violence

The duration of the battering relationship in this category is generally 8 years or longer, although the range is 2 to 35 years. The majority of these women are usually in a common-law relationship (cohabiting for 7 years or longer), a marital relationship, or recently divorced. The overwhelming majority (59.2 percent) lack a high school education and the skills to earn a decent income on their own. Almost half (47.6 percent) of the homicidal battered women had been on public assistance for many years during the battering episodes.

The 105 women in this category began at level 2, and usually escalated to either level 4 or level 5 for several years, after which the death threats became more explicit and lethal. In addition, in a number of cases, the victim had finally left the abuser and obtained a restraining order, which he violated. Most of the women in this category suffered from sleep disturbances and recurring nightmares, acute stress reactions, depression, or PTSD, and some had attempted suicide. The most significant finding related to the homicidal battered woman is that the overwhelming majority (65.7 percent) of these women had received specific lethal death threats in which the batterer specified the method, time, and/or location of their demise.

■ Limitations of This Survey

The findings of this study of 501 formerly battered women cannot be generalized to all battered women since all interviews were conducted in one region of the United States. In addition, the information on the 501 violent men comes from secondary reports based solely on the women's perceptions and recollections. Thus, it is important to note that a small number of the women may have filtered or somewhat distorted memory recall. (To increase the validity of the women's self-reports, several questions were worded slightly differently to help jog the women's memories and test for consistency.)

This survey focused on domestic violence situations in which the man was the primary aggressor against a woman. Also included were some cases of mutual combat between spouses or partners, that is, during their domestic disputes, the man and woman hit each other, but the injury inflicted by the man on the woman was usually much more severe than vice versa.

The survey did not include cases of gay and lesbian domestic violence, as well as cases in which women were the primary abusers. These types of cases do exist, but there is a much larger prevalence of relationships in which the man violently abuses the woman partner.

An important limitation of this and most other studies of domestic violence relates to the unavailability of psychiatric and medical compliance histories for the 501 women and their abusive partners. Undiagnosed or untreated (i.e., not taking prescribed medications) psychiatric disorders and the abuse of alcohol or other illegal substances can combine to result in a very lethal assault—even when the couple has been dating a short time. In addition, most young women rarely know whether a new boyfriend has been abusive with previous girlfriends. Conversely, a man who had been violent in a previous dating relationship, due to an untreated psychiatric problem and/or alcoholism or drug abuse, who then receives the proper treatment (and continues to take prescribed medications), defies the usual path of escalating violence as time goes by.

■ Summary

Predicting both the pattern of duration and the severity of battering incidents within each pattern is among the most complex issues in forensic mental health and the social sciences. Nevertheless, the courts, mental health centers, family counseling centers, intensive outpatient clinics, day treatment and residential programs, public mental hospitals, and private psychiatric facilities rely on clinicians to advise judges in civil commitment, child custody, and criminal court cases.

Practice interventions can be geared to the type of abuse pattern detected. The short-term and intermediate patterns of abuse may be more amenable to crisis intervention, brief psychotherapy, support groups, and restraining orders. The prognosis for the chronic/long-term category, whether it be intermittent or a weekly pattern of battering, is much more guarded. The chronic recidivist cases are frequently put into a life-threatening situation. However, when there are specific death threats and a loaded handgun in the house, even the short-term and intermediate battering cases can also escalate to a code blue—life-and-death—situation.

In chronic cases, the human suffering, degradation, and emotional and physical pain sometimes ends in permanent injuries to the victim or the death of the batterer or the battered woman. At other times, the chronically battered woman temporarily escapes to a shelter, a relative's home, or the police precinct. In many of the chronic cases, the victim returns to the batterer or is dragged back to the violent home. Finally, a small but growing number of chronically battered women leave the batterer and stay free of violence because they are empowered through a support group and counseling, legal aid and advocacy, or other forms of therapeutic intervention.

It has been briefly noted earlier in this book that the current study included quantitative and qualitative analysis on over 200 variables. For purposes of this professional trade book, and to maximize readability, the authors limited most of the chapters to the qualitative findings presented through the voices and stories of the abused women. For further information on the quantitative findings and statistical analysis, the reader is referred to Albert R. Roberts (2002). "Comparative Analysis of Batterred Women in the Community with Battered Women in Prison for Killing their Intimate Partners," in A. R. Roberts, editor, *Handbook of Domestic Violence Intervention Strategies: Policies, Programs, and Legal Remedies* (New York: Oxford University Press, 49–63). The statistical analysis included calculating Pearson Correlation Coefficients, creating contingency tables and computing chi-squares, using multiple-regression analysis and most important, factorial design. The statistical analysis and development of the typology was aided by Dr. Michael Camasso's valuable technical assistance. [Professor Camasso teaches and does research at the Department of Agricultural Economics, Cook College, Rutgers University. He is also the lead statistician (Johnson and Johnson Foundation sponsored New Brunswick Tomorrow project) and is supervising a team of researchers in New Brunswick, New Jersey, to determine the best ways to control crime and improve the schools, social services, and neighborhoods in the area.] Both he and/or Dr. Roberts can be contacted through the following e-mail address: Prof.albertroberts@comcast.net.

II

Practical Guidelines and Survival Strategies

9

Roberts' Seven-Stage Crisis Intervention Protocol

Consistent with the urgent need among domestic violence survivors for timely intervention, many battered women's shelters and crisis intervention programs have 24-hour crisis hotlines. Dr. Roberts developed the Seven-Stage Crisis Intervention Model (see page 133) in 1991 to provide a sequential framework for intervening on behalf of persons in acute psychological and situational crisis. In this chapter, we apply this model to battered women. Research has indicated that battered women may be more motivated to end the marital or cohabiting relationship with the abusive partner near the crisis or post-crisis period, that is, while the violence is occurring or in its immediate aftermath. The important first step for the crisis worker who answers a call from a battered woman is to assess lethality and respond to the immediate safety needs of the caller. The protocol that follows provides structure and guidelines useful for applying crisis intervention techniques to battered women.

■ Stage 1: Assessing Lethality

Assessment in the model on page 133 is ongoing and critical to effective intervention at all stages, beginning with an assessment of the lethality and safety issues for the hotline caller. With victims of family violence, child abuse, rape, or aggravated assault, it is important to assess if the caller is in any current danger, and to consider future safety concerns in treatment planning and referral. With depressed or suicidal clients it is critical to assess the person's risk for attempts, plans, or means to harm himself or herself at the current time, as well as any previous history of suicidal ideations or attempts. In addition to determining lethality and the need for emergency intervention, it is crucial to maintain active communication with the client, either by phone or in person, while emergency procedures are being initiated.

To plan and conduct a thorough assessment, the crisis worker also needs to evaluate the following issues: (1) the severity of the crisis, (2) the client's current emotional state, (3) immediate psychosocial needs, and (4) the level of the client's current coping skills and resources. In the initial contact, assessment of the client's past or precrisis level of functioning and coping skills is useful; however, past history should not be a focus of assessment, unless it is directly related to the immediate traumatic event.

The goals of this stage are assessing and identifying critical areas of intervention, while also recognizing the hazardous event or trauma and acknowledging what has happened. At the same time, the crisis survivor becomes aware of his or her state of vulnerability and initial reactions to the crisis event. It is important that the crisis worker begin to establish a relationship based on respect for and acceptance of the caller or client, while also offering support, empathy, reassurance, and reinforcement that the client has survived and that help is available.

■ Stage 2: Establishing Rapport and Communication

Survivors of acute crisis episodes and trauma may question their own safety and vulnerability, and trust may be difficult for them to establish at this time. Therefore, active listening and empathic communication skills are essential to establishing rapport and engagement of the client. Even though the need for rapid engagement is essential, the crisis worker should try to let the client set the pace of treatment. Many battered women feel out of control or powerless, and should not be coerced, confronted, or forced into action until they have stabilized and dealt with the initial trauma reactions.

Battered women may require a positive future orientation, with an understanding that they can overcome current abuse, and hope that change can occur. During this stage, clients need unconditional support, positive regard, concern, and genuineness. Empathic communication skills such as minimal encouragers, reflection of thoughts and feelings, and active listening can reassure the client and help establish trust and rapport with the client. The crisis worker needs to be attentive to the tone and level of the verbal communications to help the client calm down or deescalate from the initial trauma reactions. It is also important to remember that delayed reactions or flat affect are common with abuse victims, and not assume that these types of reaction mean that the survivor is not in crisis.

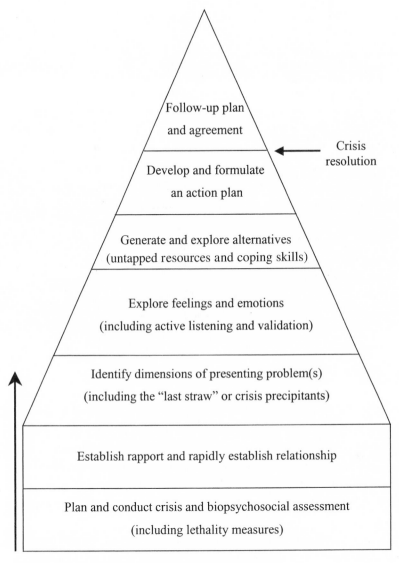

Crisis resolution

Follow-up plan and agreement

Develop and formulate an action plan

Generate and explore alternatives (untapped resources and coping skills)

Explore feelings and emotions (including active listening and validation)

Identify dimensions of presenting problem(s) (including the "last straw" or crisis precipitants)

Establish rapport and rapidly establish relationship

Plan and conduct crisis and biopsychosocial assessment (including lethality measures)

Roberts's Seven-Stage Crisis Intervention Model

■ **Stage 3: Identifying the Major Problems**

The crisis worker should help the client prioritize the most important problems or impacts by identifying these problems in terms of how they affect the survivor's current status. Encouraging the client to ventilate about the precipitating event can lead to problem identification, and some clients have an overwhelming need to talk about the specifics of the battering situation. This process enables the client to figure out the duration and severity of the event(s), which can facilitate emotional ventilation, while providing information that helps to assess and identify major problems for work.

Other crisis clients may be in denial or unable to verbalize their needs and feelings, so information may need to be obtained from collateral sources or friends. It is essential to use a systems framework during the assessment and identification of problems stages, since crisis situations may impact at all levels of practice. Family members and relatives may be important to intervention planning in supportive roles or to ensure the client's safety. However, they may be experiencing their own reactions to the crisis situation, and this should be taken into consideration in contracting and implementing the intervention plan.

The crisis worker must ensure that the client system is not overwhelmed during this stage, and the focus should be on the most immediate and safety issues needing intervention at this time. The first priority in this stage is meeting the basic needs of emotional and physical health and safety. After these have stabilized, other problems can then be addressed.

■ Stage 4: Dealing with Feelings and Providing Support

It is critical that the crisis worker demonstrate empathy and an anchored understanding of the survivor's experience, so that her or his symptoms and reactions are normalized and can be viewed as functional strategies for survival. Many victims blame themselves, and it is important to help the client accept that being a victim is not one's fault. Validation and reassurance are especially useful in this stage because survivors may be experiencing confusing and conflicting feelings.

Many clients follow the grief process when expressing and ventilating their emotions. First, survivors may be in denial about the extent of their emotional reactions and may try to avoid dealing with them in hopes that they will subside. They may be in shock and not be able to access their feelings immediately. However, significant delays in expression and ventilation of feelings can be harmful to the client in processing and resolving the trauma.

Some clients will express anger and rage about the situation and its effects, which can be healthy, as long as the client does not escalate out of control. Helping the client calm down or attending to physiological reactions such as hyperventilation are important activities for the crisis worker in this situation. Other clients may express their grief and sadness by crying or moaning, and the crisis worker needs to allow time and space for this reaction, without pressuring the client to move along too quickly. Catharsis and ventilation are critical to healthy coping, and throughout this process, the crisis worker must recognize and support the client's courage in facing and dealing with these emotional reactions and issues. The crisis worker must also be self-aware of his or her own emotional reactions and level of comfort in helping the client through this stage.

◼ Stage 5: Exploring Possible Alternatives

In this stage, effective crisis workers help clients recognize and explore a variety of alternatives, such as (1) situational supports, which are people or resources that can be helpful to the client in meeting needs and resolving crisis-related problems; (2) coping skills, which are behaviors or strategies that promote adaptive responses and help the client reach a precrisis level of functioning; and (3) positive and rational thinking patterns, which can lessen the client's levels of anxiety and stress.

The crisis worker can facilitate healthy coping skills by identifying client strengths and resources. Many crisis survivors feel they do not have a lot of choices, and the crisis worker needs to be familiar with both formal and informal community services to provide referrals. For example, working with a battered woman often requires relocation to a safe place for her and the children. The client may not have the personal resources or financial ability to move out of the home, and the crisis worker needs to be informed about the possible alternatives, which could include a shelter program, a host home or safe home, a protective order, traveler's aid, or other emergency housing services.

The crisis worker may need to be more active, directive, and confrontive in this stage, if the client has unrealistic expectations or inappropriate coping skills and strategies. The crisis worker should remember that clients are still distressed and in disequilibrium at this stage, and professional expertise and guidance could be necessary to produce positive, realistic alternatives for the client. During this potentially highly productive stage, the therapist/crisis intervenor and client collaboratively agree upon appropriate alternative coping methods.

◼ Stage 6: Formulating an Action Plan

In this stage, an active role must also be taken by the crisis worker; however, the success of any intervention plan depends on the client's level of involvement, participation, and commitment. The crisis worker must help the client look at both the short-term and long-range impacts in planning intervention. The main goals are to help the client achieve an appropriate level of functioning and maintain adaptive coping skills and resources. It is important to have a manageable intervention plan, so the client can follow through and be successful. Do not overwhelm the client with too many tasks or strategies, which may set the client up for failure.

Clients must also feel a sense of ownership in the action plan, so that they can increase the level of control and autonomy in their lives, and to ensure that they do not become dependent on other support persons or resources. Obtaining a commitment from the client to follow through with the action plan and any referrals are important activities for the crisis worker that can be maximized by using a mutual process in intervention planning. Ongoing assessment and evaluation are essential to determine whether the intervention plan is appropriate and effective in minimizing or resolving the client's identified problems. During this stage, the client should be processing and reintegrating the crisis impacts to achieve homeostasis and equilibrium in his or her life.

Termination should begin when the client has achieved the goals of the action plan, or has been referred for additional services through other service providers. It is important to realize that many survivors may need longer-term therapeutic help in working toward final crisis resolution, and referrals for individual, family, or group therapy should be considered at this stage.

■ Stage 7: Follow-up Measures

Hopefully, the sixth stage has resulted in significant changes and resolution for the client, in regard to his or her postcrisis level of functioning and coping. This last stage should help determine whether these results have been maintained, or if further work remains to be done. Typically, followup contacts should be done within two to six weeks after termination. At this stage, the four tasks of crisis resolution should have been addressed, as follows.

1. *Physical safety and survival.* Maintaining safety by being aware of one's surroundings; having a cell phone with easy access to police emergency response (911); maintaining physical health through adaptive coping skills and proper nutrition and rest

2. *Ventilation and expression of feelings.* Appropriate emotional expression/ventilation and understanding how emotional reactions impact one's mental health

3. *Cognitive mastery*. Developing a realistic understanding of the crisis event; addressing any unfinished business, irrational thoughts, or fears in regard to the crisis event(s)

4. *Interpersonal adjustments*. Adapting to changes in daily life, activities, goals, or relationships due to the crisis event, and minimizing any long-term negative effects in these areas for the future.

It is important to remember that final crisis resolution may take many months or years to achieve, and survivors should be aware that certain events, places, or dates can trigger emotional and physical reactions to the previous trauma. For example, a critical time is at the first anniversary of a crisis event, especially for crime victims, when clients may reexperience old fears, reactions, sleep disturbances, or thoughts. This is a normal part of the recovery process, and clients should be prepared to have contingency plans or supportive help through these difficult periods.

For detailed applications of this seven-stage crisis intervention model with domestic violence, divorce, adolescent suicide, substance abuse, persons diagnosed HIV-positive, school shootings, workplace violence, terrorist attacks, and community disasters, see Albert Roberts, *Crisis Intervention Handbook: Assessment, Treatment and Research*, 3rd ed. (Oxford University Press, 2005).

10

Karel Kurst-Swanger, Ph.D.

Guidelines on How to Use the Police and Courts

■ Tanya

It was a warm sunny afternoon when Tanya pulled into the parking lot of her employer. She was anxious to get back to work after her long and difficult year away at college. She thought to herself: "Being back home and back to work will be so good for me, I am so happy to be back to normal life and away from Tom." Just before she opened the door of her car, something made her glance in the rearview mirror. There she spied him. Tom, her ex-boyfriend, a young man she met while away at college, was sitting in his red Mustang in a parking spot behind where she had pulled in. "How did he find me here? Oh God, what do I do now?"

Tanya gathered up her purse, plunged out of her car, and ran into the building. Once inside the safety of the brick YMCA building, she hurried to find her supervisor, Joyce. "Joyce, my ex-boyfriend is out in the parking lot. He followed me here from school, I think he is stalking me now. We had a terrible breakup, I broke up with him in February because I couldn't take his abusive behavior anymore, but now he keeps popping up everywhere I go. I'm scared. He traveled 300 miles to follow me." Joyce said: "Let's call the police."

Officer Steve Tomilson arrived approximately 10 minutes later. Tanya explained the situation to the officer and told him she had never called the police on Tom before, but the fact that he had traveled over 300 miles to find her scared her. Because Tom had long since left the parking lot, the officer explained there was nothing he could do. Tom hadn't broken any laws, and he was nowhere to be found. The officer wrote an incident report and suggested that Tanya go to court and attempt to get a restraining order. Tanya walked slowly back to her office feeling less safe than before the police officer had arrived.

Tanya's situation is not unique. She has taken the positive step of ending the relationship with an abusive partner, however, she is still concerned that she might be hurt. She is left feeling unprotected by the police. She fully understands that the police cannot make an arrest unless a crime has been committed, yet waiting to be victimized does not feel right either.

Isn't there something the police can do to make him stop following her or to better protect her? If Tanya had experienced this abusive relationship in the 1970s the answer would probably be no, there is nothing the police can or would be willing to do regarding this situation. However, in 2003 the answer is yes, there are things both she and the police can do to interrupt this cycle of terror before it escalates into more violence. For example, today, Tanya can get a court order of protection that orders Tom not to make any contact with her. If Tom continues to follow her, he can be arrested for violating the order, or, at a minimum, be given a warning by the police that his actions constitute stalking, a criminal offense in and of itself. The police may further investigate this situation through a specialized domestic violence unit. In addition, a variety of technological applications can be used to put Tanya in immediate touch with the authorities or to track Tom's whereabouts. Some of the ways technology is being used to protect women are discussed later in this chapter.

Like Tanya, any young woman who dates is potentially at risk of becoming victimized. This chapter outlines the sources of help currently available from courts and police to assist victims and potential victims of violence. Victims no longer have to suffer alone in silence. The information presented here will help women confidently access needed services despite the maze of confusing bureaucracies and court procedures.

Police and court responses to intimate partner violence are not perfect, nor is the domestic violence law. However, in recent years, cases of abuse between intimates have been taken much more seriously by the police and the courts. Laws have evolved to better protect victims while making abusers more accountable for their behavior. The following section is an introduction to federal and state policy and their distinct role in domestic violence intervention. The next section, on the police, explores what to expect when the police are called. Next, the section on the courts reviews some basic information about the court systems. Finally, there is a review of some of the current applications of technology being used by the police and courts to combat domestic violence. (See the glossary for a detailed examination of key criminal justice and domestic violence terms and definitions.)

■ Criminal Justice Policy and the Law

If you have ever felt intimidated by the legal system, you are in excellent company. Most Americans get their knowledge about the law and the court system from the media. Television shows like *The Practice, Law and Order, NYPD Blue, CSI: Crime Scene Investigation,* and so on are realistic in many ways; however, the dramatic aspects of television often leave viewers with unrealistic expectations of what the police and courts can really do and how they really operate. The popularity of reality shows such as *COPS* and the programming on Court TV have brought the drama of crime and the courts into the family rooms of many American homes. Americans are bombarded daily with print and visual media reporting news stories related to the criminal and civil courts. In addition, blockbuster movies are often built around legal themes.

Even with the overexposure of the legal system in the media and our seemingly insatiable appetite for such stories, most Americans would find it challenging to navigate the court process without an attorney. This section provides basic information regarding the legal system to demystify the process and encourage victims and potential victims to seek assistance from the system when necessary. It should be remembered that there are many different types of professionals who can help the layperson utilize the legal system effectively. Do not hesitate to reach out and ask for assistance. Since there are many different kinds of law and courts in the United States, it is helpful to have a basic working knowledge of how the system works.

Federal policies supersede those of the states; however, they generally focus only on issues of national interest. Sometimes federal policies are developed in response to a political issue common to some or all states. At other times federal policies are developed to mandate or motivate states to initiate model policies in a particular area. Critical funding necessary for state and local implementation of the policy provisions is often included at the federal level. In terms of domestic violence legislation, a number of federal policies have been enacted in the past two decades, including the Victims of Crime Act (VOCA) of 1984; the Family Violence Prevention and Services Act of 1992; the Violence Against Women Act of 1995; and the Victims of Trafficking and Violence Protection Act of 2000. (See the glossary for further details.)

State policies provide the laws, regulations, and statutes that guide the behavior of individual state residents and organizations. Unlike federal policies, which are uniform nationwide, state policies are more diverse. They are dependent on local ideology and local needs. State policies often revolve around the following issues:

- Issuances of protective orders and their violation
- Child support and custody
- Criminal penalties and procedures
- Weapon restrictions
- Employment policies
- Service availability to victims and abusers
- Police practices and arrest policies
- Definitions of what constitutes a "domestic" case
- Funding for victim services
- The protection of victim's residential or work address
- The role of civil and criminal courts

■ State Laws and How to Access Them

State coalitions on domestic violence or local domestic violence programs will have up-to-date information regarding state polices and court processes applicable in the victim's state. Because state policies are constantly undergoing revision and new pieces of domestic violence legislation are likely to be added each year, it is important to know how to access current information on applicable state domestic violence laws. Such information can be accessed at the Violence Against Women website: www.vawmet.org, where you can access a link to your state's statewide coalition against domestic violence. The coalition may explain public policies on their website or may provide a contact address and phone number for a source of this information. You can also enter the name of your state and the key terms "domestic violence coalition" into an internet search engine (e.g., "New York state domestic violence coalition"). The statewide coalition will pop up. (For detailed information on the funding levels, goals, and accomplishments of the 50 statewide domestic violence coalitions, see Roberts and Brownell, in *Handbook of Domestic Violence Intervention Strategies* [Oxford University Press, 2002].)

   Statewide coalitions also list their numbers in local phone books. Another contact source is the National Network to End Domestic Violence, at 202-543-5566, or the National Domestic Violence Hotline, at 1-800-799-7233, for information and referral. The Family Violence Department of the National Council of Juvenile and Family Court Judges also publishes a yearly bulletin containing a state-by-state listing of newly passed legislation. They can be reached by phone at 1-800-527-3223 or on the Web at www.dvlawsearch.com.

☐ The Police

Deciding to involve the police in a case of domestic violence is likely to raise a lot of questions for the victim or potential victim. More than likely it will be a neighbor, friend, stranger, health care worker, or other family member who calls the police on behalf of the victim. Although the victim is in a state of crisis, it is important to encourage him or her to remain as calm as possible in order to help the police in their investigation and search for evidence.

What to expect when the police arrive. After the police arrive, they must conduct an investigation. They are likely to ask about injuries, bruises, and other evidence of offenses. The victim or potential victim should be honest with the police officer about what happened. When the police are called to the scene where domestic violence has occurred, the victim is often asked to:

- Describe the incident in detail
- Make a statement
- Report the presence of any witnesses
- Describe previous violent incidents
- Allow the officer to view any property damage or injuries
- Allow the officer to photograph damage or injuries for purposes of documentation
- Show the officer any court orders such as child custody, visitation orders, protection orders, etc.

Beyond fulfilling their investigative role, the police (in most instances) can also:

- Get the victim to a safe place and protect you from immediate danger
- Help locate shelter services
- Escort the victim to collect belongings
- Get medical assistance
- Provide information regarding the courts and how to file a complaint or family court petition
- Make an arrest (some are required to do so under mandatory arrest laws)
- Provide the victim with a police report

- Make a referral to victim services, that is, counseling, financial compensation, legal assistance, etc.)

- Call a victimís advocate to come and assist the victim immediately (in some communities)

- Refer the victim to an investigative unit for further followup and monitoring (specialized police domestic violence investigative units are available in some police departments)

- Explain the victim's rights

- Answer the victim's questions regarding the courts

- Take photographs to document any injuries or property damage

Things the victim should do following the investigation:

- Let the officer know if medical treatment is needed.

- Ask the police officer for a copy of the report.

- Take down the name of the responding officers and their badge numbers, in case there is a need to contact them in the future.

- If the victim expected the police to make an arrest but they did not, the victim should ask for a written explanation of their reasons. You may be able to file a warrant for arrest in a separate process.

- The victim may ask to speak to a supervisor if he or she is not satisfied with the police response.

Today police departments across the country have begun to develop innovative, community-based approaches to intimate partner violence. Your local police department may have or engage in one or all of the following:

- Specialized training regarding domestic violence

- A specialized domestic violence investigative unit

- Participation in community-wide planning around domestic violence issues

- Participation in a multidisciplinary case review team

- Formal or informal collaboration with prosecutors, domestic violence shelters, victim assistance programs, and treatment services

- Technology to use in combating intimate partner violence

- Information regarding violence on a website or in a precinct office

■ Arrest Factors

The likelihood of an arrest when the police are called is uncertain. Most states have developed specific policies to either require a police officer to make an arrest (referred to as mandatory arrest policies) or to strongly suggest an arrest (referred to as proarrest policies). Mandatory policies generally require the police officer to make an arrest, regardless of what the victim wants. Proarrest policies generally give the police officer more discretion in deciding whether or not to make an arrest, or may suggest that an arrest is to be made unless a victim specifically requests that one not be made. State policies may also be designed in vague terms, giving local police departments more latitude in how they approach such situations.

All states have now passed legislation permitting officers to make warrantless arrests when probable cause exists that a domestic crime has taken place. In the past, officers could not make an arrest on the scene of minor crimes without having had witnessed them in person, making the situation very difficult for victims and the police.

State policies generally spell out the conditions under which arrests are required or highly suggested, and these conditions are likely to include stipulations such as those listed hereafter. Check with the local domestic violence program or statewide coalition for state-specific policies. The local police department may also have a brochure, business card, or website where such policies are posted. Policies are likely to require or suggest an arrest in the following circumstances:

- There is a determination on the part of the police officer that probable cause exists to suggest a domestic offense has occurred. This might include visible harm (i.e., cuts, bruises, swelling, torn clothes, damage to personal property, threatening messages on voicemail, statements from witnesses, presence of weapons, etc.).
- The police officer witnesses a domestic offense.
- A protection order has been violated.
- The victim requests that an arrest take place and is willing to sign a formal complaint.
- A determination is made that the crime committed is a felony and not a misdemeanor. Most states now require police officers to make an arrest in felony cases, regardless of the victim's wishes.
- In cases where both parties appear to have been involved in the incident, police may need to make a determination of who is the primary physical

aggressor and arrest this person. If both persons have been injured, some police departments may arrest both parties.

■ Advantages and Disadvantages of Arresting the Batterer

Research on the effectiveness of arrest in cases of intimate partner violence is ongoing. Some researchers suggest that it is the only effective intervention, while others suggest that only particular types of abusers are impacted by such policies. Yet others argue that in some circumstances, arrest can actually provoke an escalation in the violence. It appears that one key factor in the effectiveness of arresting the batterer is whether he has had any previous involvement with the criminal justice system. Some studies show that when the abuser has never been arrested before and he cares about his reputation in the community, an arrest (sometimes combined with a counseling program) may frighten him so much that he is more likely to refrain from further violence. Conversely, when the abuser has already had some involvement with the criminal justice system, a domestic violence arrest may result in his becoming extremely angry toward his victim, and more severe violence may occur. Three additional important factors are: (1) Is the batterer unemployed or with an erratic work history? (2) What type of living arrangement does the couple have (dating and living separately vs. living together or married)? (3) How long has the violence been taking place (first or second incident vs. many years of assaults)? However, it must be emphasized that there is no guaranteed way to predict the impact that an arrest will have on the batterer, even when he is law-abiding and has roots in his community.

Although an arrest cannot guarantee the victim's long-term safety—and it may provoke the batterer to become even more violent than he had been previously—the benefits of mandatory arrest policies are as follows:

- The batterer is removed immediately from the scene, providing immediate safety and protection for you and your children.

- The decision is placed in the hands of the police. This reduces animosity toward the victim, in that the abuser knows the victim did not "have him arrested."

- The batterer is required to face the consequences of his abusive behavior with formal sanctions.

- The arrest sends a clear message that such behavior is not to be tolerated.

- A venue is provided in which the abuser can be ordered to enter into counseling or specific treatment (i.e., drug and alcohol, batterer treatment programs).

■ Orders of Protection

A restraining order or an order of protection is an official court document intended to put an immediate stop to abusive behavior. Judges grant orders in civil court, and many states also allow criminal court judges to issue such orders. Protective orders are usually granted on a temporary basis, although it may be possible to eventually be granted a permanent order after court hearings have been completed. Orders of protection generally specify or restrict an abuser's contact with the victim. States have policies that govern the procedural and eligibility requirements for obtaining orders, the timeframe in which they remain in effect, and the sanctions associated with their violation. They may be individualized to meet the unique needs of victims. Protective orders can

- Order the abuser to stop emotionally or physically abusing the partner and children
- Prevent the abuser from contacting the victim at work or at home
- Prevent the abuser from making any contact with the victim or the victim's family (no phone calls, e-mails, letters)
- Order the abuser to leave the home
- Order the abuser to have no contact with the children
- Order the abuser to enter counseling
- Order the abuser to pay child support, restitution, or attorney fees
- Restrict the abuser's custody and visitation rights
- Restrict the abuser's ability to possess or purchase firearms

Although such court orders cannot guarantee your safety, they do offer the following benefits:

- Official boundaries are set on your partner's behavior
- Consequences or sanctions are in place if the order is violated
- The order invokes more intense police services and increases the likelihood of an arrest
- Documentation is provided to the victim's employer that additional security may be required at the place of employment
- Documentation is provided to the children's school regarding the role the abuser can or cannot play in the children's school activities

■ The Courts

There are generally two types of courts available to assist victims of domestic violence: civil or criminal. The civil court system generally accepts cases in which the victim and abuser are legally married or have a child in common. These courts are often referred to as family courts. Contact your statewide coalition or local domestic violence advocacy program if you would like information regarding the civil court system in your community. The victim may choose to have her case heard in one or both courts, depending on her circumstances. If the police make a mandatory arrest, the case will be heard in criminal court. This does not necessarily preclude the victim from gaining access to a civil court and the types of services it provides.

In addition, many communities have begun to develop specialized domestic violence courts that may integrate criminal and civil cases or operate in one or the other court. Specialized courts have developed to improve the court's ability to respond to cases of intimate partner violence and to better manage the issues of protective, custody, and support orders. Although the courts can offer a certain amount of protection through restraining orders, they cannot guarantee your safety.

The police, a legal specialist, or domestic violence advocate can offer advice on which court to use, based on existing state laws and the unique facts of the situation. Assistance through the court process is provided by many communities through domestic violence advocates or legal aid offices. Such assistance is free and confidential. Some law schools even offer free legal services or clinics for women who are victims of abuse. Accessing legal assistance with the community can make the entire process of pursuing legal remedies easier and more understandable. With legal assistance, victims are more assured of knowing their rights and options. Such assistance can be found in the local phone book. In addition, contact the National Domestic Violence Hotline at 1-800-799-7233 for the closest program.

☐ Civil Court

Civil courts have been designed to resolve issues or problems between individuals. The outcome in a civil case is usually a court order or monetary settlement. The court is held to a lower standard of proof and therefore can process cases that do not meet the prerequisites for criminal prosecution. Benefits of the civil court include:

- Issuance of orders of protection
- Private proceedings

- Issuance of custody, visitation, and child support orders
- Issuance of orders mandating counseling or treatment for the abuser
- Divorce proceedings
- Issuance of orders of spousal support

One needs to file a petition to be heard in a civil court, and one must meet the court's eligibility requirements. Someone who is legally married and is pregnant or has a child in common with the abuser is likely to be able to access the civil court process. Many communities have specialized intake workers that can help with the petition process and explain court procedures. Contact the local domestic violence advocacy program or shelter, victim assistance agency, legal aid office, or a private attorney to assist with the process. In some instances the court may appoint an attorney for the victim or a law guardian for the child.

☐ Criminal Court

Criminal court action begins with an arrest made by the police or a warrant issued by the court for an arrest or an appearance ticket. If the police do not make an arrest, especially in the case of misdemeanors or violations, you may be able to issue a petition for a warrant or appearance ticket by talking with the city court or the district attorney's office. Judges or magistrates can issue warrants that the police or sheriff's officers must execute.

Once an arrest has been made, it is the decision of the prosecutor, generally referred to as the district attorney, to decide whether or not to prosecute the case. Criminal cases are considered offenses against the state, not offenses against victims. District attorneys, therefore, represent the community to seek redress for crimes committed against the state. The victim does not need to hire an attorney, for the district attorney serves this role in criminal court. The criminal court requires a higher standard of proof, beyond a reasonable doubt, and therefore may not be a viable option for all cases.

Criminal law designates different types of crimes by placing them in one of three different categories. The category of the crime usually defines how the court will proceed once the case has been formally brought forth to the court. Each state is responsible for developing its penal code, which specifies and defines crimes as felonies, misdemeanors, or violations.

Felonies: Considered to be the most serious crimes, felonies are defined as offenses that are punishable by one year or more of imprisonment or death. Felonies are classified by their level of seriousness, using either a number or letter. For example, assaults in the first or second degree might be considered felonies, while assault in the third degree is considered a misdemeanor. The punishment for individuals convicted of felony crimes can range from death to a term of imprisonment to a wide range of community-based correctional programs. State policy is likely to require the police to make arrests in felony cases. Felony level crimes are generally processed in a county level court, with a district attorney or assistant district attorney (prosecutor) bringing forth formal charges.

Misdemeanors: Considered less serious crimes than felonies, misdemeanors are punishable by local incarceration for a period of up to one year or less. Although jail time can be ordered, misdemeanors often involve a wide range of community-based sanctions. The vast majority of domestic offenses are misdemeanor-level crimes. These crimes are likely to be disposed of in a city, town, or village court. They generally do not result in a long trial process.

Violations: Also referred to as petty offenses or infractions, violations are considered less serious than misdemeanors. Individuals who commit violations are likely to receive an appearance ticket to attend a court hearing and are generally sanctioned with a fine. Offenders are usually ticketed and released, meaning jail time is very unlikely.

☐ **Criminal Justice Process**

The vast majority of cases coming into the criminal justice system never go to trial and are formally disposed of through plea bargaining. Many states, through crime victims rights legislation, require prosecutors to keep victims informed of every stage of the criminal process. They are required to inform a victim when an abuser has been released from jail on bail or has been released on his own recognizance (ROR). A domestic violence advocate or victim assistance worker is helpful in explaining the details of what is likely to occur during the criminal justice process and in assuring that your individual rights are preserved. Many prosecutors' offices have victim assistance staff available upon request. It is important to be familiar with the language used in the court system, especially the following commonly used terms, which are defined in the glossary:

- Bail

- Released on their own recognizance (ROR)

- Arraignment

- Grand jury hearing

- Preliminary hearing

- Plea bargaining
- Sentencing
  - Jail terms
  - Prison
  - Parole
  - Probation

☐   **Benefits Derived from Criminal Court Proceedings**

The criminal court cannot guarantee the victim's safety; however, it does offer some of the following benefits:

- It sends a clear message that abusive behavior is illegal and will not be tolerated by our society.
- It can result in a formal sanction of jail, prison, fine, probation, and so on.
- It holds the state responsible for pressing charges and processing the case, not the victim.
- It eliminates the need for the victim to hire an attorney.
- It can issue orders of protection.
- It can order the offender to attend specialized treatment programs.
- It is an open, public process.

☐   **The Role of Technology in Protection**

Technology can be used by the police and by the courts to protect battered women and hold the offender more accountable for behavioral compliance. There are a number of technological advancements that serve as a resource for police and the courts. Here are some of the most common technologies available and their benefits:

- *Criminal investigation*: A number of forensic technological advancements have revolutionized the way the police investigate and solve crimes. Forensic techniques such as DNA profiling, advancements in photography, fingerprinting, and so on are very helpful in providing the physical evidence to solve a crime. The collection of physical evidence at the scene of domestic incidents is becoming more commonplace.
- *Surveillance equipment*: Technological advancements have been applied to improve the ability of the police to conduct surveillance activities. For

example, in cases of domestic violence, surveillance cameras, GPSs (global positioning systems), tracking devices, phone taps, caller IDs, and so on are popular devices used to document the behavior of offenders and to protect victims.

- *Cellular phones, pagers, panic alarms*: Victims may be better protected by carrying a preprogrammed cellular phone, pager, or panic alarm. Many domestic violence advocacy programs or police departments provide these free of charge to victims. They can give victims an immediate contact with the police when they are threatened. Some communities and college campuses offer GPSs with alarms that alert authorities with a victim's exact location.

- *Electronic monitoring devices* are used to monitor an offender's location in proximity to his victim. Courts can order such devices to be used in conjunction with court protection orders. Offenders are given a transmitter that emits a signal if it comes into contact with the receiver unit given to the victim. The signal is sent to the authorities and notifies them that the offender has violated the order of protection.

- *Electronic databases*: Improvements in electronic information systems have provided the police and the courts with immediate information regarding court orders, arrest records, and court records. For example, information-tracking alerts can be placed on various addresses, so when a call for service is received from that address, the police immediately put their domestic violence specialized police unit into action.

■ Summary

The police and courts can be used effectively to stop battering; however, navigating the legal process is understandably a scary and frustrating experience. This chapter provides the support of some basic information regarding the role of the police and the courts and how they can be used to better protect victims and their children. I cannot stress enough the helpful role that domestic violence advocates, victim assistance counselors, or police officers can play in helping the victim through this process. The victim should be aware that she does not have to face the criminal justice system alone.

■ **Suggested Additional Readings**

Buzawa, E. S., & Buzawa, C. (2002). *Domestic violence: The criminal justice response*. Sage.

Kurst-Swanger, K., & Petcosky, J. (2003). *Violence in the home: Multidisciplinary perspectives*. New York: Oxford University Press.

Pleck, E. (1987). *Domestic tyranny: The making of American social policy against family violence from colonial times to the present*. New York: Oxford University Press.

Roberts, A. (2002). *Handbook of domestic violence intervention strategies: Policies, programs, and legal remedies*. New York: Oxford University Press.

Sherman, L., & Berk, R. (1984). The specific deterrent effects of arrest for domestic assault. *American Sociological Review, 49,* 261–272.

11

Karen S. Knox, Ph.D., LMSW-ACP
and Eileen Kelley, LMSW

Drug-Facilitated Sexual Assault

Acquaintance Rape and Date Rape Drugs

Linda went clubbing with her girlfriends to celebrate a birthday, even though her boyfriend had asked her not to go. She met Steve, who was a friend of one of her girlfriends from school. Everybody was drinking and dancing when Linda started feeling woozy, and she decided to go home. Steve offered to walk her to her car and help drive her home. At her apartment, Steve sexually assaulted Linda; she was only partially conscious at the time. She has few memories about the incident. She did not suspect that Steve had used date rape drugs, and she was reluctant to report it to the police, since she couldn't recall what had happened. Linda feels guilty about going out after her boyfriend told her not to and about getting drunk. She has not told anyone what happened.

Carla and Mary were at a restaurant having dinner and drinks. When they left, Carla started having difficulty driving and pulled over to the side of the road. Unknown to them, two men sitting at the bar of the restaurant had slipped some drugs into the women's drinks when the bartender and the waiter were not watching. The two men followed Carla and Mary. Both women were sexually assaulted. Carla regained consciousness first and began to drive home, not realizing what had happened. On the way, a police car pulled her over and arrested her for driving while intoxicated (DWI). Mary recalled some memories the next day, and reported it to the police in hopes of getting Carla out of jail. The police officers had not suspected drug-facilitated sexual assault (DFSA) and thought the women were making up the incident to get out of legal trouble.

Mark and his friends were on spring break, partying and drinking with their fraternity brothers at the beach house. Mark had too much beer and decided to go into one of the bedrooms, where he passed out. He awoke to find one of the most popular fraternity brothers performing oral sex on him. Mark pretended to be unconscious, not knowing how to react and scared that his friends would find out. He refused to report the incident out of shame and thought nobody would believe him anyway.

■ Introduction

The foregoing stories illustrate some of the many different types of drug-facilitated sexual assault and acquaintance/date rape. Fortunately, the public's awareness of DFSA and acquaintance/date rape has dramatically increased over the past 10 years. According to the medical social worker Gail Abarbanel, at Santa Monica Medical Center, media reports, research studies, and scholarly publications have contributed to public and professional knowledge about the types of drugs used and how they are administered.[1] The dynamics and critical issues associated with acquaintance/date rape have also received attention. As documented by Professor Ullman and her associates at the University of Arizona Medical Center, date rape is closely associated with DFSA, in that the perpetrator may use drugs and alcohol to sedate his victims.[2]

This chapter looks at the types of drugs commonly used and their effects, focuses on the dynamics associated with DFSA and acquaintance/date rape, and offers practical advice on the best legal responses, prevention, and how to access support from law enforcement, the court system, victim services, rape crisis centers, and family violence programs.

■ Drug-Facilitated Sexual Assault

In the past few years, there has been an increase in the number of reports of sexual assault where drugs or other substances have been slipped into a victim's beverage. For centuries, perpetrators of sex crimes have used alcohol to sedate their victims. The psychologist Alice Abbey and associates have pointed out that perpetrators use a wide variety of substances to commit crimes of assault. Alcohol is one of the most common factors associated with the risk of sexual assault, with both victims and perpetrators reporting greater consumption than their peers.[3] The dangers and realities of sexual assault are exacerbated when drugs and alcohol become involved. Alcohol and drugs can inhibit resistance, increase aggression, and impair decision-making skills. Alcohol and drug use can also exaggerate problems with misinterpretation of sexual intent and can be used to justify assault.

The relatively new term "drug-facilitated sexual assault" (DFSA) is used to describe a sexual assault where alcohol and/or drugs are used to incapacitate or render the victim unconscious and incapable of consent (1). The drugs and/or alcohol may be ingested voluntarily or without the victim's knowledge or consent. In DFSA, the victim may not recall any of the sexual assault or the events preceding it; may have partial memories; or may regain consciousness during the sexual assault. Survivors may experience the added trauma of not remembering what happened, as well as the typical reactions and feelings that sexual assault survivors share.

This lack of recall is referred to as "mind rape," in that the offender controls the victim's consciousness and memories, which, unfortunately, may have an impact on the reporting and prosecution of DFSA. As illustrated in the case scenarios at the beginning of this chapter, Linda did not report the sexual assault due to her lack of memory of the event. When Carla and Mary started piecing together what had happened and reported it to the police, doubt was raised as to the survivors' version and motives for the allegations.

■ Acquaintance/Date Rape

A number of studies have looked at the prevalence of sexual assault with adult women. According to Patricia Tjaden and Nancy Thoennes at the Center for Women Policy Research in Denver, Colorado, in the National Women's Survey, one in eight women reported being raped (4). Other studies have found that 3–10 percent of reported sexual offenses are made by male victims. Most rapes are committed by someone the victim knows, and 80 percent of the rapes reported in the National Women's Survey were acquaintance/date rapes (1, 4).

Professor Mary Koss and associates reported that female college students are at great risk for sexual assault. Studies show that the rates are three times higher than for similar age cohorts in the general population, with more than half of the women (54 percent) surveyed nationally on college campuses experiencing some form of forced sexual contact (5). Although there is little research on college men, studies indicate that 32–45 percent have experienced coerced sexual advances (6).

Victims are more likely to report stranger rapes than acquaintance/date rapes for a variety of reasons. Victims of acquaintance/date rape vary as to the prior relationship with the perpetrator. A perpetrator can be a friend, coworker, neighbor, date, fellow student, business associate, teacher, or service provider. Usually the prior relationship is a socially acceptable one before the sexual assault incident. The degree of the relationship also varies, with some perpetrators being well-known or longstanding acquaintances and others being relatively new or infrequent associates.

Survivors of acquaintence/date rape feel a betrayal that does not exist with stranger rapes, since the victim previously had some degree of trust, or at least no reason to fear the person, before the rape. The perpetrator may have been seen as "safe," and this leads the victim to distrust his or her sense of judgment. Survivors frequently blame themselves for not being suspicious or failing to see the dangerousness of the perpetrator. Therefore, many survivors do not report, and when they do, may experience discriminatory treatment. Victims of stranger rape may also receive more empathy and support than do victims of acquaintance rape, who are frequently blamed or disbelieved (1).

However, studies show that victims do not differ in the severity of trauma reactions based on whether the perpetrator is known to them (5). Survivors of acquaintance/date rape experience trauma reactions that are similar to stranger rape. These reactions include physical/somatic problems, PTSD symptoms, and psychological/emotional reactions. The survivor's social adjustment can be affected by withdrawing from or avoiding work, friends, school, or leisure activities. Feelings of powerlessness and isolation are also common.

Acquaintance/date rape survivors are more likely to experience self-blame and to second-guess how things could have been different if they had been more observant or careful. If drugs or alcohol are involved, women experience increased guilt because they blame themselves for their incapacitation. In the case of Linda, she experienced self-blame and guilt for drinking and passing out, as well as for going out with her friends despite her boyfriend's objections. According to the school social worker Mary Beth Williams, self-blame has been highly correlated with PTSD symptoms, with victims who blame themselves for the sexual assault experiencing more severe symptoms than those who do not (7).

Given the prevalence of acquaintence/date rape, especially on college campuses, it is important for entering freshpersons to know how to prevent its occurrence. Fourteen tips follow to help prevent acquaintance/date rape (8).

How to Prevent Acquaintance/Date Rape

- Communicate up front with your date. If there is to be no sex, say so.
- Be assertive—no one can read your mind.
- Make sure your body language matches your words.
- Wear clothes that allow you a full range of motion and in which you can move quickly, if necessary.
- Introduce your date to your family or roommates and let them know the approximate time of your return.
- On first dates, meet during daylight hours and take your own car.
- Remember that isolated spots are dangerous—meet in public and stay around other people.
- Parties with excessive alcohol and drug consumption are dangerous—do not go to bedrooms or allow yourself to be alone with men with no other females present.
- Don't get drunk or high—this makes you more vulnerable to rape and your escape more difficult.
- At a party, always pour your own drinks and never leave your drink unattended. Never let someone else watch your drink, for example, while you are dancing or in the ladies' room.
- Always have a cell phone and cash handy to get help and get home.
- Never leave a bar or party with a man you do not know or have just met for the first time.
- Take a self-defense class to learn as many precautions as you can.
- Be aware of what is happening around you and trust your instincts.

■ Characteristics of Perpetrators

Acquaintance/date rapists and those who use drugs and alcohol to rape share many characteristics. They usually have good social skills and can be charming and persuasive. They are manipulative, rather than violent, depending on a planned attack that is well-thought-out in advance. Whether the plan is an opportunistic one, where the offender stages an encounter at a bar, party, or club to find a victim, or the offender has set up a date with the victim, there is always some planning involved, characterized by an intent to commit a sexual offense. Professor Irving Weiner, at the University of South Florida Psychology Department, has identified the following four components of a perpetrator's modus operandi (9).

- *Means*: Knowledge and access to drugs or alcohol and a victim
- *Setting*: Any place where the perpetrator is in control and can isolate the victim
- *Opportunity*: How the perpetrator sets up the victim to gain trust and access
- *Plan to avoid arrest*: How the perpetrator tries to excuse himself or to confuse the victim and dissuade him or her from reporting

According to the literature, with acquaintance/date rape and DFSA, the perpetrator has usually managed to develop some degree of trust in the victim, often by being friendly, helpful, and polite so that the woman lets her guard down. An offender may be in a position of authority or trust, for example, he may be a police officer, doctor, teacher, or mental health provider, so that the victim might not be naturally suspicious. Of course, there are perpetrators who are strangers to their victims, as in the case of Carla and Mary's situation.

Once the perpetrator manages to gain access to the victim, some type of isolation must be found before the sexual offense can be committed. Often witnesses or bystanders are unaware of what is really happening because the perpetrator "appears" to be helping the victim, as in Linda's case.

These first three components are integral to the fourth, how not to get caught, which is very important to the perpetrator. Most acquaintance/date rapists and DFSA perpetrators are repeat offenders (9). Incapacitating the victim so she cannot remember what happened or cannot resist an attack is the primary purpose of the drugs and alcohol. But there can be another motive, which is to destroy the victim's credibility, either by the voluntary ingestion of the drugs or alcohol or by using a combination of drugs so that it will appear that the victim is a drug abuser if tests are run by the police. Implying that the sexual act was consensual is also common, since the victim is confused and may not remember the sequence of events leading up to the sexual assault. Sometimes the victim may not even be aware that a rape occurred, until noticing that clothes are not on correctly or have been disarranged.

Coconspirators, as in the second example, are not uncommon, and these can be multiple perpetrators, as in gang rapes. Sometimes trophies or souvenirs are kept, such as underwear or hair. Photos and videotapes are other ways to "keep the memory" of the assault, either for narcissistic reasons or to fantasize and masturbate.

This type of offender does not ordinarily show any remorse or guilt, or empathy toward the victim, even after he has been criminally charged, prosecuted, imprisoned, and treated clinically. This lack of empathy, coupled with a well-developed set of cognitive distortions or "thinking errors" about one's self and the sexually offending behaviors, make it possible for the offender to continue raping and denying responsibility. *Thinking errors* are ways that offenders make excuses or blame the victim for the sexual assault. Such errors in thinking and deficits in the capacity for empathy are associated with a high risk of recidivism.

A list follows of behavioral warning signs that are associated with the characteristics of men who have been perpetrators of sexual assaults with acquaintances or in a dating relationship.

■ Warning Signals

The crime prevention specialist Scott Lindquist describes some behavioral warning signals that a perpetrator may exhibit (8). One should be on the lookout for these behaviors but remember that they should be regarded merely as possible warning signs of a possible problem—there are no guarantees that a man who does not exhibit these characteristics will not commit a sexual assault, just as there are no guarantees that a man who does exhibit some of these characteristics will commit an assault.

- He behaves as if the two of you are more intimate than you really are.

- He appears to be working too hard to get you to trust him.

- He appears to be too charming or ingratiating in an attempt to disarm any suspicions.

- He attempts to manipulate or control you.

- He shares too many stories that appear be lies, in an attempt to impress or mislead you.

- He spends lavishly on you and appears to expect something in return.

- He makes slight criticisms or derogatory remarks about you or women in general.

- When you want to end the evening, he refuses to leave, or he makes excuses when you try to leave, such as "let's have just one more drink."

- He does not accept "no" for an answer.

■ Types of Drugs Used

Drug-facilitated sexual assaults are closely associated with raves, dance parties, bars, and nightclubs. Raves and dance parties attract young adults and teens with the pulsating beat of the techno music that puts listeners into a trance-like state. The physical closeness of dancing and mosh pits and the intensified sensations of instant drug-induced friendships add to the attraction. Young people today have a preference for "noncalorie drugs," with MDMA (Ecstasy) being the most commonly abused drug at raves (10).

Ecstasy is a hallucinogenic stimulant that can be in the form of a powder or small pill that comes in a wide variety of colors, shapes, and logos. This drug is popular because its users can dance for hours and do not typically have powerful hallucinations. Users report that the drug intensifies colors, lights, and one's sense of smell and touch. These heightened sensations may cause the victim to be more vulnerable to sexual assault, since users tend to be passive and highly susceptible to being touched and caressed (10).

Another commonly used sexual assault drug is Rohypnol, commonly known as "Roofies." Perpetrators reportedly slip it into the victim's drink, also known as *scooping*, causing him or her to black out. Rohypnol is the brand name for flunitrazepam, which is in the class of drugs called benzodiazepines that also includes Xanax, Librium, Klonopin, Valium, and Ativan. Flunitrazepam was introduced in the mid-1970s in Europe, South America, and Asia. It was primarily used in hospitals prior to anesthesia to decrease patient anxiety and to produce a dose-dependent amnesia while keeping an awake, compliant patient. This drug has never been approved by the U.S. Food and Drug Administration (FDA), and its distribution has been curtailed through increased drug enforcement on the Mexico-U.S. border in recent years. It is either a white, dime-sized pill or a grayish-green oval tablet and is odorless and tasteless.

Rohypnol takes away a victim's normal inhibitions, leaving the victim helpless and blocking the memory of a rape or assault. The effects of this drug begin about 30 minutes after ingesting it, peak within two hours, and usually last up to eight hours. Combined with alcohol, Rohypnol can be fatal. Side effects include:

- Blackouts and loss of memory
- Aggressive behaviors
- Decreased blood pressure
- Muscle relaxation

- Disorientation

- Dizziness

- Nausea

In recent years, use of gamma hydroxybutyrate (GHB) has increased, due to the difficulty of obtaining Rohypnol (since it is not FDA approved). First studied and used for sleep disorders such as narcolepsy, GHB began to appear in health food stores in the early 1990s as a food supplement with claims that it aided in weight loss and acted as a sleep enhancer. It also gained popularity in health clubs and with body builders who believed it stimulated the growth of muscles. As more people became familiar with its euphoric effects, it began to make its way to the party and club scenes.

Synthesized from a chemical used to clean electronic circuit boards, GHB is odorless and tasteless and is available in clear liquid, white powder, tablet, and capsule forms. It is known on the street by the names G, Liquid X, Scoop, Easy Lay, Grievous Bodily Harm, and Salty Water. The FDA banned GHB in 1990, following reports of seizures and coma attributed to its use. It has been implicated in several deaths and is now a Schedule I drug. Possession, manufacture, or distribution of GHB could result in prison terms of up to 20 years.

Since the liquid is odorless and tasteless, it has been used as a date rape drug. It can have effects similar to Rohypnol, producing euphoria and extreme relaxation, sometimes to the point of unconsciousness. Coma and seizures often occur, especially when GHB is combined with other drugs or alcohol. When GHB is used with alcohol, nausea and difficulty breathing might be the first sign of problems. Users may present with insomnia, anxiety, tremors, drooling, and respiratory failure. Gamma hydroxybutyrate can be made at home using legal precursor drugs that are readily available. There are numerous websites with information on how to make these illegal drugs. As a result of an error in mixing, dosage, or using a bad recipe, the user may end up drinking a toxic or fatal dose.

Side effects of GHB are usually felt within 5 to 20 minutes after ingestion and they usually last no more than two to three hours. The effects of GHB are unpredictable and very dose dependent. Side effects include:

- Abrupt, intense drowsiness

- Dizziness

- Temporary amnesia

- Seizures

- Sleep paralysis

- Agitation

- Delusions

- Hallucinations

- Excessive salivation

- Decreased gag reflex and vomiting

When combined with alcohol, benzodiazepines, opiates, anticonvulsants, and allergy remedies, GHB can cause severe reactions. Dizziness may occur for up to two weeks after ingestion. Often GHB users present with abrupt onset of coma, requiring intubation. There have been reports of intubated patients suddenly becoming awake and oriented to the point of being extubated, at which time they sign out against medical advice. There is no specific treatment for GHB overdose. Some thrill-seekers deliberately ingest GHB to get high. Since GHB is addictive, the user may increase the chance of overdose by taking more and more to get the same high. This drug also produces withdrawal effects, including insomnia, anxiety, tremors, and sweating.

Ketamine, another relatively new drug, is a veterinarian tranquilizer. It is known as Special K and is usually a liquid that cigarettes or marijuana joints are dipped in and then smoked. It can also be dried into a powder and snorted. Ketamine's effects include slurred speech, slowed responses, elevated vital signs, hallucinations, agitated behavior, attention impairment, flashbacks, and depressed respiration. It causes the victim to become detached, disoriented, uncoordinated, and confused (8). Other hallucinogenic drugs sometimes used in drug-facilitated sexual assaults include LSD, mescaline, peyote, and psilocybin.

■ Physical Signs of Drug Inducement

There are several telltale signs that a person has been drugged. If a person appears disproportionately inebriated in relation to the amount of alcohol she has consumed, she may have unknowingly ingested one of any number of substances. Sedating substances can temporarily inhibit a person's ability to remain awake and conscious. Someone who has been sedated may experience sudden and unexplained drowsiness and have trouble with motor coordination. Other possible effects include impaired judgment, disinhibition, dizziness, and confusion.

Brief periods of impaired memory also may result from the misuse of sedating substances. This means the person who has been raped may not remember the details of what happened while under the drug's influence. Depending on the drug and the presence of other substances in the person's system, more dangerous side effects may occur. Someone who experiences dizziness, confusion, or other sudden and unexplained symptoms after drinking a beverage should call a family member, a friend, the police, a doctor, or 911 for help in getting to a hospital emergency room.

The following steps will reduce the risk of sexual assault associated with parties, drugs, and alcohol.

■ How to Reduce the Risk of a Drug-Induced Sexual Assault

- Do not leave beverages unattended.

- Do not take any beverage from someone you do not know well and trust. Watch the pourer, even if it's a friend or a bartender. Better yet, don't drink what you don't open or pour yourself. Don't drink from punch bowls and shared containers.

- Don't ever leave a drink unattended. Before dancing, using the restroom, or making a phone call, either finish the drink in your glass and remove that glass, or pour the half-finished drink down the sink. If you slip up, toss the drink.

- Even if you are holding your own drink, develop the habit of keeping your hand over the container's openings whenever you are having a conversation or when glancing in other directions.

- Appoint a sober friend to check up on you at parties, bars, and clubs.

- Call 911 if a friend seems very drunk or sick after a drink and has trouble breathing.

- At a bar or club, accept drinks only from the bartender, waiter, or waitress.

- At parties, do not accept open container drinks from anyone.

- Do not give your drink to anyone else to watch. Even if it is a friend you trust to not put an illegal substance into your drink, the friend may not be as cautious as you would be about covering your drink to prevent someone else from tampering with it.

- Be alert to the behavior of friends. Anyone appearing disproportionately inebriated in relation to the amount of alcohol has consumed may be in danger.

Anyone who believes he or she has consumed a sedative-like substance should be driven immediately to a hospital emergency room or should call 911 for an ambulance. If at all possible, a sample of the suspicious beverage should be kept for analysis.

In the case of an assault, it is important to seek prompt medical treatment for the negative (perhaps life-threatening) effects of the ingested drug, in addition to receiving medical attention for the rape. Legal recourse for the assault often begins in the hospital emergency room. The next section discusses the steps that should be taken by anyone who is a victim of sexual assault.

■ Steps to Take If Sexually Assaulted

If someone believes she has been raped or sexually assaulted (either with or without a date rape drug), the following information is vitally important for her to know.

- If a date-rape drug is suspected, you should request a urine test for the presence of sedating substances as soon as possible. The screening should test for GHB, Rohypnol, and other drugs. Every hour matters. Chances of getting proof are best when the sample is obtained soon after the substance has been ingested.

- Get to a safe place and call a rape crisis center. For a toll-free rape crisis hotline, victims can call 1-800-656-4673.

- If there is any chance you want to report the assault, you should not shower, bathe, douche, change clothes, or straighten up the area until the medical and legal evidence has been collected. It is suggested that you report the sexual assault to the police right away, because the evidence of the sexual assault must be collected quickly.

- If you choose to report, you should first call the police and then cooperate with the investigation by going to the hospital to have the medical evidence collected (semen sample and any other DNA evidence).

- At the hospital, clinic, or private doctorís office, you will receive treatment for external or internal injuries, get tested for pregnancy and sexually transmitted diseases, and be referred to support services.

■ Aftermath for Survivors

Rape survivors assaulted under the influence of a sedating substance will have additional issues that are likely to affect their recovery, particularly about their inability to recall the incident. Since survivors will have been heavily sedated, they may not have complete recall of the assault. It is likely that they will be uncertain about exactly what happened and who was involved. The "unknowns" may create tremendous anxiety as survivors are left to fill in the gaps with their imagination. This dynamic increases the loss of control that most survivors feel and that they must deal with in their healing process.

Survivors may not know the identity of their assailants, so added to their concerns is the question "Whom should I fear?" While most survivors have fears regarding their perpetrator, someone assaulted under the influence of a sedating substance will have more generalized fear. They may find themselves looking at people in various settings, wondering "Is that the person that assaulted me?" They may have additional concerns about stalking, fearing that the perpetrator may be someone known to them who may try to drug and sexually assault them in the future.

In situations such as that of Carla and Mary, they may fear that the perpetrators have information on where they live and work from having gone through their purses and car. The women don't know what the perpetrators look like or what public places they frequent, so Carla and Mary might avoid socializing and going out in the future, afraid their perpetrators may be around them. On the other hand, if police follow through with the investigation, information might be gathered from the restaurant employees or other patrons, if the perpetrators frequent that location or neighborhood. At the very least, the restaurant or bar manager and employees need to be aware of what happened to be on the alert to try to prevent other incidents.

Eventually, most survivors must come to terms with the fact that they probably will never be able to fill in those missing pieces. The questions may remain unanswered. Memory may be completely gone or partially erased. Coming to this resolution is not unlike the process experienced by adult survivors of childhood sexual abuse who have only partial recall of repressed memories.

Unfortunately, the inability to recall important facts makes prosecution of these crimes extremely difficult. While law enforcement personnel are becoming more aware of the misuse of sedating substances and their effects on victims, skepticism may continue on the part of those who are unfamiliar with or inexperienced in dealing with these types of crimes. More education and public awareness programs are needed for legal professionals and law enforcement personnel working with sexual assault, and for the general public to become more aware of and learn how to prevent DFSA.

To combat substance-related sexual assault, it is important for colleges to adopt programs of prevention and early intervention. According to the psychologists Alan Ottens and Kathy Hotelling at the counseling center at Northern Illinois University, sexual assault prevention and drug education programs are mandated at all colleges and universities that receive federal funding (11). Many campuses have presentations and reading materials for incoming freshmen as part of their orientation process. Rape crisis centers and family violence agencies are also sources of information and services, both for prevention and intervention.

Clearly, substance-related sexual assault poses unique difficulties both for survivors and for those trying to reduce their risk of assault. School counselors, mental health providers, and medical professionals need to be educated and have information about DFSA in order to help survivors and reduce the risk of this crime for others in their care. Though intervention services vary in communities, there are usually crisis intervention programs available through law enforcement victim services, the local rape crisis center, or family violence agencies. Victim services counselors who work within law enforcement agencies usually intervene on the scene of the offense, or at the hospital if the victim is transported there. Victim services counselors help the survivor through the initial stages of the reporting and investigation procedures. The primary goals of intervention at this initial stage are to:

- Assess the health needs and the well-being of the victim
- Establish rapport and trust
- Provide information on the medical and investigative procedures
- Address safety issues and develop a safety plan
- Identify sources of support and ongoing services
- Provide crisis counseling and short-term therapy
- Follow up with the victim as the case goes through the criminal justice system

■ Victim Services

Victim services counselors would have been beneficial for Carla and Mary, even if no police report or charges were filed. The victim services counselors would have the opportunity to support and validate the victims' experiences and to try to prevent further revictimization of the women by the criminal justice system, which occurs when victims are not treated professionally and with empathy by police officers and the courts. Imagine how Carla felt after being arrested, when she was the innocent victim of a sexual predator. The disbelief of the police officers and reluctance to investigate also revictimize the survivor, and physical evidence that could substantiate the case could be lost with a delay of the investigation and medical exam. The victim services counselors would encourage the women to have a medical exam to ensure their health, check for pregnancy, drugs, and sexually transmitted diseases, and collect a rape kit.

Law enforcement victim services counselors usually work with survivors for a period of four to six weeks until the victim returns to a pre–crisis incident level of functioning. At that time, victims may be referred for ongoing therapeutic services, such as individual counseling or survivors' groups, and their family members or loved ones may participate in counseling as well. Most local communities provide long-term treatment through rape crisis centers, nonprofit counseling agencies, or private clinical practitioners. The goals of long-term treatment are to:

- Identify unresolved issues and problems associated with the sexual assault
- Deal with feelings and emotional reactions
- Explore alternatives and options to address major concerns or needs
- Provide support and counseling services as needed
- Assist the survivor in trying to achieve resolution and insight

Sexual assault survivors who never file a report (as in the cases of Linda and Mark) may find the need for counseling at a later time. This happens when emotional, social, and physical problems stemming from the sexual assault impact so negatively on their functioning and coping skills that they seek help. Often family and loved ones notice changes and have enough concerns to suggest the need for treatment. Many victims think that if they do not talk about the sexual assault, it will go away or they can put it in the past. However, this does not work for most survivors. While some sexual assault survivors have the support and coping skills to resolve their trauma in their own ways and timeframes, many find that support groups or individual counseling help their recovery.

It is important to remember that sexual assault affects not only the victims but also those close to them. Many loved ones don't know what to say or how to respond to the physical and emotional needs of the survivor. They can be a valuable support to the survivor, but they also need support themselves.

If community-based services are not available, many bookstores and the internet can be sources of support, providing self-help books, reference materials, and information helpful to those involved. A list of internet sources is provided at the end of this chapter. Scott Lindquist, a crime prevention specialist, suggests the following ways to support a victim of sexual assault (8)

- Believe her regardless of the circumstances. Do not question her even if the story does not seem to make sense.

- Reassure her and let her know that what she is feeling is normal for someone who has been raped.

- Listen to her, even if she wants to talk about the same events over and over again—do not try to minimize her feelings and what has happened.

- Let her know how you feel—but don't tell her you understand or know how she feels.

- Don't take control—reassure her that you are there for her, but have confidence that she is capable and in control of her own life.

- Be patient—don't expect too much too soon. Recovery timeframes vary among survivors.

- Encourage her to seek professional counseling and agree to go for help with her.

■ Sources of Information

□ Drugs of Abuse

The National Institute on Drug Abuse (NIDA) sponsors several websites:
- www.clubdrugs.org has information on club drugs, methamphetamine, LSD, ketamine, and other recently popular drugs
- NIDA Notes
- NIDA Infofax
- Dr. Kenneth Yager's "Drug Facts"; www.crisisinterventionnetwork.com

Substance Abuse and Mental Health Services Administration
www.samhsa.gov
Provides counseling services, lists of treatment facilities, faxes, and mails printed materials; NHSDA survey available online

National Clearinghouse for Alcohol and Drug Information (NCADI)
www.health.org
Library of information with subject searches and statistics

Drug Enforcement Agency
www.usdoj.gov/dea
Information on specific drugs and drug trafficking

Norchem Drug Testing Laboratories
www.norchemlab.com
Online newsletter *Drug Testing Quarterly*

☐ **Sexual Assault**

Antistalking Website
www.antistalking.com

Security on Campus
www.securityoncampus.org

Men's Rape Prevention Project
www.mencanstoprape.org

Victim Services Network
www.safehorizon.org

Rape, Abuse, and Incest National Network
www.rainn.org

■ **Suggested Readings**

Adams, C., & Fay, J. (1984). *Nobody told me it was rape: A parent's guide to talking with teenagers about acquaintance rape and sexual exploitation.* Santa Cruz, CA: Network.

Goring, R. (1996). *Date rape.* Downersgrove, IL: Intervarsity Press.

Johnson, S. (1992). *Man to man: When your partner says no: Pressured sex and date rape.* Brandon, VT: Safer Society Press.

Landau, E. (1993). *Sexual harassment.* New York: Walker.

Lindquist, S. (2000). *The date rape prevention handbook: The essential guide for girls and women.* Napierville, IL: Sourcebooks.

McColgan, A. (1994). *The case for taking the date out of rape.* New York: New York University Press.

Miller, M. (1995). *Drugs and date rape.* Baltimore: Rosen.

Parrot, A. (1993). *Sexual assault on campus.* Lexington, MA: Lexington Books.

Parrot, A. (1999). *Coping with date and acquaintance rape.* New York: Rosen.

■ **References**

(1) Abarbanel, G. (2000). Assessing drug-facilitated rape: Learning from victims. *National Institute of Justice Journal,* April, 11–12. Abarbanel, G. (2001). The victim. In M. A. LeBeau & A. Mozayani (Eds.), *Drug-facilitated sexual assault: A forensic handbook* (pp. 1–37). San Diego, CA: Academic Press.

(2) Ullman, S.E., Karabatsos, G., & Koss, M.P. (1999). Alcohol and sexual assault in a national sample of college women. *Journal of Interpersonal Violence,* 14(6), 603–625.

(3) Abbey, A., Ross, L. T., McDuffie, D., & McAustan, P. (1996). Alcohol and dating risk factors for sexual assault among college women. *Psychology of Women Quarterly*, 20, 147–169.

(4) Tjaden, P. & Thoennes, N. (1998) *Prevalence, incidence, and consequences of violence against women: Findings from the National Violence Against Women Survey*. Washington, DC: U.S. Department of Justice, Office of Justice Programs.

(5) Koss, M.P., Gidyez, C.A., & Wisniewski, N. (1987). The scope of rape: Incidence and prevalence of sexual aggression and victimization in a national sample of higher education students. *Journal of Consulting and Clinical Psychology*, 55, 162–170.

Koss, M. P., & Harvey, M. R. (1991). *The rape victim: Clinical and community interventions*, 2nd ed. Newbury Park, CA: Sage.

(6) Lottes, I. I. (1991). The relationship between nontraditional gender roles and sexual coercion. *Journal of Psychology and Human Sexuality*, 4, 89–109. Stuckman-Johnson, D., & Stuckman-Johnson, C. (1994). College men's reactions to hypothetical forceful sexual advances from women. In E.S. Byers & L.F. O'Sullivan (Eds.), *Sexual coercion in dating relationships*. New York: Haworth Press.

(7) Mary Beth Williams, Ph.D., school social worker, Fairfax, Virginia.

(8) Lindquist, S. (2000). *The date rape prevention book: The essential guide for girls and women*. Napierville, IL: Sourcebooks.

(9) Weiner, I. (2001). The perpetrators and their modus operandi. In M.A. LeBeau & A. Mozayani (Eds.), *Drug-facilitated sexual assault: A forensic handbook* (pp. 39–71). San Diego: Academic Press.

(10) Dr. Kenneth Yeager, director of the outpatient clinic, Ohio State University Medical Center. See website: www.crisisinterventionnetwork.com.

(11) Ottens, A. J., & Hotelling, K. (2001). *Sexual violence on campus: Policy, programs and perspectives*. New York: Springer.

Evelyn Roberts Levine and Albert R. Roberts

Glossary

Adjourn To postpone a court appearance to an alternate date.

Adjournment in Contemplation of Dismissal (ACD) An order given by a judge to dismiss charges, scheduled to take effect in one year, provided there has been no criminal activity, and if certain specified conditions have been satisfied. If the ACD is granted, there is no criminal record. In a case where there is a violation, the judge may schedule a trial on the original crime.

Administrative law Regulations established by the government to govern the actions of public agencies, industry, businesses and individuals. Examples include environmental law, tax laws, health and safety regulations, vehicle registration, product safety, social insurance, legislative committee powers, public authorities, and so on. Violations of administrative law are likely to be resolved through settlements; however, violations may also lead to criminal action. In the case of domestic violence, administrative law may play a role in state regulations and mandates guiding child and adult protection agencies.

Affidavit of service A sworn statement that gives the time, date, place, and manner in which the summons or subpoena is served on the defendant.

Acquaintance/date rape Rape in which the victim has a prior relationship with the perpetrator. A perpetrator can be a friend, coworker, neighbor, date, fellow student, business associate, teacher, or service provider. Usually the prior relationship is a socially acceptable one before the sexual assault incident.

Arraignment The formal charging of the defendant by the court. Offenders are notified of the charges against them and are required to enter a plea.

Arraignment In criminal court, the proceeding in which a defendant in a criminal case is brought before a judge and formally charged with a crime. At this time, the defendant's rights are explained, an attorney is assigned, and future hearing dates are determined. The **court intake hearing** is the equivalent in family court.

Arrest Occurs when a police officer takes a person into custody for the purpose of charging them with a specific crime. According to the Constitution, this act requires **probable cause.**

Assault in the first degree An offense that consists of causing serious physical injury to a person, committed by means of a deadly weapon or dangerous instrument; intending to seriously and permanently disfigure; or recklessly engaging in conduct that causes a grave risk of death.

Assault in the second degree An offense that consists of intentionally causing serious physical injury to another person or causing physical injury by means of a deadly weapon or dangerous instrument.

Assault in the third degree An offense that consists of intentionally or recklessly causing injury to another person.

Bail A form of pretrial release in which a defendant puts up a specific amount of money to the court to ensure that he or she returns to court for all court appearances. If the defendant does not appear for court appearances, the money is forfeited to the court.

Booking After an arrest, the process that includes the photographing, fingerprinting, and positive identification of the arrested individual.

Case law A body of law developed over time based on past judicial decisions. Judicial precedents occur in written decisions on unique cases. Reasoning developed in written court opinions is then considered in future cases. Case law on domestic violence continues to develop.

Cellular phones, pagers, panic alarms Devices used to better protect victims. Many domestic violence advocacy programs or police departments provide these free of charge to victims. They can give victims an immediate contact with the police when they are threatened. Some communities and college campuses offer global positioning systems (GPSs) with alarms to alert authorities to the victim's exact location.

Charge An accusation of criminal behavior, usually the first step in a criminal prosecution. Charges are formally drawn up in a complaint and sworn to by the arresting officer or the person pressing charges.

Civil court Courts that have been designed to resolve issues or problems between individuals. The outcome in a civil case is usually a court order or monetary settlement. The court is held to a lower standard of proof and therefore can process cases that do not meet the elements necessary for criminal prosecution. Benefits of the civil court include issuance of orders of protection; private proceedings; issuance of custody; visitation and child support orders; issuance of orders mandating counseling or treatment for the abuser; divorce proceedings; and issuance of orders of spousal support.

Civil law Law that governs the relationships between various parties of people, that is, families, businesses, public agencies, and other organizations that are noncriminal in nature. Civil law regulates contracts, divorce, child support, child custody, wills, property, actions of liability, and so on. Violations of civil law result in lawsuits in which compensation for losses or damages are sought.

Coalitions against domestic violence As of 2001, all 50 states had statewide domestic violence coalitions with responsibility for preparing and advocating for new domestic violence policies and legislation and training police, prosecutors, social service agency staff, school guidance counselors and social workers, and other community leaders on domestic violence facts and issues. Women's advocacy groups and statewide domestic violence coalitions emerged in the late 1970s and early 1980s. These highly organized and dedicated advocacy groups/coalitions helped community members, community leaders, and legislators to recognize that domestic violence is a serious public health and social problem.

Command The special unit or precinct where a police officer is assigned.

Complainant The person who makes a complaint in a criminal action.

Complaint A document that contains criminal charges alleged against a defendant.

Concurrent jurisdiction This occurs when a case can be heard in either criminal court or family court, or when both courts have jurisdiction over the same subject matter within the same territory.

Conviction Determination that a defendant is guilty as charged; results from defendant either having pleaded guilty or been found guilty, by a jury or judge, of one or more crimes.

Costs of domestic violence Woman-battering costs society over 1.3 billion dollars each year in the form of medical bills and lost wages due to absenteeism and disabilities. The long-term health and mental health costs to the children who witness marital violence are significant, and impossible to measure.

Court intake hearing In family court, the respondent's initial appearance before a judge, at which time the petition is read, the respondent's rights are explained, attorneys are assigned, charges are explained, and future hearing dates are set. In criminal court, the equivalent of the arraignment.

Criminal court Court that has jurisdiction over misdemeanors and violations. The goal of the criminal court is to punish an offender against the law.

Criminal investigation A number of forensic technological advancements have revolutionized the way the police investigate and solve crimes. Forensic techniques such as DNA profiling, advancements in photography, fingerprinting, and so on are very helpful in providing the physical evidence to solve a crime. The collection of physical evidence at the scene of domestic incidents is becoming more commonplace.

Criminal law, penal law Laws that govern the behavior of individuals and organizations by defining and identifying sanctions for offenses that are considered wrongs against society. Violations of criminal law result in a variety of sanctions that include fines, imprisonment, community service, custodial supervision, mandated treatment, and so on.

Criminal procedural law Type of statutory law that guides the processing of criminal complaints through the criminal justice system; dictates the specific methods or procedures to which the court must adhere in criminal cases; governs the actions of the police and court personnel.

Criminal term supreme court Court that has jurisdiction over felony cases.

Date abuse Unwanted physical abuse and/or a pattern of emotional abuse in dating relationships. Abusive acts include pushing, shoving, slapping, throwing objects at the person, punching, hair pulling, kicking, biting, scratching, choking, head banging, whipping with a belt, striking with a knife, and cutting with a nail file or scissor, or hitting with a heavy object (e.g., a lamp, a baseball bat, or a golf club).

Date rape Any form of forced sexual intercourse between people who are in a dating relationship. The laws vary from state to state, and as a result of extensive reform of the rape laws in recent years, rape can include sexual assault, criminal sexual conduct, gross sexual imposition, and attempts to commit sexual penetration by force or threat of serious harm. The rape reform statutes also appropriately include as rape nonconsensual sexual penetration of a youth or adult incapable of giving consent, such as a mentally retarded, mentally ill, intoxicated, or drugged individual.

Defendant Person who is charged with having committed a crime or is named in a civil lawsuit.

Defense counsel An attorney who prepares the materials and arguments to refute the charges against his or her client (the defendant).

Desk appearance ticket (DAT) A type of arrest where a notice is given to an individual by a police officer to return to court at a later date. A DAT is not an arraignment; however, the individual is fingerprinted.

Disposition The judge's resolution of a case.

District attorney An elected or appointed official who prosecutes those charged with crimes.

Docket The list of cases that a court hears on a given day.

Drug-facilitated sexual assault (DFSA) A sexual assault where alcohol and/or drugs are used to incapacitate or render the victim unconscious and incapable of consent. The drugs and/or alcohol may be ingested voluntarily or without the victim's knowledge or consent. In DFSA, the victim may not recall any of the sexual assault or the events preceding it; some victims may have partial memories; and some victims regain consciousness during the sexual assault. Survivors experience this added trauma of not remembering what happened, as well as the typical reactions and feelings that sexual assault survivors share. This lack of recall is referred to as "mind rape," where the offender controls the victim's consciousness and memories, which, unfortunately, may have an impact on the reporting and prosecution of DFSA.

Electronic databases Improvements in electronic information systems now provide the police and the courts with immediate information regarding court orders, arrest records, and court records. For example, information-tracking alerts can be placed on various addresses, so when a call for service is received from that address, the police immediately put their domestic violence specialized police unit into action.

Electronic monitoring Electronic technology that monitors an offender's location in proximity to his victim. Courts can order such devices to be used in conjunction with court protection orders. Offenders are given a transmitter that emits a signal if it comes into contact with the receiver unit given to the victim. The signal is sent to the authorities and notifies them that the offender has violated the order of protection.

Emotional abuse/mental abuse A pattern of intense insults, degrading statements, long harangues, threats of repeat abuse, and aversive and intimidating demands on one's intimate partner. The emotional abuse usually is intense and is repeated on a daily or weekend pattern. The mental abuse becomes psychologically debilitating when it includes sleep deprivation, food deprivation, prolonged and repeated questioning, malicious mischief, and terroristic threats.

Evidence Information or objects that tend to either disprove or establish a fact. Types of evidence include testimony, documents, and other tangible objects, for example, a bloody knife.

Ex-parte A court proceeding where only one side of a given dispute is presented. An example where only one party is present is when a judge grants a temporary order of protection to a victim without the alleged batterer being present.

Family court Court that has jurisdiction over cases involving visitation, child custody and support, paternity, domestic violence, juvenile delinquency and family offenses. Also known as the civil court system, family court generally accepts cases in which the victim and abuser are legally married or have a child in common.

Family Violence Prevention and Service Act of 1992 Also known as the Child Abuse, Domestic Violence, Adoption and Family Services Act of 1992, this Act supports the maintenance and expansion of programs designed to prevent incidents of family violence. It provides immediate shelter and related assistance for victims of family violence and their children.

Felonies Considered to be the most serious crimes; offenses that are punishable by one year or more of imprisonment or death. Felonies are classified by their level of seriousness, using either a number or letter. For example, assaults in the first or second degree might be considered felonies, while assault in the third degree is considered a misdemeanor. The punishment for individuals convicted of felony crimes can range from death to a term of imprisonment to a wide range of community-based correctional programs. State policy is likely to require the police to make arrests in felony cases. Felony-level crimes are generally processed in a county level court, with a district attorney or assistant district attorney (the prosecutor) bringing forth formal charges.

Full stay-away order (exclusionary) An order of protection that prohibits the respondent from communication with the petitioner and excludes the respondent from the petitioner's home, school, place of employment, and so on.

Gamma hydroxybutyrate (GHB) Drug that is synthesized from a chemical used to clean electronic circuit boards. It is odorless and tasteless, and is available in clear liquid, white powder, tablet, and capsule forms, also known on the street by the names G, Liquid X, Scoop, Easy Lay, Grievous Bodily Harm, and Salty Water. Since the liquid is odorless and tasteless, it has been used as a date rape drug.

Grand jury hearing A pretrial process to ensure that there is enough evidence in a case to proceed with a criminal trial. Not all states use the grand jury system. An **indictment** is the formal document issued by the grand jury to support formal criminal charges. Grand juries are presented with information provided by the prosecutor, generally only in felony cases. Victims may be required to testify in front of the grand jury. Neither the defendant nor the defense attorney are allowed into these secret proceedings.

Grand jury A group of 21 people called together by the district attorney to determine if there is sufficient evidence in existence to charge a defendant with a crime.

Indictment A written accusation presented by a grand jury, based on evidence presented to it, that an individual has committed a crime and that there is enough evidence to prosecute. An indictment only applies to felonies.

Jail term Incarceration in a local jail facility for a term of not more than a year. Jail terms may be used in conjunction with other correctional strategies and is usually reserved for misdemeanor level offenses.

Judicial conduct panel Most campuses have a code of conduct for student behavior and have a process for dealing with students who violate the code. Often referred to as judicial conduct panels or boards, they generally function to examine student behavior and have the authority to remove a student from the college community. Judicial conduct boards are generally made up of faculty and staff with student representation and operate like a quasi court. Victims of abuse can access their campus judicial conduct boards for assistance, whether or not the police have been involved in a particular situation.

Jurisdiction A particular court's legal authority to hear and decide a case.

Ketamine A relatively new drug that is a veterinarian tranquilizer. Known as "Special K," it is usually a liquid that cigarettes or marijuana joints are dipped in and then smoked. It can also be dried into a powder and snorted. Ketamine's effects include slurred speech, slowed responses, elevated vital signs, hallucinations, agitated behavior, attention impairment, flashbacks, and depressed respiration. It causes the victim to become detached, disoriented, uncoordinated, and confused.

Law guardian An attorney admitted to practice law in New York state and designated by the court to represent a minor who is the subject of court proceedings. An attorney who is a law guardian works "on behalf of the child." New York state pays for the cost of a law guardian.

Lifetime prevalence rate Domestic violence has a lifetime prevalence rate estimate of one in every four couples in America. As a result, it is viewed as a pervasive and severe social and public health problem in American society today.

Marital rape, partner rape Forced sexual intercourse (vaginal-penile penetration), or sexual intercourse obtained by intimidation and/or threat of force. In addition, in chronic battering relationships, the abusive partner intermittently or on a regular basis controls the type and frequency of oral, genital, and/or anal sexual activity. Chronically and severely battered women have reported that their husbands frequently forced them to perform degrading and sadistic sexual acts, such as forcible anal intercourse and/or forcing objects into their vagina.

MDMA Also known as "Ecstasy"; a hallucinogenic stimulant that can be in the form of a powder or small pill that comes in a wide variety of colors, shapes, and logos. This drug is popular because its users can dance for hours and do not typically have powerful hallucinations. Users report that the drug intensifies colors, lights, and one's sense of smell and touch. These heightened sensations may cause the victim to be more vulnerable to sexual assault, since users tend to be passive and highly susceptible to being touched and caressed.

Menacing The act of intentionally placing another person in fear of imminent serious physical injury.

Misdemeanor Crimes that are considered less serious crimes than felonies and are punishable by local incarceration for a period of up to one year or less. Although jail time can be ordered, misdemeanors often involve a wide range of community-based sanctions. The vast majority of domestic offenses are misdemeanor-level crimes. These crimes are likely to be disposed of in a city, town, or village court. They generally do not result in a long trial process.

Modification petition A request made by the petitioner (usually the victim) to change a part of the judge's order. Usually a modification is requested when some circumstances of the petitioner have changed, for example, the petitioner now desires to have the father of her children pick the children up at a neutral location for visitation. The petitioner would request that the judge modify the original order of protection to include this new condition.

Order of protection A court order that sets forth reasonable conditions of behavior to be observed for a specific time period. The behavior usually includes refraining from menacing or harassing members of a household. In criminal court, an order is valid for up to five years for felony cases and up to three years for class A misdemeanors. In family court, a final order of protection is valid for up to three years. Temporary orders of protection can be valid for shorter periods of time. For example, a temporary order of protection could last until a specific phase of a case is completed.

Parole The conditional release of an offender from prison, prior to the completion of his or her prison sentence. Granted by a parole authority, parolees are placed under the correctional supervision of a parole officer and must abide by a contact. If the parole contract has been violated, the parolee may be sent back to prison to complete his or her full term. Parole can also be the release of a person from custody without bail, in the course of a criminal action.

Part The specific courtroom where a case will be heard.

Partner abuse Intentional abuse of an intimate partner by methods that cause bruises, scratches, cuts, bleeding, injuries, pain, and/or suffering. The most frequent types of physical battering include slapping, grabbing, pushing, shoving, punching, hair pulling, kicking, choking, biting, head-banging, throwing objects at the person, whipping with a belt, and striking with a bat. The most severe abuse usually involves weapons, such as hot objects, chains, knives, cars, guns, and rifles. Recent studies indicate that 80–90 percent of spouse/partner abuse victims are women.

Petition Written application to a court requesting some action or relief.

Petitioner Party who begins a court proceeding in family court. Often this is the victim seeking relief.

Plaintiff Party who commences a civil action in any court except family court.

Plea bargaining It is the process of negotiating an agreement between the defense and the prosecution regarding the appropriate plea (usually a guilty plea in return for a lesser charge and sentence) and associated sentence for a case, bypassing the trial process; occurs in the majority of cases presented in the criminal justice system. A state crime victims' rights legislation may require prosecutors to seek victim input in this process.

Preliminary hearing Hearing to determine sufficiency of evidence for a trial. In a preliminary hearing the court hears evidence and testimony presented by both the defense and the prosecution. The court then determines whether or not there is enough evidence to hold the defendant over for trial. Victims may have to testify at the preliminary hearing.

Prison Incarceration of an individual in a state prison facility, usually for a term of more than one year. Reserved for felony-level crimes.

Probable cause Based on the Fourth Amendment of the United States Constitution; the minimum standard that a police officer uses to make an arrest. Probable cause requires that facts and circumstances taken together lead a police officer to believe that a crime has been committed and that the person who is the subject of the arrest committed the crime.

Probation A sentence of incarceration that has been formally suspended by the court. Instead the defendant is placed in the custody of a probation officer. The probationer must meet with a probation officer on a regular basis and abide by a formal contract. If a defendant violates the terms of the probation, he or she is likely to be sent back to the court and may have to fulfill the rest of the sentence incarcerated. This community-based correctional alternative is very popular and is likely to be the preferred correctional method in many criminal cases in a given community. For example, treatment programs for batterers, if available, are likely to be linked to such a probation contract.

Rape trauma syndrome Long-term maladaptive, traumatic, and self-destructive responses in the aftermath of being a victim of forcible rape. Dr. Ann Wolbert Burgess coined the term "rape trauma syndrome" in 1974 in conjunction with the publication of her classic research study on rape trauma victims at Boston City Hospital. Dr. Burgess was the first researcher to document adaptive as well as maladaptive responses in the aftermath of rape. Specifically, almost one-fourth of the rape victims from Dr. Burgess' study reported that they either attempted suicide and/or seriously abused drugs or alcohol in the long-term aftermath of the rape. This longitudinal study documented the importance of short-term crisis intervention and longer-term psychotherapy for rape victims, especially those individuals with a history of depression, previous suicide attempts, substance abuse, and/or other preexisting psychiatric disorders.

Reckless endangerment in the first degree The offense of recklessly engaging in conduct that creates a grave risk of death to another person.

Reckless endangerment in the second degree The offense of reckless engaging in conduct that creates a substantial risk of serious injury to another person.

Release on own recognizance (ROR) A defendant's release from custody without having to pay bail, during the course of a criminal action. This is allowed because the court believes the defendant has enough community ties to keep him or her from fleeing before the trial.

Respondent The party against whom a proceeding is brought in family court.

Restitution A sum of money paid to the crime victim by the defendant to compensate for loss of property and/or other expenses incurred as a result of a crime.

Restraining order, Order of protection Court order signed by a judge that usually forbids the alleged batterer from making contact with the victim and, in some cases, specifies the distance the abuser must maintain from the victim who requested the order. Depending on the state law, the restraining order may mandate that the abusive spouse/partner immediately vacate the residence, refrain from terroristic threats of abuse or further abusive acts, pay support for the victim and minor children, and/or be court mandated to participate in a group counseling program aimed at ending the violence or a chemical dependency treatment program (both the abusive partner and the victim may be mandated to attend and complete treatment).

Rohypnol A commonly used sexual assault drug, commonly known as "Roofies." Perpetrators reportedly slip it into the victim's drink, also known as "scooping," causing her to black out. Rohypnol is the brand name for flunitrazepam, which is in the class of drugs called benzodiazepines that also includes Xanax, Librium, Klonopin, Valium, and Ativan. Either a white, dime-sized pill or a grayish-green oval tablet, odorless and tasteless, Rohypnol takes away a victim's normal inhibitions, leaving the victim helpless, and blocking the memory of a rape or assault. Combined with alcohol, Rohypnol can be fatal.

Roll call A procedure conducted within a police department before each tour of duty. Names are called out for attendance purposes, and assignments are given out.

Sentencing Sentences are the formal punishments doled out to offenders after a plea of guilty has been entered or an individual has been found guilty after a trial. Judges issue sentences, usually after a probation department has conducted a PSI or presentence investigation. Victims may have input into this process through a *victim impact statement.* Depending on state policy, victims may have the right to include a statement in the PSI report or actually provide an oral or written statement to the judge during the sentencing phase. State policy dictates what sentences are available to judges based on the type of crime committed and mitigating or aggravating circumstances. Some of the basic sentences include jail, prison, and probation. A variety of creative sentencing approaches have been adopted by many communities. Specialized courts may also use specific types of sentences and often are heavily weighted toward ensuring that an offender receives appropriate treatment.

Shelters for battered women and their children First and foremost, shelters provide a safe place for the abused women and their children to stay for a few days to three months. Second, they provide crisis counseling, as well as food, toiletries, clothing, and toys for the children. Once the woman is stabilized, a domestic violence advocate helps her with applying for emergency and interim financial assistance applications and connecting up with legal aid, and vocational rehabilitation. Almost half of all shelters now have a legal advocate on staff. The first emergency shelters for battered women opened their doors in the mid-1970s. During the past three decades, as a result of increased awareness of the chronic and severe nature of battering relationships, short-term shelters have grown in both numbers and the scope of services provided. In 1975, there were only a half dozen shelters for battered women; by January 2003 there were over 2,200 such shelters throughout the United States. In the late 1970s, the most frequent type of services available in shelters was a 24-hour crisis hotline and emergency housing. Once a woman was ready to leave the shelter, she was usually given referrals to welfare and/or legal advocacy, depending on her individual needs, but little else. Services as of 2003 have been expanded to include additional components, particularly support groups and legal advocacy for the women; education, crisis counseling, and trauma treatment for the children;

and transitional and congregate housing placement upon leaving the shelter. In addition, executive directors of family crisis programs and shelters are hiring clinical social workers and licensed master's level counselors to provide mental health treatment to the battered women. Outreach has been expanded to include specialized training to police officers, and prevention efforts at local middle schools, high schools, and colleges on date abuse and acquaintance rape. Major changes in the staffing of shelters has taken place in the past two decades from the original grassroots movement of former battered women and paraprofessionals to the utilization of trained clinicians and managers, many of whom have bachelor's and/or master's degrees. By 2002, approximately 300 comprehensive family crisis programs secured funding for transitional second-stage communal housing, usually lasting from six months to one year, and vocational training and job placement services.

Social isolation of battered women When the abusive partner prevents the abused women from contacting all of her relatives, friends, and neighbors. Some batterers go so far as to put a lock on the phone and not allow the victim to have a cell phone. These women are rarely left alone when the batterer is home, and he escorts and shadows her to any medical appointments or the supermarket. These women report being locked in closets, bedrooms, or basements, chained to the bed, and/or held captive with a rifle or handgun pointed at their head. Others have access to a car, but their mileage is carefully scrutinized and clocked to make sure they only went to work, the local supermarket, or the hospital or intermediate care facility, for example, to visit a frail grandmother.

Subpoena Legal order requiring a person's attendance at a particular place and time in order to testify as a witness.

Supreme court A court of general jurisdiction that hears both felony criminal cases (criminal term) and civil cases (e.g., divorce and negligence cases).

Surveillance equipment In cases of domestic violence, surveillance cameras, tracking devices, phone taps, caller IDs, and so on are popular devices now used to document the behavior of offenders and to protect victims.

Temporary order of protection (TOP) Court order that defines conditions of behavior that a person who harms another person must follow for a limited period of time. The order is temporary because the alleged batterer is not present when it is issued. The order remains in effect until the victim and the batterer are scheduled to return to court. A TOP does not take effect until the battery is served with a copy. Also known as a temporary restraining order.

Testify To give verbal statements under oath while serving as a witness.

Tour of duty A law enforcement officers' scheduled hours to work.

Types of law Laws governing domestic violence intervention fall under three general categories: criminal, civil, and administrative. It might be helpful to have an understanding of how each type of law impacts intervention practices of the police, the courts, and other government entities.

UF-(61) The name and number of the complaint form that is registered at the local police precinct when an incident is reported.

Verdict The final decision or finding made by the jury at the conclusion of a trial.

Victim service programs Crisis intervention programs for crime victims, not as common as victim/witness assistance programs, usually located in a police department, sheriff's office, hospital, probation department, or nonprofit social service agency. Typically, these programs attempt to intervene within the first 24 hours after the victimization. The primary objectives of victim service programs include providing early and timely intervention and aid to crime victims through a 24-hour telephone hotline; crisis intervention at the crime scene, the hospital, or local battered women's shelter; emergency lock repairs; assistance in completing victim compensation award applications; helping the victim complete forms for replacing lost documents; and referral to the prosecutor's domestic violence and sexual assault intake unit as well as community mental health centers. Providing victim assistance and support services that will facilitate the crime victim's recovery is difficult and complex. Several research studies have indicated that the most effective methods of lessening psychological consequences, including fear and distress, are: restoring tarnished beliefs and correcting negative cognitions and irrational beliefs, and building on inner strengths and positive coping skills through both crisis intervention and cognitive-behavioral therapy. A small number of victim service programs, such as Safe Horizons in New York, have full-time therapists on staff. Most other programs refer to family counseling agencies and community mental health centers.

Victim/witness assistance programs Usually located either within the local county prosecutor's suite of offices, the county courthouse, or across the street from the court building, these programs are designed to encourage witness cooperation in the filing of criminal charges as well as testifying in court. In general, these programs include a witness notification and case monitoring system in which staff keep witnesses advised of indictment, continuances, and postponements; specific trial and hearing dates; negotiated pleas; and trial outcomes. In addition, many of these programs provide secure and comfortable reception rooms for witnesses waiting to testify in court, transportation services, and court escort in the form of accompanying the witness to court and remaining with the individual in order to explain and interpret the court proceedings. Typically these programs also prepare and distribute court orientation pamphlets about the adjudication process on topics such as "The Crime Victims' Bill of Rights," "Witness Guidelines for Courtroom Testimony," "What You Should Know about Your Criminal Court and the Court Process," and "Information Guide for Crime Victims." According to Dr. Roberts's national organizational survey of victim service and witness assistance programs, approximately one-third of these programs reported having some form of childcare for the children of victims and witnesses while the parents testified in court. Providing responsible and structured childcare for a parent while they are testifying in court can be an important service. The overriding objectives of victim/witness assistance programs and units are to assist witnesses in overcoming the anxiety and trauma associated with testifying in court, while encouraging witness cooperation in the prosecution of criminal cases. The primary objectives of these programs are as follows: (1) providing victims and witnesses with the message that their cooperation is essential to crime control efforts and successful criminal prosecution; (2) informing victims and witnesses of their rights to receive dignified and compassionate treatment by criminal justice authorities; (3) providing information to witnesses on the court process, the scheduling of the case, the trial, and the disposition; and (4) providing orientation to the court and tips on how best to accurately recall the crime scene and testify.

Victims of Crime Act (VOCA) of 1984 This federal legislation provides the authorization for the collection of federal fines and fees through a fund established by the U.S. Treasury to subsidize state crime victim compensation programs nationwide; VOCA also funds staff training and technical assistance for those managing such programs. The state crime victim compensation fund should be easily accessible to the victim through the local police department or victim assistance program.

Victims of Trafficking and Violence Protection Act of 2000 This act reauthorizes the **Violence Against Women Act** of 1994.

Violation Petition Written notice that informs the court that a defendant has disobeyed or violated of an order of protection.

Violations Also referred to as **petty offenses** or **infractions,** violations are considered less serious than misdemeanors. Individuals who commit violations are likely to receive an appearance ticket to attend a court hearing and are generally sanctioned with a fine. Offenders are usually ticketed and released; jail time is very unlikely.

Violence Against Women Act A landmark piece of legislation included in Title IV of the Violent Crime Control and Law Enforcement Act of 1994. The reauthorization provides for the strengthening of law enforcement approaches to domestic violence. It strengthens services to victims of violence by providing legal assistance, shelter services, transitional housing, national hotline, victim counselors, and services to reduce the effects of violence on children, and strengthens education and training to combat violence against women. It provides funds to encourage arrest policies, and the enforcement of domestic violence and child abuse laws in rural communities. The Act also provides amendments to domestic violence and stalking offenses and addresses school, campus, and dating violence. In addition, the Act provides a full faith and credit provision in which courts in one state must recognize the issuance of protective orders issued in another state and supports research to study state laws regarding the discrimination against victims of violence regarding insurance and unemployment compensation and the workplace effects from violence against women. Under this Act, the U.S. Congress earmarked $1.3 billion to be allocated to statewide and local domestic violence and rape crisis programs beginning in 1995 and ending in October 2000. In addition, President Clinton helped establish a federal office on Violence Against Women in the U.S. Department of Justice. It seemed appropriate for President Bill Clinton to have authorized significant funding and program developments for expanding domestic violence programs, since as a young boy growing up in Arkansas, President Clinton observed his mother being battered by his sometimes drunken stepfather. In October 2000 President Clinton signed the reauthorization of VAWA, known as VAWA II, which provides $3.3 billion in state and local funding to state domestic violence coalitions, shelters for battered women, police and prosecutor's offices, and three national domestic violence resource centers—the Health Resource Center on Domestic Violence, located in California; the Battered Women's Justice Project, with administrative offices at the Pennsylvania Coalition Against Domestic Violence; and the National Resource Center to End Violence Against Native American Women.

Warrant Court order allowing the police to search a specific place or directing police to arrest a certain person.

Directory of National and Statewide Domestic Violence Crisis Hotlines, Resource Centers, and the Fifty Statewide Coalitions Against Domestic Violence

■ National Toll-Free Telephone Hotline Numbers and Resources

Battered Women's Justice Project
800-903-0111

Bureau of Indian Affairs Indian
Country Child Abuse Hotline
800-633-5155

Childhelp USA National Hotline
800-4-A-CHILD

Family Violence Prevention
Fund/Health Resource Center
888-RX-ABUSE

Mothers Against Drunk Driving
800-GET-MADD

National Center for Missing and
Exploited Children
TDD Hotline
800-843-5678
800-826-7653

National Center for Victims of Crime
TTY Helpline
800-FYI-CALL
800-211-7996

National Children's Alliance
800-239-9950

National Clearinghouse for Alcohol
and Drug Information
TDD Hotline
Hearing Impaired
800-729-6686
800-487-4889
800-735-2258

National Clearinghouse on Child
Abuse and Neglect
800-394-3366

National Criminal Justice Reference
Service (provider of juvenile
justice statistics and information
and victims of crime resources)
800-851-3420

National Domestic Violence Hotline
TTY Hotline
800-799-7233
800-787-3224

National Fraud Information Hotline
800-876-7060

National Organization for Victim
Assistance
800-TRY-NOVA

National Resource Center on
Domestic Violence
TTY Hotline
800-537-2238
800-553-2508

National Violence Against Women
Prevention Research Center
800-472-8824

Office for Victims of Crime Training
and Technical Assistance Center
TTY Telephone
800-OVC-TTAC
866-682-8880

Parents of Murdered Children
888-818-POMC

Rape, Abuse, and Incest National
Network
800-656-4673

Resource Center on Domestic
Violence, Child Protection,
and Custody
800-527-3223

VALOR/National Victim Assistance
Academy
877-748-NVAA

■ **State Coalitions Against
Domestic Violence**

Alabama Coalition Against Domestic
Violence
P.O. Box 4762
Montgomery, AL 36101
Phone: 334-832-4842
Fax: 334-832-4803

Alaska Network on Domestic
Violence and Sexual Assault
130 Seward Street, Room 501
Juneau, AK 99801
Phone: 907-586-3650
Fax: 907-463-4493

Council on Domestic Violence and
Sexual Assault
(907) 465-4356

State of Alaska Division of Adult
Abuse Reporting and Adult
Protective Services
Juneau - 907-563-5654

Arizona Coalition against Domestic
Violence
100 West Camelback Street,
Suite 109
Phoenix, AZ 85013
602-279-2900
602-279-2980

Southern Arizona Task Force
Stop Domestic Violence
Phone: 888-0111 or 800-782-6400
800-786-7380/800-STOPDV0

Arkansas Coalition against Domestic
Violence
1 Sheriff Lane, Suite C
Little Rock, AR 72114
Phone: 501-812-0571
Fax: 501-371-0450

California Alliance against Domestic
Violence
619 13th Street, Suite I
Modesto, CA 95354
Phone: 209-524-1888
Fax: 209-524-0616

Colorado Domestic Violence Coali-
tion
P.O. Box 18902
Denver, CO 80218
Phone: 303-831-9632
Fax: 303-832-7067

Connecticut Coalition Against
Domestic Violence
106 Pitkin Street
East Hartford, CT 06108
(860) 282-7899

Delaware Coalition against Domestic
Violence
P.O. Box 847
Wilmington, DE 19899
Phone: 302-658-2958
Fax: 302-658-5049

D.C. Coalition against Domestic
Violence
P.O. Box 76069
Washington, DC 20013
Phone: 202-783-5332
Fax: 202-387-5684

Florida Coalition against Domestic
Violence
1535 C-5 Killearn Center Boulevard
Tallahassee, FL 32308
Phone: 904-668-6862, 800-500-1119
Fax: 904-668-0364

Georgia Advocates for Battered
Women & Children
250 Georgia Avenue, S.E., Suite 308
Atlanta, GA 30312
Phone: 404-524-3847, 800-643-1212
Fax: 404-524-5959

Hawaii State Coalition against
Domestic Violence
Aiea, HI 96701-5012
Phone: 808-486-5072
Fax: 808-486-5169

Idaho Coalition against Sexual/
Domestic Violence
200 North Fourth Street, Suite 10-K
Boise, ID 83702
Phone: 208-384-0419

Illinois Coalition against Domestic
Violence
730 East Vine Street, Suite 109
Springfield, Illinois 62703
Phone: 217-789-2830
Fax: 217-789-1939

Indiana Coalition against Domestic
Violence
2511 E. 46th Street, Suite N-3
Indianapolis, IN 46205
Phone: 317-543-3908, 800-332-7385
Fax: 317-568-4045

Iowa Coalition against Domestic
Violence
1540 High Street, Suite 100
Des Moines, IA 50309-3123
Phone: 515-244-8028, 800-942-0333
Fax: 515-244-7417

Kansas Coalition against Sexual &
Domestic Violence
820 S.E. Quincy, Suite 416
Topeka, KS 66612
Phone: 913-232-9784
Fax: 913-232-9937

Kentucky Domestic Violence
Association
P.O. Box 356
Frankfort, KY 40602
Phone: 502-875-4132
Fax: 502-875-4268

Louisiana Coalition against Domestic
Violence
P.O. Box 3053
Hammond, LA 70404-3053
Phone: 504-542-4446
Fax: 504-542-6561

Maine Coalition for Family
Crisis Services
128 Main Street
Bangor, ME 04401
Phone: 207-941-1194
Fax: 207-941-2327

Maryland Network against Domestic
Violence
11501 Georgia Avenue, Suite 403
Silver Spring, MD 20902-1955
Phone: 301-352-4574,
800-MD-HELPS

Massachusetts Coalition Of Battered
Women Services Group
14 Beacon Street, Suite 507
Boston, MA 02108
Phone: 617-248-0922
Fax: 617-248-0902

Michigan Coalition against Domestic
  Violence
P.O. Box 16009
Lansing, MI 48901
Phone: 517-484-2924
Fax: 517-372-0024

Minnesota Coalition for Battered
  Women
450 North Syndicate Street, Suite 122
St. Paul, MN 55104
Phone: 573-646-6177
Fax: 573-646-1527

Mississippi Coalition Against
  Domestic Violence
P.O. Box 4703
Jackson, MS 39296-4703
Phone: 601-981-9196,
  800-898-3234
Fax: 601-982-7372

Missouri Coalition Against Domestic
  Violence
331 Madison
Jefferson City, MO 65101
Phone: 314-634-4161

Montana Coalition against Domestic
  Violence
P.O. Box 633
Helena, MT 59624
Phone: 406-443-7794
Fax: 406-449-8193

Nebraska Domestic Violence/Sexual
  Assault Coalition
315 South 9th, No. 18
Lincoln, NE 68508-2253
Phone: 402-476-6256, 800-876-6238

Nevada Network against Domestic
  Violence
2100 Capurro Way, Suite E
Sparks, NV 89431
Phone: 702-358-1171, 800-500-1556
Fax: 702-358-0546

New Hampshire Coalition against
  Domestic and Sexual Violence
P.O. Box 353
Concord, NH 03302-0353
Phone: 603-224-8893, 800-852-3388
Fax: 603-228-6096

New Jersey Coalition for Battered
  Women
2620 Whitehorse/Hamilton Square
  Road
Trenton, NJ 08690
Phone: 609-584-8107
Fax: 609-584-9750

New Mexico Coalition against
  Domestic Violence
P.O. Box 25363
Albuquerque, NM 87125
Phone: 505-246-9240
Fax: 505-246-9434
State hotline: 800-773-3645

New York State Coalition Against
  Domestic Violence
Women's Bldg., 79 Central Ave.
Albany, NY 12206
518-432-4864
Eng. 800-942-6906
Span. 800-942-6908

North Carolina Coalition against
  Domestic Violence
P.O. Box 51875
Durham, NC 27717
Phone: 919-956-9124
Fax: 919-682-1449

North Dakota Council on Abused
  Women's Services
State Networking Office
418 East Rosser Avenue, Suite 320
Bismarck, ND 58501
Phone: 701-255-6240
Fax: 701-255-1904
State hotline: 800-472-2911

Ohio Domestic Violence Network
4041 N High St., No. 101
Columbus, OH 43214
614-784-0023

Oklahoma Coalition on Domestic
  Violence/Sexual Assault
2200 N Classen Blvd, Suite 610
Oklahoma City, OK 73801
Phone: 405-557-1210
Fax: 405-557-1296
State hotline: 800-522-9054

Oregon Coalition against
  Domestic/Sexual Violence
520 N.W. Davis, Suite 310
Portland, OR 97204
Phone: 503-223-7411
Fax: 503-223-7490

Pennsylvania Coalition against
  Domestic Violence
National Resource Center on
  Domestic Violence
6440 Flank Drive, Suite 1300
Harrisburg, PA 17112-2778
Phone: 717-545-6400, 800-932-4632
Fax: 717-545-9456

Rhode Island Coalition Against
  Domestic Violence
422 Post Road, Suite 104
Warwick, RI 02888
Phone: 401-467-9940, 800-494-8100
Fax: 401-467-9943

South Carolina Coalition Against
  Domestic Violence and Sexual
  Assault
P.O. Box 7776
Columbia, SC 29202
Phone: 803-750-1222 or
  803-254-3699, 800-260-9293
Fax: 803-750-1246

South Dakota Coalition Against
  Domestic Violence and Sexual
  Assault
P.O. Box 141
Pierre, SD 57401
Phone: 605-945-0869, 800-572-9196
Fax: 605-945-0870

Texas Council on Family Violence
8701 North Mopac Expressway, Suite
  450
Austin, TX 78759
Phone: 512-794-1133
Fax: 512-794-1199

Utah Domestic Violence Advisory
  Council
120 North 200 West
Salt Lake City, UT 84145
Phone: 801-538-4100, 800-897-LINK
Fax: 801-538-3993

Vermont Network Against Domestic
  Violence and Sexual Assault
P.O. Box 405
Montpelier, VT 05601
Phone: 802-223-1302
Fax: 802-223-6943

Virginiaians against Domestic
  Violence
2850 Sandy Bay Road, Suite 101
Williamsburg, VA 23185
Phone: 804-221-0990,
  800-838-VADV
Fax: 804-229-1553

Washington State Coalition against
  Domestic Violence
2101 4th Avenue E, Suite 103
Olympia, WA 98506
Phone: 360-352-4029, 800-562-6025
Fax: 360-352-4078

West Virginia Coalition against
  Domestic Violence
P.O. Box 85
181B Main Street
Sutton, WV 26601-0085
Phone: 304-765-2250
Fax: 304-765-5071

Wisconsin Coalition Against
  Domestic Violence
1400 E. Washington Ave., No. 103
Madison, WI 53703
608-255-0539

Wyoming Coalition Against
  Domestic Violence and Sexual
  Assault
341 East E. Street, Suite 135A
Pinedale, WY 82601
Phone: 307-367-4296, 800-990-3877
Fax: 307-235-4796

Directory of World Wide Web Resources on Domestic Violence

Web Address	**Title & Description of Specific Focus**
www.abanet.org	**The American Bar Association Commission on Domestic Violence** Publishes the *Lawyer's Handbook on the Impact of Domestic Violence* and other legal materials; also provides legal booklets and help for domestic violence law school clinics and the public.
www.acponline.org	**American College of Physicians Site and Annals of Internal Medicine** Search for tips to recognize and respond to domestic violence.
www.cdc.gov/ncipc	**Centers for Disease Control and Prevention, National Center for Injury Prevention and Control** These centers provide federal funding and leadership in epidemiological research and intimate partner violence prevention programs and evidence-based studies. CDC's research on preventing IPV complements the work of other federal agencies to broaden the understanding of the causes of violence and ways to prevent it.
www.cpsdv.org	**Center for the Prevention of Sexual and Domestic Violence/ Faith Trust Institute** Addresses specific groups, including Asian/ Pacific Islands and religious orientations, including Muslim and Jewish.
www.crisisintervention network.com	**Crisis Intervention Network** Provides detailed information on crisis intervention protocols for domestic violence survivors and suicidal individuals, the woman battering continuum; and Dr. Roberts's books on evidence-based practices, domestic violence, criminal justice, and social work interventions.

www.divorcesource.com	**Divorce Source** Offers online information and state-wide referrals to legal resources; allows you to search violence for specific information; a resource center for divorce-related articles and case law.
www.stoptheviolence.org	**Domestic Violence Clearinghouse and Legal Resource Center** Provides a listing and description of legal services for survivors of domestic violence.
www.ucis.unc.edu/about/pubs/carolina/abuse/appendix.html	**Fact sheet** on the abuse of women in countries throughout the world.
www.endabuse.org	**Family Violence Prevention Fund** A national organization that places emphasis on the legal and medical community and international and domestic policy initiatives.
www.hsph.harvard.edu	**Harvard School of Public Health** Advances the public's health through learning, research, and communication. It provides the highest level of education to public health scientists, practitioners, and leaders; fosters new evidence-based studies on domestic violence leading to improved health for the victims and survivors in this country and all nations; strengthens health capacities and services for communities; informs policy debate, and disseminates healthcare research findings.
www.leavingabuse.com	**Leaving Abuse** Written by a survivor, it addresses the details of leaving, including safety plans, and so forth.
www.menstoppingviolence.org	**Men Stopping Violence Center** Founded in 1982, it is based on the belief that men can collaborate and work together with the battered women's movement to end violence against women. Online guide to services and information.
www.ncadv.org	**NCADV—The National Coalition Against Domestic Violence** Formally organized in January 1978 when over 100 battered women's advocates attended the U.S. Civil rights Commission hearings on battered women in Washington D.C., it provides a center for resources, policy, and shelters with great links.
www.ncjfcj.org	**National Council of Juvenile and Family Court Judges** Dedicated to serving the nation's children and families by advocating for updates on domestic violence legislation and improving the courts of juvenile and family jurisdictions. Their mission is to improve the justice system for domestic violence victims and their children through education, policy analysis, and improving the standards and practices of the juvenile court system.
www.NDVH.org Toll-free Hotline 1-800-799-SAFE (7233) TTY 1-800-787-3224, Translators in 139 languages available; for e-mail assistance ndvh@ndvh.org	**National Domestic Violence Hotline** The national domestic violence hotline continues to answer one call at a time until the violence stops. Great links to other sites.

www.nnedv.org

National Network to End Domestic Violence
This is the national organization consisting of all 50 state domestic violence coalitions. The NNEDV mission is to create a social, political, and economic environment in which violence against women no longer exists and to provide more direct support to local programs and the state coalitions through public awareness, outreach, funding, and training.

www.trynova.org/

National Organization for Victim Assistance (NOVA)
This organization was founded in 1970. Its members include victim/witness advocates, prosecutors, mental health professionals, professors, researchers, and crisis responders.

www.now.org/issues/violence/

National Organization for Women-Violence Against Women
Focuses on political activism, including recent articles pertaining to domestic violence, legislative updates, and links to important legislation.

www.4women.gov/violence/

National Women's Health Information Center
Includes resources on family violence, elder abuse, and sexual assault; checklist on leaving relationship; and links to state resources.

www.opdv.state.ny.us/

New York State Office on Prevention of Domestic Violence
Governor's cabinet-level office that oversees the funding, monitoring, and improvements in shelters and batterer's counseling programs throughout the state; conducts legislative planning and updates, research, policy analysis, and safety audits.

www.ending violence.com

Information about **Non-Violence Alliance**, the **Domestic Violence Training Institute**, and issues related to work with batterers.

www.ojp.usdoj.gov/ovc
Victim Assistance Programs
nationwide: Toll free
1-800-FYI-Call

Office for Victims of Crime
Enhances the nation's capacity to assist crime victims and to provide leadership in changing attitudes, policies, and practices to promote justice and healing for all victims. Funds and monitors victim assistance, victim compensation, and domestic violence programs throughout the United States.

www.menweb.org

Online Journal of Men's Voices
A quarterly journal that includes links to discussions of anger, grief, depression, and men's groups in the popular press.

www.pavnet.org

Partnerships Against Violence Network
An online electronic library of articles on domestic violence and links to relevant legislation.

www.pvs.org

Physicians for a Violence Free Society
Resources for physicians to aid in early detection and medical intervention in domestic violence.

www.safehorizon.org
24-hour Crime Victim Hotline:
212-577-7777, in NYC
DV Hotline: 1-800-621-HOPE
Rape and sexual assault:
212-227-3000

Safe Horizons (formerly Victim Services Agency-VSA)
Operates a city-wide, 24-hours-a-day crime victims hotline; domestic violence shelters throughout NYC; batterers counseling; storefront victim assistance programs in all 5 boroughs; and domestic violence social worker/detective teams in 44 police precincts.

www.silentwitness.net	**Silent Witness National Initiative**
	This organization honors battered women murdered by their partners in community-wide and college student center conferences. The goal is to advocate for the prevention of domestic violence.
www.tcfv.org	**Texas Council on Family Violence**
	A bilingual website with facts, history, resources, and links to shelters throughout Texas and other areas of the United States. They also operate the national toll-free hotline.
www.therapistfinder.net/ Domestic Violence/Spouse-Abuse.html	**Therapist Finder**
	Links to mental health professionals specializing in family violence intervention and recovery.
www.infoline.org	**2-1-1 Infoline** is a Connecticut integrated system of help via the telephone—a single source for information about crisis intervention hotlines, community services, and referrals to human services. It operates 24 hours a day, 365 days a year. Multilingual case workers and TDD access is available.
www.vaw.umn.edu	**Violence Against Women Online Resources**
	Provides legal, criminal justice, social work advocacy information—including standards for batterers counseling programs.
www.whiteribbon.ca/default .asp	**The White Ribbon Campaign**
	Started in 1991 by a small group of Canadian men working internationally to end men's violence against women, it contains links to key issues, activism, and coalitions.

Prepared by Dianne Orenstein, M.S.W., Anne Flitcraft, M.D., and Albert R. Roberts, Ph.D.

Directory of Shelters and Victim Services for Domestic Violence Survivors

Alabama

DOMESTIC VIOLENCE INTERVENTION CENTER PO BOX 1104 Ph: 334-749-1515	Auburn	Domestic Violence	Shelter	Crisis Counseling, Crisis Hotline Counseling, Emergency Financial Assistance, Emergency Legal Advocacy, Follow-up Contact, Group Therapy, Information and Referral, Personal Advocacy, Shelter/Safe House, Telephone Contacts, Assistance in Filing Compensation Claims, Criminal Justice Support Advocacy
EAST ALABAMA TASK FORCE FOR BATTERED WOMEN, INC. PO BOX 1104 Ph: 334-749-1515	Auburn	Domestic Violence	Shelter	Crisis Counseling, Crisis Hotline Counseling, Emergency Financial Assistance, Emergency Legal Advocacy, Group Therapy, Information and Referral, Personal Advocacy, Shelter/Safe House, Assistance in Filing Compensation Claims, Criminal Justice Support Advocacy
YWCA Ph: 205-322-9912	Birmingham 35203	Domestic Violence	Shelter	Crisis Counseling, Crisis Hotline Counseling, Emergency Financial Assistance, Emergency Legal Advocacy, Follow-up Contact, Group Therapy, Information and Referral, Personal Advocacy, Shelter/Safe House, Telephone Contacts, Assistance in Filing Compensation Claims, Criminal Justice Support Advocacy

HARRIET'S HOUSE, INC. PO BOX 569 Ph: 334-289-8988	Demopolis	Adult Sexual Assault, Adults Molested as Children, Assault, Child Physical Abuse, Child Sexual Abuse, Domestic Violence, Elder Abuse, Non-Violent Crimes, Survivors of Homicide	Shelter	Crisis Counseling, Crisis Hotline Counseling, Emergency Financial Assistance, Emergency Legal Advocacy, Follow-up Contact, Group Therapy, Information and Referral, Personal Advocacy, Shelter/Safe House, Telephone Contacts, Assistance in Filing Compensation Claims, Criminal Justice Support Advocacy

Alaska

ABUSED WOMEN'S AID IN CRISIS Ph: 907-279-9581	Anchorage 99501	Domestic Violence	Shelter	Crisis Counseling, Crisis Hotline Counseling, Emergency Financial Assistance, Emergency Legal Advocacy, Follow-up Contact, Information and Referral, Personal Advocacy, Shelter/Safe House, Telephone Contacts, Assistance in Filing Compensation Claims, Criminal Justice Support Advocacy
AIDING WOMEN IN ABUSE AND RAPE EMERGENCIES PO BOX 20809 Ph: 907-586-6623	Juneau	Adult Sexual Assault, Adults Molested as Children, Child Physical Abuse, Child Sexual Abuse, Domestic Violence, Elder Abuse	Shelter	Crisis Counseling, Crisis Hotline Counseling, Emergency Legal Advocacy, Follow-up Contact, Information and Referral, Personal Advocacy, Shelter/Safe House, Telephone Contacts, Therapy, Assistance in Filing Compensation Claims, Criminal Justice Support Advocacy
KENAISOL-DOTNA WOMEN'S RESOURCE AND CRISIS CENTER Ph: 907-283-9473	Kenai 99611	Adult Sexual Assault, Adults Molested as Children, Child Physical Abuse, Child Sexual Abuse, Domestic Violence, Elder Abuse	Shelter	Crisis Counseling, Crisis Hotline Counseling, Emergency Financial Legal Advocacy, Follow-up Contact, Group Therapy, Information and Referral, Personal Advocacy, Shelter/Safe House, Telephone Contacts, Assistance in Filing Compensation Claims, Criminal Justice Support Advocacy

Arizona

CHRYSALIS SHELTER Ph: 602-955-9059	Phoenix 85006	Domestic Violence	Shelter	Crisis Counseling, Crisis Hotline Counseling, Emergency Financial Assistance, Group Therapy, Information and Referral, Personal Advocacy, Shelter/Safe House, Telephone Contacts, Therapy, Assistance in Filing Compensation Claims
CHICANOS POR LA CAUSA, INC. Ph: 602-257-0700	Phoenix 85034	Domestic Violence	Shelter	Crisis Counseling, Crisis Hotline Counseling, Emergency Legal Advocacy, Follow-up Contact, Group Therapy, Information and Referral, Personal Advocacy, Shelter/Safe House, Telephone Contacts, Assistance in Filing Compensation Claims, Criminal Justice Support Advocacy
BREWSTER CENTER Ph: 520-320-7556	Tucson 85716	Domestic Violence	Shelter	Crisis Counseling, Crisis Hotline Counseling, Emergency Legal Advocacy, Follow-up Contact, Group Therapy, Information and Referral, Personal Advocacy, Shelter/Safe House, Telephone Contacts, Assistance in Filing Compensation Claims, Criminal Justice Support Advocacy
TUCSON CENTERS FOR WOMEN AND CHILDREN PO BOX 40878 Ph: 520-795-8001	Tucson	Domestic Violence	Shelter	Crisis Counseling, Crisis Hotline, Group Therapy, Information and Referral, Personal Advocacy, Shelter/Safe House, Telephone Contacts, Therapy, Assistance in Filing Compensation Claims
MT GRAHAM SAFE HOUSE PO BOX 1202 Ph: 928-348-9104	Safford	Adult Sexual Assault, Domestic Violence	Shelter	Crisis Counseling, Crisis Hotline, Follow-up Contact, Group Therapy, Information and Referral, Personal Advocacy, Shelter/Safe House, Telephone Contacts, Assistance in Filing Compensation Claims, Criminal Justice Support Advocacy

Arkansas

ABUSED WOMEN AND CHILDREN, INC. DBA COURAGE HOUSE PO BOX 924 Ph: 870-246-3122	Arkadelphia	Domestic Violence	Shelter	Crisis Counseling, Crisis Hotline Counseling, Follow-up Contact, Information and Referral, Shelter/Safe House, Assistance in Filing Compensation Claims
HARMONY HOUSE, INC. PO BOX 1901 Ph: 870-743-3393	Harrison	Domestic Violence	Shelter	Crisis Counseling, Follow-up Contact, Information and Referral, Personal Advocacy, Shelter/Safe House, Telephone Contacts, Assistance in Filing Compensation Claims,
SANCTUARY, INC. PO BOX 762 Ph: 870-741-2121	Harrison	Domestic Violence	Shelter	Crisis Counseling, Follow-up Contact, Information and Referral, Personal Advocacy, Shelter/Safe House, Telephone Contacts, Assistance in Filing Compensation Claims
WOMEN AND CHILDREN FIRST: THE CENTER AGAINST DOMESTIC VIOLENCE PO BOX 1954 Ph: 501-376-3219	Little Rock	Domestic Violence	Shelter	Crisis Counseling, Crisis Hotline, Follow-up Contact, Information and Referral, Personal Advocacy, Shelter/Safe House, Telephone Contacts, Assistance in Filing Compensation Claims

California

WOMEN-SHELTER OF LONG BEACH PO BOX 32107 Ph: 562-988-1187	Long Beach	Domestic Violence	Shelter	Crisis Counseling, Crisis Hotline, Emergency Legal Advocacy, Follow-up Contact, Group Therapy, Information and Referral, Personal Advocacy, Shelter/Safe House, Telephone Contacts, Assistance in Filing Compensation Claims, Criminal Justice Support Advocacy

1736 FAMILY CRISIS CENTER Ph: 323-737-3900	Los Angeles 90018	Domestic Violence	Shelter	Crisis Counseling, Crisis Hotline, Emergency Legal Advocacy, Follow-up Contact, Group Therapy, Information and Referral, Personal Advocacy, Shelter/Safe House, Telephone Contacts, Assistance in Filing Compensation Claims, Criminal Justice Support Advocacy
CENTER FOR THE PACIFIC ASIAN Ph: 323-653-4045	Los Angeles 90036	Domestic Violence	Shelter	Crisis Counseling, Crisis Hotline, Emergency Financial Assistance, Emergency Legal Advocacy, Follow-up Contact, Group Therapy, Information and Referral, Personal Advocacy, Shelter/Safe House, Telephone Contacts, Therapy, Assistance in Filing Compensation Claims
JEWISH FAMILY SERVICES Ph: 323-761-8800	Los Angeles 90048	Domestic Violence	Shelter	Crisis Counseling, Crisis Hotline, Emergency Financial Assistance, Emergency Legal Advocacy, Follow-up Contact, Group Therapy, Information and Referral, Personal Advocacy, Shelter/Safe House, Telephone Contacts, Therapy, Assistance in Filing Compensation Claims, Criminal Justice Support Advocacy
WEAVE PO BOX 161389 Ph: 916-319-4923	Sacramento	Domestic Violence	Shelter	Crisis Counseling, Crisis Hotline Counseling, Emergency Financial Assistance, Emergency Legal Advocacy, Follow-up Contact, Group Therapy, Information and Referral, Personal Advocacy, Shelter/Safe House, Telephone Contacts, Therapy, Assistance in Filing Compensation Claims, Criminal Justice Support Advocacy

WOMEN ESCAPING A VIOLENT ENVIRONMENT, INC. WEAVE PO BOX 161389 Ph: 916-319-4987	Sacramento	Domestic Violence	Shelter	Crisis Counseling, Crisis Hotline Counseling, Emergency Legal Advocacy, Group Therapy, Information and Referral, Personal Advocacy, Shelter/Safe House, Telephone Contacts, Assistance in Filing Compensation Claims, Criminal Justice Support Advocacy

Colorado

DOVE: ADVOCACY SERVICES FOR ABUSED DEAF WOMEN AND CHILDREN PO BOX 44191 Ph: 303-831-7932	Denver	Adult Sexual Assault, Adults Molested as Children, Child Physical Abuse, Child Sexual Abuse, Domestic Violence, Non-Violent Crimes	Advo-cacy Ctr.	Crisis Counseling, Crisis Hotline Counseling, Follow-up Contact, Group Therapy, Information and Referral, Personal Advocacy, Shelter/Safe House, Telephone Contacts, Assistance in Filing Compensation Claims, Criminal Justice Support Advocacy
SAFEHOUSE DENVER, INC. Ph: 303-318-9959	Denver 80218	Adult Sexual Assault, Adults Molested as Children, Assault, Child Physical Abuse, Child Sexual Abuse, Domestic Violence, Non-Violent Crimes	Shelter	Crisis Counseling, Crisis Hotline Counseling, Follow-up Contact, Group Therapy, Information and Referral, Personal Advocacy, Shelter/Safe House, Telephone Contacts, Assistance in Filing Compensation Claims
CROSSROADS SAFEHOUSE PO BOX 993 Ph: 970-482-3535	Fort Collins	Domestic Violence	Shelter	Crisis Counseling, Crisis Hotline Counseling, Emergency Financial Assistance, Emergency Legal Advocacy, Follow-up Contact, Group Therapy, Information and Referral, Personal Advocacy, Shelter/Safe House, Telephone Contacts, Assistance in Filing Compensation Claims, Criminal Justice Support Advocacy

SAFE SHELTER OF ST VRAIN VALLEY PO BOX 231 Ph: 303-772-0432	Longmont	Domestic Violence	Shelter	Crisis Counseling, Crisis Hotline Counseling, Emergency Legal Advocacy, Follow-up Contact, Group Therapy, Information and Referral, Personal Advocacy, Shelter/Safe House, Telephone Contacts, Assistance in Filing Compensation Claims, Criminal Justice Support Advocacy

Connecticut

CENTER FOR WOMEN AND FAMILES OF EASTERN FAIRFIELD COUNTY Ph: 203-334-6154	Bridgeport 06604	Domestic Violence	Shelter	Crisis Counseling, Crisis Hotline Counseling, Group Therapy, Information and Referral, Personal Advocacy, Shelter/Safe House, Telephone Contacts, Assistance in Filing Compensation Claims
WOMENS CENTER OF GREATER DANBURY Ph: 203-731-5200	Danbury 06810	Domestic Violence	Shelter	Crisis Counseling, Crisis Hotline Counseling, Group Therapy, Information and Referral, Personal Advocacy, Shelter/Safe House, Telephone Contacts, Assistance in Filing Compensation Claims
PRUDENCE CRANDALL CENTER FOR WOMEN PO BOX 895 Ph: 860-225-5187	New Britain	Domestic Violence	Shelter	Crisis Counseling, Crisis Hotline Counseling, Group Therapy, Information and Referral, Personal Advocacy, Shelter/Safe House, Telephone Contacts, Assistance in Filing Compensation Claims

Delaware

PEOPLE'S PLACE II, INC. Ph: 302-422-8058	Milford 19963	Domestic Violence	Shelter	Crisis Counseling, Crisis Hotline Counseling, Follow-up Contact, Information and Referral, Personal Advocacy, Shelter/Safe House, Assistance in Filing Compensation Claims, Criminal Justice Support Advocacy

YWCA OF NEW CASTLE COUNTY 233 KING STREET Ph: 302-658-7161	Wilmington 19801	Adult Sexual Assault, Child Physical Abuse, Child Sexual Abuse, Domestic Violence		Crisis Counseling, Follow-up Contact, Group Therapy, Information and Referral, Telephone Contacts, Therapy, Assistance in Filing Compensation Claims, Criminal Justice Support Advocacy
SURVIVORS OF ABUSE RECOVERY (SOAR) Ph: 302-655-3953	Wilmington 19803	Adult Sexual Assault	Rape Crisis	Crisis Counseling, Follow-up Contact, Group Therapy, Information and Referral, Telephone Contacts, Therapy, Assistance in Filing Compensation Claims, Criminal Justice Support Advocacy
NORTHEAST TREATMENT CENTERS 287 CHRISTIANA ROAD Ph: 302-368-2070	New Castle 19720	Child Physical Abuse, Child Sexual Abuse	Mental Health Agency	Information and Referral, Therapy, Assistance in Filing Compensation Claims

Washington, DC

| AYUDA, INC.

Ph: 202-387-0434 | 20009 | Domestic Violence | Shelter | Crisis Counseling, Emergency Financial Assistance, Emergency Legal Advocacy, Follow-up Contact, Group Therapy, Information and Referral, Personal Advocacy, Shelter/Safe House, Telephone Contacts, Assistance in Filing Compensation Claims, Criminal Justice Support Advocacy |
| HOUSE OF RUTH

Ph: 202-745-2326 | 20005 | Domestic Violence | Shelter | Crisis Counseling, Emergency Financial Assistance, Follow-up Contact, Group Therapy, Information and Referral, Personal Advocacy, Shelter/Safe House, Telephone Contacts, Therapy, Assistance in Filing Compensation Claims, Criminal Justice Support Advocacy |

MY SISTER'S PLACE PO BOX 29596 Ph: 202-529-5261		Domestic Violence	Shelter	Crisis Counseling, Crisis Hotline Counseling, Emergency Financial Assistance, Emergency Legal Advocacy, Follow-up Contact, Group Therapy, Information and Referral, Personal Advocacy, Shelter/Safe House, Telephone Contacts, Therapy, Assistance in Filing Compensation Claims, Criminal Justice Support Advocacy

Florida

WOMEN IN DISTRESS OF BROWARD COUNTY, INC. PO BOX 676 Ph: 954-760-9800	Fort Lauderdale	Domestic Violence	Shelter	Crisis Counseling, Crisis Hotline Counseling, Information and Referral, Shelter/Safe House, Assistance in Filing Compensation Claims
SPOUSE ABUSE, INC. D/B/A HARBOR HOUSE PO BOX 680748 Ph: 409-886-2244	Orlando	Domestic Violence	Shelter	Crisis Counseling, Crisis Hotline Counseling, Follow-up Contact, Group Therapy, Information and Referral, Personal Advocacy, Shelter/Safe House, Therapy, Criminal Justice Support Advocacy
PALM BEACH COUNTY DIVISION OF VICTIM SERVICES Ph: 561-355-4409	West Palm Beach 33401	Adult Sexual Assault, Adults Molested as Children, Assault, Child Physical Abuse, Child Sexual Abuse, Domestic Violence, DUI/DWI Crashes, Elder Abuse, Non-Violent Crimes, Robbery, Survivors of Homicide	Victim Service	Crisis Counseling, Crisis Hotline Counseling, Emergency Financial Assistance, Emergency Legal Advocacy, Follow-up Contact, Group Therapy, Information and Referral, Personal Advocacy, Shelter/Safe House, Telephone Contacts, Therapy, Assistance in Filing Compensation Claims, Criminal Justice Support Advocacy

YMCA OF PALM BEACH COUNTY Ph: 546-164-0005	West Palm Beach 33409	Domestic Violence	Shelter	Crisis Counseling, Crisis Hotline Counseling, Emergency Financial Assistance, Emergency Legal Advocacy, Follow-up Contact, Group Therapy, Information and Referral, Personal Advocacy, Shelter/Safe House, Telephone Contacts, Therapy, Assistance in Filing Compensation Claims, Criminal Justice Support Advocacy

Georgia

WOMEN MOVING ON PO BOX 171 Ph: 404-508-9717	Decatur	Domestic Violence	Shelter	Crisis Counseling, Crisis Hotline Counseling, Emergency Financial Assistance, Emergency Legal Advocacy, Follow-up Contact, Group Therapy, Information and Referral, Personal Advocacy, Shelter/Safe House, Telephone Contacts, Therapy, Assistance in Filing Compensation Claims, Criminal Justice Support Advocacy
SALVATION ARMY OF GEORGIA Ph: 478-742-0037	Atlanta 30329	Domestic Violence	Shelter	Crisis Counseling, Crisis Hotline Counseling, Emergency Legal Advocacy, Follow-up Contact, Information and Referral, Personal Advocacy, Shelter/Safe House, Telephone Contacts, Assistance in Filing Compensation Claims
ASSOCIATION OF BATTERED WOMEN OF CLAYTON COUNTY, INC. POST OFFICE BOX 870386 Ph: 770-960-7153	Morrow	Domestic Violence	Shelter	Crisis Counseling, Crisis Hotline Counseling, Emergency Financial Assistance, Follow-up Contact, Group Therapy, Information and Referral, Personal Advocacy, Shelter/Safe House, Telephone Contacts, Assistance in Filing Compensation Claims, Criminal Justice Support Advocacy

Hawaii

TURNING POINT FOR FAMILIES, INC. PO BOX 612 Ph: 808-935-8229	Hilo	Domestic Violence	Shelter	Crisis Counseling, Crisis Hotline Counseling, Follow-up Contact, Group Therapy, Shelter/Safe House, Assistance in Filing Compensation Claims,
YWCA OF HAWAII ISLAND Ph: 808-935-7141	Hilo 96720	Adult Sexual Assault, Adults Molested as Children, Child Sexual Abuse	Rape Crisis	Crisis Counseling, Crisis Hotline Counseling, Follow-up Contact, Group Therapy, Information and Referral, Telephone Contacts, Therapy, Assistance in Filing Compensation Claims,
KAPIOLANI MEDICAL CENTER FOR WOMEN AND CHILDREN/SEX ABUSE TREAT-MENT CENTER 55 MERCHANT STREET 22ND FLOOR Ph: 808-535-7600	Honolulu 96813	Adult Sexual Assault, Adults Molested as Children, Child Sexual Abuse	Shelter	Crisis Counseling, Crisis Hotline Counseling, Follow-up Contact, Information and Referral, Therapy, Assistance in Filing Compensation Claims, Criminal Justice Support Advocacy
FAMILY VIOLENCE SHELTER YWCA Ph: 808-245-5959	Lihue 96766	Child Physical Abuse, Domestic Violence	Shelter	Crisis Counseling, Crisis Hotline Counseling, Emergency Legal Advocacy, Follow-up Contact, Group Therapy, Information and Referral, Personal Advocacy, Telephone Contacts, Therapy, Assistance in Filing Compensation Claims, Criminal Justice Support Advocacy
BOISE WOMEN'S AND CHILDREN'S ALLIANCE Ph: 208-343-3688	Boise 83702	Adult Sexual Assault, Adults Molested as Children, Assault, Child Physical Abuse, Child Sexual Abuse, Domestic Violence, DUI/DWI Crashes, Elder Abuse, Non-Violent Crimes, Robbery, Survivors of Homicide	Shelter	Crisis Counseling, Crisis Hotline Counseling, Emergency Financial Assistance, Emergency Legal Advocacy, Follow-up Contact, Group Therapy, Information and Referral, Personal Advocacy, Shelter/Safe House, Telephone Contacts, Therapy, Assistance in Filing Compensation Claims, Criminal Justice Support Advocacy

SAFE PLACE MINISTRIES PO BOX 4892 Ph: 208-323-2169	Boise	Adult Sexual Assault, Adults Molested as Children, Domestic Violence	Religious Organization	Crisis Counseling, Emergency Financial Assistance, Emergency Legal Advocacy, Follow-up Contact, Group Therapy, Information and Referral, Personal Advocacy, Shelter/Safe House, Telephone Contacts, Assistance in Filing Compensation Claims
WOMEN'S RESOURCE CENTER Ph: 208-784-6841	Kellogg 83837	Adult Sexual Assault, Child Physical Abuse, Child Sexual Abuse, Domestic Violence, Non-Violent Crimes, Robbery, Survivors of Homicide	Resource and Referral Center	Crisis Counseling, Crisis Hotline, Emergency Financial Assistance, Emergency Legal Advocacy, Follow-up Contact, Group Therapy, Information and Referral, Personal Advocacy, Shelter/Safe House, Telephone Contacts, Assist. in Filing Compensation Claims
COEUR WOMEN'S CENTER Ph: 208-664-9303	Coeurd Alene 83814	Adult Sexual Assault, Adults Molested as Children, Child Physical Abuse, Child Sexual Abuse, Domestic Violence, Elder Abuse	Shelter	Crisis Counseling, Crisis Hotline Counseling, Emergency Financial Assistance, Emergency Legal Advocacy, Follow-up Contact, Group Therapy, Information and Referral, Personal Advocacy, Shelter/Safe House, Telephone Contacts, Therapy, Assistance in Filing Compensation Claims, Criminal Justice Support Advocacy

Illinois

APNA GHAR, INC. Ph: 773-334-0173	Chicago 60640	Domestic Violence	Shelter	Crisis Counseling, Crisis Hotline Counseling, Emergency Legal Advocacy, Follow-up Contact, Information and Referral, Personal Advocacy, Shelter/Safe House, Telephone Contacts Criminal Justice Support Advocacy
FREEDOM HOUSE Ph: 815-872-0087	Princeton 61356	Domestic Violence	Shelter	Follow-up Contact, Information and Referral, Personal Advocacy, Shelter/Safe House, Telephone Contacts, Assistance in Filing Compensation Claims, Criminal Justice Support Advocacy

| HAMDARD CENTER FOR HEALTH AND HUMAN SERVICES

Ph: 630-860-9122 | Wood Dale 60191 | Domestic Violence | Women's Service Center | Crisis Counseling, Crisis Hotline Counseling, Emergency Legal Advocacy, Follow-up Contact, Group Therapy, Information and Referral, Personal Advocacy, Shelter/Safe House, Telephone Contacts, Criminal Justice Support Advocacy |

Indiana

FORT WAYNE WOMEN'S BUREAU, INC. Ph: 219-424-7977	Fort Wayne 46805	Adult Sexual Assault, Adults Molested as Children, Child Sexual Abuse, Domestic Violence, Non-Violent Crimes	Shelter	Crisis Counseling, Crisis Hotline Counseling, Emergency Financial Assistance, Emergency Legal Advocacy, Follow-up Contact, Group Therapy, Information and Referral, Shelter/Safe House, Telephone Contacts, Therapy, Assistance in Filing Compensation Claims, Criminal Justice Support Advocacy
YOUNG WOMEN'S CHRISTIAN ASSOCIATION OF FORT WAYNE, INC. Ph: 219-424-4908	Fort Wayne 46808	Domestic Violence	Shelter	Crisis Counseling, Crisis Hotline Counseling, Emergency Financial Assistance, Emergency Legal Advocacy, Group Therapy, Information and Referral, Personal Advocacy, Shelter/Safe House, Telephone Contacts, Assistance in Filing Compensation Claims, Criminal Justice Support Advocacy
YWCA OF FORT WAYNE, INC. 219-424-4908	Fort Wayne 46808	Adult Sexual Assault, Adults Molested as Children, Assault, Child Physical Abuse, Child Sexual Abuse, Domestic Violence, Elder Abuse, Non-Violent Crimes, Robbery, Survivors of Homicide	Shelter	Crisis Counseling, Emergency Financial Assistance, Emergency Ph: Legal Advocacy, Group Therapy, Information and Referral, Personal Advocacy, Shelter/Safe House, Telephone Contacts, Assistance in Filing Compensation Claims, Criminal Justice Support Advocacy

INDIANA COALITION AGAINST DOMESTIC VIOLENCE, INC. Ph: 317-543-3908	Indianapolis 46205	Domestic Violence	Shelter Coalit-ion	Emergency Legal Advocacy, Follow-up Contact, Information and Referral, Shelter/Safe House, Telephone Contacts, Assistance in Filing Compensation Claims, Criminal Justice Support Advocacy
HAVEN HOUSE, INC. PO BOX 508 Ph: 219-931-2090	Hammond	Adult Sexual Assault, Domestic Violence, Elder Abuse	Shelter	Crisis Counseling, Crisis Hotline Counseling, Emergency Legal Advocacy, Follow-up Contact, Group Therapy, Information and Referral, Personal Advocacy, Shelter/Safe House, Telephone Contacts, Assistance in Filing Compensation Claims, Criminal Justice Support Advocacy

Iowa

YWCA DOMESTIC VIOLENCE & SEXUAL ASSAULT CENTER Ph: 319-753-6734	Burlington 52601	Adult Sexual Assault, Adults Molested as Children, Assault, Child Physical Abuse, Child Sexual Abuse, Domestic Violence, Elder Abuse, Non-Violent Crimes	Shelter	Crisis Counseling, Crisis Hotline Counseling, Emergency Legal Advocacy, Follow-up Contact, Group Therapy, Information and Referral, Personal Advocacy, Shelter/Safe House, Telephone Contacts, Assistance in Filing Compensation Claims, Criminal Justice Support Advocacy
DOMESTIC VIOLENCE INTERVENTION PROGRAM PO BOX 3170 Ph: 319-351-1042	Iowa City	Domestic Violence	Shelter	Crisis Counseling, Crisis Hotline Counseling, Emergency Financial Assistance, Emergency Legal Advocacy, Follow-up Contact, Group Therapy, Information and Referral, Personal Advocacy, Shelter/Safe House, Telephone Contacts, Assistance in Filing Compensation Claims, Criminal Justice Support Advocacy

Organization	City	Victim Type		Services
CRISIS CENTER & WOMEN'S SHELTER PO BOX 446 Ph: 641-683-1750	Ottumwa	Adult Sexual Assault, Adults Molested as Children, Child Physical Abuse, Child Sexual Abuse, Domestic Violence, Non-Violent Crimes	Shelter	Crisis Counseling, Crisis Hotline Counseling, Emergency Legal Advocacy, Follow-up Contact, Group Therapy, Information and Referral, Personal Advocacy, Shelter/Safe House, Telephone Contacts, Assistance in Filing Compensation Claims, Criminal Justice Support Advocacy

Kansas

Organization	City	Victim Type		Services
FRIENDS OF YATES Ph: 913-321-1566	Kansas City 66102	Domestic Violence	Shelter	Crisis Counseling, Crisis Hotline Counseling, Follow-up Contact, Information and Referral, Personal Advocacy, Shelter/Safe House, Telephone Contacts, Assistance in Filing Compensation Claims
WOMEN'S TRANSITIONAL CARE SERVICES PO BOX 633 Ph: 785-331-2034	Lawrence	Domestic Violence	Shelter	Crisis Counseling, Crisis Hotline Counseling, Information and Referral, Shelter/Safe House, Telephone Contacts, Assistance in Filing Compensation Claims
CRISIS RESOURCE CENTER OF SOUTHEAST KANSAS, FORMERLY SAFEHOUSE Ph: 316-231-8692	Pittsburg 66762	Adult Sexual Assault, Child Physical Abuse, Child Sexual Abuse, Domestic Violence	Shelter	Crisis Counseling, Crisis Hotline Counseling, Emergency Financial Assistance, Emergency Legal Advocacy, Follow-up Contact, Group Therapy, Information and Referral, Personal Advocacy, Shelter/Safe House, Telephone Contacts, Assistance in Filing Compensation Claims
SAFE HARBOR PO BOX 2163 Ph: 606-329-9304	Ashland	Adult Sexual Assault, Adults Molested as Children, Assault, Child Physical Abuse, Child Sexual Abuse, Domestic Violence, Elder Abuse, Non-Violent Crimes, Survivors of Homicide	Shelter	Crisis Counseling, Crisis Assistance, Emergency Legal Advocacy, Follow-up Group Therapy, Information and Referral, Personal Advocacy, Shelter/Safe House, Telephone Contacts, Therapy, Assistance in Filing Compensation Claims, Criminal Justice Hotline, Emergency Financial Contact, Support Advocacy

CENTER FOR WOMEN CHILDREN & FAMILIES Ph: 859-259-1974	Lexington 40508	Adult Sexual Assault, Adults Molested as Children, Assault, Child Physical Abuse, Child Sexual Abuse, Domestic Violence, Elder Abuse, Survivors of Homicide	Shelter	Crisis Counseling, Emergency Financial Assistance, Follow-up Contact, Group Therapy, Information and Referral, Personal Advocacy, Shelter/Safe House Referals, Telephone Contacts, Compensation Claims, Therapy, Assistance in Filing Criminal Justice Support Advocacy
YWCA OF LEXINGTON PO BOX 8028 Ph: 859-233-9927	Lexington	Domestic Violence	Shelter	Crisis Counseling, Crisis Hotline Counseling, Emergency Financial Assistance, Emergency Legal Advocacy, Follow-up Contact, Group Therapy, Information and Referral, Personal Advocacy, Shelter/Safe House, Telephone Contacts, Assistance in Filing Compensation Claims, Criminal Justice Support Advocacy

Kentucky

BETHANY HOUSE PO BOX 864 Ph: 606-679-1553	Somerset	Domestic Violence	Shelter	Crisis Counseling, Crisis Hotline Counseling, Emergency Financial Assistance, Emergency Legal Advocacy, Follow-up Contact, Information and Referral, Personal Advocacy, Shelter/Safe House, Telephone Contacts, Assistance in Filing Compensation Claims, Criminal Justice Support Advocacy
FAITH HOUSE PO BOX 93145 Ph: 337-267-9422	Lafayette	Domestic Violence	Shelter	Crisis Counseling, Crisis Hotline Counseling, Emergency Legal Advocacy, Information and Referral, Personal Advocacy, Shelter/Safe House, Telephone Contacts, Criminal Justice Support Advocacy

CALCASIEU WOMEN'S SHELTER, INC. PO BOX 276 Ph: 337-436-4552	Lake Charles	Domestic Violence, Elder Abuse	Shelter	Crisis Counseling, Crisis Hotline Counseling, Emergency Financial Assistance, Emergency Legal Advocacy, Follow-up Contact, Group Therapy, Information and Referral, Personal Advocacy, Shelter/Safe House, Telephone Contacts, Assistance in Filing Compensation Claims, Criminal Justice Support Advocacy

Louisiana

METROPOLI-TIAN BATTERED WOMEN'S PROGRAM PO BOX 10775 Ph: 504-837-5400	New Orleans	Domestic Violence	Shelter	Crisis Counseling, Crisis Hotline Counseling, Emergency Financial Assistance, Emergency Legal Advocacy, Follow-up Contact, Group Therapy, Information and Referral, Personal Advocacy, Shelter/Safe House, Telephone Contacts, Criminal Justice Support Advocacy
BATTERED WOMEN'S PROJECT Ph: 207-764-2977	Presque Isle 04769	Domestic Violence	Shelter	Crisis Hotline Counseling, Follow-up Contact, Group Therapy, Information and Referral, Personal Advocacy, Shelter/Safe House, Telephone Contacts, Assistance in Filing Compensation Claims, Criminal Justice Support Advocacy

Maine

NEW HOPE FOR WOMEN PO BOX A Ph: 207-594-2128	Rockland	Domestic Violence	Shelter	Crisis Hotline Counseling, Follow-up Contact, Group Therapy, Information and Referral, Personal Advocacy, Shelter/Safe House, Telephone Contacts, Assistance in Filing Compensation Claims, Criminal Justice Support Advocacy

WOMANCARE/ AEGIS ASSOCIATION PO BOX 192 Ph: 207-564-8165	Dover, Foxcroft	Domestic Violence	Shelter	Crisis Hotline Counseling, Follow-up Contact, Group Therapy, Information and Referral, Personal Advocacy, Shelter/Safe House, Telephone Contacts, Assistance in Filing Compensation Claims, Criminal Justice Support Advocacy

Maryland

HOUSE OF RUTH Ph: 410-889-0840	Baltimore 21218	Domestic Violence	Shelter	Crisis Counseling, Crisis Hotline Counseling, Emergency Legal Advocacy, Follow-up Contact, Group Therapy, Information and Referral, Personal Advocacy, Shelter/Safe House, Telephone Contacts, Therapy, Assistance in Filing Compensation Claims
WOMEN'S HOUSING COALITION, INC. Ph: 410-235-5782	Baltimore 21218	Domestic Violence	Shelter	Crisis Counseling, Emergency Legal Advocacy, Information and Referral, Personal Advocacy, Shelter/Safe House, Telephone Contacts, Assistance in Filing Compensation Claims, Criminal Justice Support Advocacy
DOMESTIC VIOLENCE CENTER OF HOWARD COUNTY Ph: 410-997-0304	Columbia 21045	Domestic Violence	Shelter	Crisis Counseling, Crisis Hotline Counseling, Emergency Legal Advocacy, Group Therapy, Information and Referral, Shelter/Safe House, Criminal Justice Support Advocacy
DOMESTIC VIOLENCE/ SEXUAL ASSAULT RESOURCE CENTER, INC. Ph: 301-334-6255	Oakland 21550	Domestic Violence	Shelter	Crisis Counseling, Crisis Hotline Counseling, Emergency Financial Assistance, Emergency Legal Advocacy, Follow-up Contact, Group Therapy, Information and Referral, Personal Advocacy, Shelter/Safe House, Telephone Contacts, Assistance in Filing Compensation Claims, Criminal Justice Support Advocacy

Massachusetts

ASIAN TASK FORCE AGAINST DOMESTIC VIOLENCE PO BOX 120108 Ph: 617-338-2350	Boston	Domestic Violence	Shelter	Assistance in Filing Compensation Claims, Group Therapy, Information and Referral, Shelter/Safe House, Therapy
NEW BEDFORD WOMENS CENTER Ph: 508-996-3343	New Bedford 09740	Assault, Child Physical Abuse, Child Sexual Abuse, Violence, Survivors of Homicide	Shelter	Crisis Counseling, Crisis Hotline Counseling, Emergency Legal Advocacy, Follow-up Contact, Group Therapy, Information and Referral, Personal Advocacy, Shelter/Safe House, Telephone Contacts, Therapy, Criminal Justice Support Advocacy
SAFELINK-24 Hour Statewide Domestic Violence Hotline 877-785-2020	Boston	Multilingual Statewide Hotline	Crisis Hotline	Counseling, Information and Refferal, Crisis Intervention
BOSTON MEDICAL CENTER Ph: 617-534-4075	Boston			Emergency Medical Services and Crisis Intervention for Domestic Violence and Sexual Assault Survivors
BRIGHAM AND WOMEN'S HOSPITAL Ph: 617-732-5636	Boston			Emergency Medical Services and Crisis Intervention for Domestic Violence and Sexual Assault Survivors
RENEWAL HOUSE Ph: 617-566-6881	Boston		Shelter	Child Advocacy, Court Advocacy, Support Groups, Emergency Shelter, Legal and Welfare Advocacy,
TRANSITION HOUSE Ph: 617-661-7203	Cambridge		Shelter	Crisis Hotline, Crisis Counseling, Emergency Shelter, Emergency Financial Aid, Haitian Services
VOICES AGAINST VIOLENCE	Framingham		Shelter	Crisis Hotline, Crisis Counseling, Emergency Shelter, Support Groups, Legal Advocacy

Michigan

SAFE SHELTER PO BOX 808 Ph: 269-925-9500	Benton Harbor	Adult Sexual Assault, Child Sexual Abuse, Domestic Violence, Non- Violent Crimes	Shelter	Crisis Counseling, Crisis Hotline Counseling, Emergency Legal Advocacy, Follow-up Contact, Group Therapy, Information and Referral, Personal Advocacy, Shelter/Safe House, Telephone Contacts, Assistance in Filing Compensation Claims, Criminal Justice Support Advocacy
WOMEN'S JUSTICE CENTER PO BOX 13500 Ph: 313-371-3985	Detroit	Domestic Violence	Shelter/ Com- munity Services	Shelter/Safe House, Therapy
YWCA OF GRAND RAPIDS Ph: 616-459-4681	Grand Rapids 49503	Adult Sexual Assault, Adults Molested as Children, Child Sexual Abuse, Domestic Violence	Shelter	Crisis Counseling, Crisis Hotline Counseling, Emergency Financial Assistance, Emergency Legal Advocacy, Follow-up Contact, Group, Assistance in Filing Compensation Claims

Minnesota

MIDMINNESOTA WOMEN'S CENTER PO BOX 602 Ph: 218-828-1216	Brainerd	Child Physical Abuse, Domestic Violence, Elder Abuse	Shelter	Crisis Counseling, Crisis Hotline, Emergency Financial Assistance, Emergency Legal Advocacy, Follow-up Contact, Group Therapy, Information and Referral, Personal Advocacy, Shelter/Safe House, Telephone Contacts, Assistance in Filing Compensation Claims, Criminal Justice Support Advocacy
BATTERED WOMEN'S LEGAL ADVOCACY PROGRAM Ph: 612-343-9844	Minneapolis 55404	Domestic Violence	Legal Aid/ Advoc- acy	Divorce Counseling, Assistance with Protective Order, Emergency Financial Assistance, Emergency Legal Advocacy, Follow-up Contact, Information and Referral, Personal Advocacy, Shelter/Safe House Referrals, Assistance in Filing Compensation Claims

CORNERSTONE ADVOCACY SERVICES Ph: 952-884-0376	Minneapolis 55431	Child Physical Abuse, Domestic Violence	Shelter	Crisis Counseling, Crisis Hotline Counseling, Emergency Financial Assistance, Emergency Legal Advocacy, Follow-up Contact, Group Therapy, Information and Referral, Personal Advocacy, Shelter/Safe House, Assistance in Filing Compensation Claims
HARRIET TUBMAN CENTER, INC. Ph: 612-825-3333	Minneapolis 55408	Domestic Violence	Shelter	Crisis Counseling, Crisis Hotline, Emergency Financial Assistance, Emergency Legal Advocacy, Follow-up Contact, Group Therapy, Information and Referral, Personal Advocacy, Shelter/Safe House, Telephone Contacts, Assistance in Filing Compensation Claims, Criminal Justice Support Advocacy
HOME FREE SHELTER MISSIONS, INC. Ph: 763-545-7072	Minneapolis 55441	Child Physical Abuse, Child Sexual Abuse, Domestic Violence	Shelter	Crisis Counseling, Crisis Hotline Counseling, Emergency Financial Assistance, Emergency Legal Advocacy, Follow-up Contact, Group Therapy, Information and Referral, Personal Advocacy, Shelter/Safe House, Assistance in Filing Compensation Claims
WOMEN OF NATIONS Ph: 651-222-5830	St. Paul 55104	Domestic Violence	Shelter	Crisis Counseling, Crisis Hotline Counseling, Emergency Financial Assistance, Emergency Legal Advocacy, Follow-up Contact, Group Therapy, Information and Referral, Personal Advocacy, Shelter/Safe House, Telephone Contacts, Assistance in Filing Compensation Claims
WOMEN'S ADVOCATES Ph: 651-227-9966	St. Paul 55102	Child Physical Abuse, Child Sexual Abuse, Domestic Violence	Shelter	Crisis Counseling, Crisis Hotline, Emergency Legal Advocacy, Follow-up Contact, Group Therapy, Personal Advocacy, Shelter/Safe House, Assistance in Filing Compensation Claims

ARLINGTON HOUSE Ph: 651-771-3040	St. Paul 55117	Child Physical Abuse, Child Sexual Abuse, Domestic Violence	Shelter	Crisis Counseling, Emergency Financial Assistance, Follow-up Contact, Group Therapy, Information and Referral, Shelter/Safe House, Telephone Contacts, Assistance in Filing Compensation Claims, Criminal Justice Support Advocacy
ASIAN WOMEN UNITED OF MINNESOTA Ph: 651-646-2118	St. Paul 55104	Domestic Violence	Shelter	Crisis Counseling, Crisis Hotline Counseling, Emergency Financial Assistance, Emergency Legal Advocacy, Follow-up Contact, Group Therapy, Information and Referral, Personal Advocacy, Shelter/Safe House, Telephone Contacts, Assistance in Filing Compensation Claims

Mississippi

CATHOLIC CHARITIES, INC. Ph: 601-355-8634	Jackson 39202	Adult Sexual Assault, Adults Molested as Children, Child Sexual Abuse, Domestic Violence	Social Service and Shelter	Crisis Counseling, Crisis Hotline Counseling, Emergency Financial Assistance, Emergency Legal Advocacy, Follow-up Contact, Group Therapy, Information and Referral, Personal Advocacy, Shelter/Safe House, Telephone Contacts, Therapy, Assistance in Filing Compensation Claims, Criminal Justice Support Advocacy
CATHOLICS CHARITIES, INC.; DOMESTIC VIOLENCE/RAPE CRISIS PO BOX 2248 Ph: 601-355-8634	Jackson	Adult Sexual Assault, Domestic Violence	Shelter	Crisis Counseling, Crisis Hotline Counseling, Emergency Financial Assistance, Emergency Legal Advocacy, Follow-up Contact, Group Therapy, Information and Referral, Personal Advocacy, Shelter/Safe House, Telephone Contacts, Therapy, Assistance in Filing Compensation Claims, Criminal Justice Support Advocacy

SALVATION ARMY DOMESTIC VIOLENCE SHELTER PO BOX 1144	Greenville	Domestic Violence	Social Hotline Service and Shelter	Crisis Counseling, Crisis Counseling, Emergency Financial Assistance, Emergency Legal Advocacy, Follow-up Contact, Group Therapy, Ph: 662-334-3280 Information and Referral, Personal Advocacy, Shelter/Safe House, Telephone Contacts, Assistance in Filing Compensation Claims, Criminal Justice Support Advocacy
GULF COAST WOMEN'S CENTER FOR NONVIOLENCE PO BOX 333 Ph: 228-436-3809	Biloxi	Adult Sexual Assault, Adults Molested as Children, Child Physical Abuse, Child Sexual Abuse, Domestic Violence, Survivors of Homicide	Shelter	Crisis Counseling, Crisis Hotline Counseling, Emergency Financial Assistance, Emergency Legal Advocacy, Follow-up Contact, Group Therapy, Information and Referral, Personal Advocacy, Shelter/ Safe House, Telephone Contacts, Therapy, Assistance in Filing Compensation Claims, Criminal Justice Support Advocacy

Missouri

ALIVE PO BOX 11201 Ph: 314-993-7080	St. Louis	Domestic Violence, Elder Abuse	Shelter	Crisis Counseling, Crisis Hotline Counseling, Emergency Legal Advocacy, Follow-up Contact, Group Therapy, Information and Referral, Personal Advocacy, Shelter/Safe House, Telephone Contacts, Therapy, Assistance in Filing Compensation Claims, Criminal Justice Support Advocacy
FAMILY RESOURCE CENTER 3309 SOUTH KINGS HIGHWAY Ph: 314-534-9350	St. Louis 63108	Child Physical Abuse, Child Sexual Abuse, Domestic Violence	Family Service Agency	Crisis Counseling, Information and Referral, Personal Advocacy, Telephone Contacts, Therapy, Assistance in Filing Compensation Claims
FAMILY RESOURCE CENTER 3309 S KINGS HIGHWAY Ph: 314-534-9350	St. Louis 63139	Child Physical Abuse, Child Sexual Abuse, Domestic Violence	Family Service Agency	Crisis Counseling, Information and Referral, Personal Advocacy, Therapy, Assistance in Filing Compensation Claims

LYDIA'S HOUSE PO BOX 2722 Ph: 314-771-4411	St. Louis	Domestic Violence	Shelter	Crisis Counseling, Follow-up Contact, Group Therapy, Information and Referral, Personal Advocacy, Shelter/Safe House, Telephone Contacts
ST LOUIS, COUNTY OF Ph: 314-615-4485	St. Louis 63105	Adult Sexual Assault, Adults Molested as Children, Child Physical Abuse, Child Sexual Abuse, Domestic Violence	Social Service Agency	Crisis Hotline Counseling, Information and Referral, Shelter/Safe House referrals, Telephone Contacts, Assistance in Filing Compensation Claims
ST MARTHA'S HALL PO BOX 4950 Ph: 314-533-1313	St. Louis	Domestic Violence	Shelter	Crisis Counseling, Crisis Hotline Counseling, Emergency Financial Assistance, Emergency Legal Advocacy, Follow-up Contact, Group Therapy, Information and Referral, Personal Advocacy, Shelter/Safe House, Telephone Contacts, Assistance in Filing Compensation Claims, Criminal Justice Support Advocacy
THE WOMEN'S SAFE HOUSE PO BOX 63010 Ph: 314-772-4535	St. Louis	Domestic Violence	Shelter	Crisis Counseling, Crisis Hotline Counseling, Information and Referral, Personal Advocacy, Shelter/Safe House, Telephone Contacts
THE WOMEN'S SAFE HOUSE PO BOX 63010 Ph: 314-772-4535	St. Louis	Domestic Violence	Shelter	Crisis Counseling, Crisis Hotline Counseling, Group Therapy, Shelter/Safe House
MATTIE RHODES MEMORIAL SOCIETY Ph: 816-471-2536	Kansas City 64108	Adult Sexual Assault, Adults Molested as Children, Assault, Child Physical Abuse, Child Sexual Abuse, Domestic Violence, Non-Violent Crimes	Shelter	Crisis Counseling, Emergency Legal Advocacy, Follow-up Contact, Group Therapy, Information and Referral, Personal Advocacy, Shelter/Safe House, Telephone Contacts, Therapy, Assistance in Filing Compensation Claims, Criminal Justice Support Advocacy

NEWHOUSE, INC. PO BOX 240019 Ph: 816-474-6446	Kansas City	Domestic Violence	Shelter	Crisis Counseling, Crisis Hotline Counseling, Information and Referral, Personal Advocacy, Shelter/Safe House, Telephone Contacts, Assistance in Filing Compensation Claims
ROSE BROOKS CENTER, INC. PO BOX 320599 Ph: 816-523-5550	Kansas City	Adult Sexual Assault, Child Physical Abuse, Child Sexual Abuse, Domestic Violence, Elder Abuse	Shelter	Crisis Counseling, Crisis Hotline Counseling, Emergency Legal Advocacy, Follow-up Contact, Information and Referral, Personal Advocacy, Shelter/Safe House, Telephone Contacts, Assistance in Filing Compensation Claims
SYNERGY SERVICES, INC. Ph: 816-587-4100	Kansas City 64152	Domestic Violence	Shelter	Crisis Hotline Counseling, Emergency Legal Advocacy, Follow-up Contact, Group Therapy, Information and Referral, Personal Advocacy, Shelter/Safe House, Telephone Contacts, Therapy, Assistance in Filing Compensation Claims, Criminal Justice Support Advocacy
SYNERGY SERVICES, INC. Ph: 816-587-4100	Kansas City 64152	Domestic Violence	Shelter	Crisis Hotline Counseling, Emergency Legal Advocacy, Follow-up Contact, Group Therapy, Information and Referral, Personal Advocacy, Shelter/Safe House, Telephone Contacts, Therapy, Assistance in Filing Compensation Claims, Criminal Justice Support Advocacy
COMPREHEN-SIVE HUMAN SERVICES, THE SHELTER PO BOX 1367 Ph: 573-875-1369	Columbia	Adult Sexual Assault, Domestic Violence Rape Crisis	Shelter	Crisis Counseling, Crisis Hotline Counseling, Emergency Financial Assistance, Group Therapy, Information and Referral, Personal Advocacy, Shelter/Safe House, Telephone Contacts, Therapy, Assistance in Filing Victim Compensation Claims

Montana

BILLINGS YWCA GATEWAY HOUSE Ph: 406-252-6303	Billings 59101	Adult Sexual Assault, Adults Molested as Children, Child Physical Abuse, Child Sexual Abuse, Domestic Violence, Elder Abuse	Shelter	Crisis Counseling, Crisis Hotline Counseling, Emergency Financial Assistance, Emergency Legal Advocacy, Follow-up Contact, Group Therapy, Information and Referral, Personal Advocacy, Shelter/ Safe House, Telephone Contacts, Assistance in Filing Compensation Claims, Criminal Justice Support Advocacy
YWCA GREAT FALLS/ MERCY HOME Ph: 406-452-1315	Great Falls 59401	Adult Sexual Assault, Adults Molested as Children, Assault, Child Physical Abuse, Child Sexual Abuse, Domestic Violence	Shelter	Crisis Counseling, Crisis Hotline Counseling, Emergency Legal Advocacy, Follow-up Contact, Group Therapy, Information and Referral, Personal Advocacy, Shelter/Safe House, Telephone Contacts, Assistance in Filing Compensation Claims, Criminal Justice Support Advocacy
YWCA OF MISSOULA PATHWAYS Ph: 406-543-6691	Missoula 59802	Adult Sexual Assault, Adults Molested as Children, Assault, Child Physical Abuse, Child Sexual Abuse, Domestic Violence, Elder Abuse, Non-Violent Crimes, Survivors of Homicide	Shelter	Crisis Counseling, Crisis Hotline Counseling, Emergency Financial Assistance, Emergency Legal Advocacy, Follow-up Contact, Group Therapy, Information and Referral, Personal Advocacy, Shelter/ Safe House, Telephone Contacts, Assistance in Filing Compensation Claims, Criminal Justice Support Advocacy

Nebraska

FRIENDSHIP HOME PO BOX 85358 Ph: 402-434-0161	Lincoln	Adult Sexual Assault, Adults Molested as Children, Child Physical Abuse, Child Sexual Abuse, Domestic Violence, Elder Abuse	Shelter	Crisis Counseling, Crisis Hotline Counseling, Emergency Financial Assistance, Emergency Legal Advocacy, Group Therapy, Information and Referral, Personal Advocacy, Shelter/ Safe House, Telephone Contacts, Assistance in Filing Compensation Claims, Criminal Justice Support Advocacy

| CRISIS CENTER

P O BOX 1008
Ph: 308-382-8250 | Grand Island | Adult Sexual Assault, Adults Molested as Children, Domestic Violence, Non-Violent Crimes | Shelter | Crisis Counseling, Crisis Hotline Counseling, Emergency Financial Assistance, Emergency Legal Advocacy, Follow-up Contact, Group Therapy, Information and Referral, Personal Advocacy, Shelter/Safe House, Telephone Contacts, Therapy, Assistance in Filing Compensation Claims |
| CATHOLIC CHARITIES

Ph: 402-558-5708 | Omaha 68104 | Child Physical Abuse, Child Sexual Abuse, Domestic Violence | Shelter | Crisis Counseling, Follow-up Contact, Group Therapy, Information and Referral, Personal Advocacy, Shelter/Safe House, Telephone Contacts, Therapy, Assistance in Filing Compensation Claims |

Nevada

ADVOCATES TO END DOMESTIC VIOLENCE SEXUAL ASSAULT PO BOX 2529 Ph: 702-883-7654	Carson City	Domestic Violence	Shelter	Crisis Counseling, Crisis Hotline Counseling, Follow-up Contact, Group Therapy, Information and Referral, Personal Advocacy, Shelter/Safe House, Telephone Contacts, Assistance in Filing Compensation Claims, Criminal Justice Support Advocacy
SAFE HOUSE Ph: 775-451-4203	Las Vegas 89014	Domestic Violence	Shelter	Crisis Counseling, Crisis Hotline Counseling, Follow-up Contact, Group Therapy, Information and Referral, Personal Advocacy, Shelter/Safe House, Telephone Contacts, Assistance in Filing Compensation Claims, Criminal Justice Support Advocacy
THE SHADE TREE PO BOX 669 Ph: 702-385-0073	Las Vegas	Domestic Violence	Shelter	Crisis Counseling, Follow-up Contact, Group Therapy, Shelter/Safe House, Assistance in Filing Compensation Claims
STEP 2 PO BOX 40674 Ph: 775-787-9411	Reno	Domestic Violence	Mental Health Agency Shelter	Crisis Counseling, Follow-up Contact, Group Therapy, Information and Referral, Personal Advocacy, Shelter/Safe House, Therapy, Assistance in Filing Compensation Claims, Criminal Justice Support Advocacy

New Hampshire

RAPE AND DOMESTIC VIOLENCE CRISIS CENTER PO BOX 1344 Ph: 603-225-7376	Concord	Adult Sexual Assault, Adults Molested as Children, Child Physical Abuse, Child Sexual Abuse, Domestic Violence, Elder Abuse, Non-Violent Crimes	Rape Crisis Shelter	Assistance in Filing Compensation Claims, Criminal Justice Support Advocacy, Crisis Counseling, Crisis Hotline Counseling, Emergency Financial Assistance, Emergency Legal Advocacy, Follow-up Contact, Group Therapy, Information and Referral, Personal Advocacy, Shelter/Safe House, Telephone Contacts, Therapy
YWCA CRISIS SERVICES Ph: 603-625-5785	Manchester 03101	Adult Sexual Assault, Adults Molested as Children, Child Physical Abuse, Child Sexual Abuse, Domestic Violence, Elder Abuse, Non-Violent Crimes	Rape Crisis Shelter	Crisis Counseling, Crisis Hotline Counseling, Emergency Legal Advocacy, Follow-up Contact, Group Therapy, Information and Referral, Personal Advocacy, Shelter/Safe House, Telephone Contacts, Assistance in Filing Compensation Claims, Criminal Justice Support Advocacy
BRIDGES PO BOX 217 Ph: 603-889-0858	Nashua	Adult Sexual Assault, Adults Molested as Children, Assault, Child Physical Abuse, Child Sexual Abuse, Domestic Violence, Elder Abuse, Non-Violent Crimes	Rape Crisis Shelter	Crisis Counseling, Crisis Hotline Counseling, Emergency Financial Assistance, Emergency Legal Advocacy, Follow-up Contact, Group Therapy, Information and Referral, Personal Advocacy, Shelter/Safe House, Telephone Contacts, Therapy, Assistance in Filing Compensation Claims, Criminal Justice Support Advocacy

New Jersey

JERSEY BATTERED WOMEN'S SERVICE PO BOX 1437 Ph: 973-262-7520	Morristown	Domestic Violence	Shelter	Crisis Counseling, Crisis Hotline, Shelter/Safe House, Childcare and Play Therapy for Children of Battered Women, Emergency Legal Advocacy, Court Advocacy, Transitional Housing, Community Education
WOMEN AWARE, INC. PO BOX 312 Ph: 732-249-4900	New Brunswick	Domestic Violence		Crisis Counseling, Crisis Hotline Counseling, Emergency Legal Advocacy, Referral, Shelter/Safe House, Community Education

WOMANSPACE, INC. 1212 Stuyvesant Avenue 609-394-0136	Trenton	Domestic Violence		Crisis Counseling, Crisis Hotline, Bilingual Advocates, Emergency Legal Advocacy, Follow-up Contact, Referrals, Shelter/Safe Ph: House, Therapy, Assistance in Filing Compensation Claims
PROVIDENCE HOUSE-WILLINGBORO SHELTER OF CATHOLIC CHARITIES and OCEAN COUNTY DOMESTIC VIOLENCE SERVICES PO BOX 496 Ph: 732-244-8259 or 856-824-0599	Willingboro and Toms River Catholic Charities Diocese of Trenton	Domestic Violence	Shelter	Crisis Counseling, Crisis Hotline, Emergency Legal Advocacy, Information and Referral , Shelter/Safe House, Support Groups for Battered Women, DV Safety Plans, Child Care and Play Therapy for Children of Battered Women, and Community Education
SHELTER OUR SISTERS Ph: 201-498-9247	Hackensack 07601	Domestic Violence	Shelter	Crisis Counseling, Crisis Hotline, Emergency Financial Assistance, Emergency Legal Advocacy, Referrals, Shelter/Safe House, Court Advocacy, and Childcare

New York

EQUINOX, INC. Ph: 518-434-6135	Albany 12206	Domestic Violence	Shelter	Crisis Counseling, Crisis Hotline Counseling, Emergency Financial Assistance, Follow-up Contact, Group Therapy, Information and Referral, Personal Advocacy, Telephone Contacts, Assistance in Filing Compensation Claims, Criminal Justice Support Advocacy
CROWN HEIGHTS JEWISH COMMUNITY COUNCIL Ph: 718-778-8808	Brooklyn 11225	Assault, Child Physical Abuse, Child Sexual Abuse, Domestic Violence, Elder Abuse, Non-Violent Crimes, Robbery	Shelter/ Safe Homes	Crisis Counseling, Crisis Hotline, Emergency Financial Assistance, Follow-up Contact, Group Therapy, Information and Referral, Personal Advocacy, Shelter/Safe Homes, Telephone Contacts, Assistance in Filing Compensation Claims, Criminal Justice Support Advocacy

KINGS COUNTY DISTRICT ATTORNEY Ph: 718-250-3820	Brooklyn 11201	Adult Sexual Assault, Assault, Child Physical Abuse, Child Sexual Abuse, Domestic Violence, Elder Abuse, Non-Violent Crimes, Robbery, Survivors of Homicide	Victim/ Witness Assist-ance	Assistance in Filing Compensation Claims, Witness Notification, Preparation for Court, and Court Advocacy, Follow-up Contact
GOOD SHEPHERD SERVICES Ph: 213-243-7070	New York 10001	Domestic Violence	Shelter	Crisis Counseling, Crisis Hotline, Emergency Financial Assistance, Emergency Legal Advocacy, Follow-up Contact, Group Therapy, Information and Referral, Personal Advocacy, Shelter/ Safe House, Telephone Contacts, Assistance in Filing Compensation Claims, Criminal Justice Support Advocacy
NEW YORK CITY GAY & LESBIAN ANTI-VIOLENCE PROJECT Ph: 212-714-1184 Ph: 212-714-1141 Fax: 212-714-2627 TTY: 212-714-1134	New York 10001	Adult Sexual Assault, Aggravated Battery, Arson, Assault, Domestic Violence, Economic/ Elder Abuse, Gang Violence, Non-Violent Crimes, Stalking, Survivors of Homicide, and Hate Crimes	Mental Health Agency, Rape Crisis Shelter	Crisis Counseling, Crisis Hotline, Emergency Financial Assistance, Follow-up Contact, Group Therapy, Information and Referral, Personal Advocacy, Safety Plans (DV), Shelter/ Safe House, Transportation, Assistance in Filing Compensation Claims, Criminal Justice Support Advocacy
NEW YORK PRESBYTERIAN HOSPITAL Ph: 212-305-9060	New York 10032	Adult Sexual Assault, Adults Molested as Children, Assault, Child Physical Abuse, Child Sexual Abuse, Domestic Violence, Elder Abuse, Survivors of Homicide	Hospital Based Crisis Inter-vention	Crisis Counseling, Emergency Financial Assistance, Follow-up Contact, Group Therapy, Information and Referral, Personal Advocacy, Shelter/ Safe House, Assistance in Filing Compensation Claims, Criminal Justice Support Advocacy

SANCTUARY FOR FAMILIES PO BOX 1406 WALL ST STATION Ph: 212-349-6009 Ph:212-234-9600	New York	Domestic Violence	Shelter	Crisis Counseling, Emergency Financial Assistance, Follow-up Contact, Group Therapy, Information and Referral, Personal Advocacy, Shelter/ Safe House, Assistance in Filing Compensation Claims
VIOLENCE INTERVENTION PROGRAM PO BOX 1161 TRIBOROUGH STATION Ph: 212-360-5090	New York	Domestic Violence	Shelter	Crisis Counseling, Crisis Hotline Counseling, Emergency Financial Assistance, Follow-up Contact, Group Therapy, Information and Referral, Personal Advocacy, Shelter/ Safe House, Telephone Contacts, Assistance in Filing Compensation Claims, Criminal Justice Support Advocacy
CENTER AGAINST DOMESTIC VIOLENCE Ph: 718-254-9134	Brooklyn 11201	Domestic Violence		Crisis Counseling, Follow-up Contact, Group Therapy, Information and Referral, Personal Advocacy, Telephone Contacts, Therapy, Assistance in Filing Compensation Claims, Criminal Justice Support Advocacy
TRIPACT 2575 Coney Island Ave. Ph: 718-627-5088	Brooklyn 11223	Adult Sexual Assault, Assault, Domestic Violence, Robbery		Crisis Counseling, Follow-up Contact, Information and Referral, Personal Advocacy, Telephone Contacts, Assistance in Filing Compensation Claims, Court Advocacy
ROCKLAND FAMILY SHELTER Ph: 914-634-3391	New City 10956	Adult Sexual Assault, Domestic Violence	Shelter	Crisis Counseling, Crisis Hotline Counseling, Emergency Legal Advocacy, Follow-up Contact, Group Therapy, Information and Referral, Shelter/Safe House, Therapy, Assistance in Filing Compensation Claims, Court Advocacy
GOOD SHEPHERD Ph: 213-243-7070	Manhattan 10001	Domestic Violence	Shelter	Crisis Counseling, Crisis Hotline Counseling, Emergency Financial Assistance, Emergency Legal Advocacy, Follow-up Contact, Group Therapy, Information and Referral, Shelter/Safe House, Assistance in Filing Compensation Claims, Criminal Justice Support Advocacy

| WOMEN'S SURVIVAL SPACE

Ph: 718-923-1400
11231 | Brooklyn | Adult Sexual Assault, Child Physical Abuse, Child Sexual Abuse, Domestic Violence, Stalking | Shelter | Battered Women's Shelter, DV Safety Plans, Children's Advocacy Centers, Family Visitation Center, Rape Crisis |

North Carolina

VICTIM ASSISTANCE Ph: 704-336-4126	Charlotte 28202	Domestic Violence	Victim/ Witness Assist- ance	Crisis Counseling, Emergency Legal Advocacy, Witness Notification, Follow-up Contact, Information and Referral, Court Advocacy, Telephone Contacts, Assistance in Filing Compensation Claims, Criminal Justice Support Advocacy
FAMILY VIOLENCE PREVENTION CENTER DBA INTERACT Ph: 919-828-7501	Raleigh 27605	Domestic Violence	Shelter	Crisis Counseling, Emergency Legal Advocacy, Follow-up Contact, Group Therapy, Information and Referral, Shelter/Safe House, Telephone Contacts, Assistance in Filing Compensation Claims, Criminal Justice Support Advocacy
FAMILY SERVICES, INC. Ph: 336-722-8173	Winston-Salem 27107	Domestic Violence	Family Service Agency	Crisis Counseling, Crisis Hotline Counseling, Follow-up Contact, Group Therapy, Information and Referral, Shelter/Safe House, Telephone Contacts, Therapy, Assistance in Filing Compensation Claims, Criminal Justice Support Advocacy
ALBERMARLE HOPELINE PO BOX 2064 Ph: 252-338-5338	Elizabeth City	Domestic Violence	Shelter	Crisis Counseling, Crisis Hotline Counseling, Emergency Legal Advocacy, Follow-up Contact, Group Therapy, Information and Referral, Personal Advocacy, Telephone Contacts, Therapy, Assistance in Filing Compensation Claims, Criminal Justice Support Advocacy

ALBERMARLE HOPELINE PO BOX 2064 Ph: 252-338-5338	Elizabeth City	Domestic Violence	Crisis Hotline	Crisis Counseling, Crisis Hotline Counseling, Emergency Legal Advocacy, Follow-up Contact, Information and Referral, Personal Advocacy, Assistance in Filing Victim Compensation Claims

Ohio

LIGHTHOUSE YOUTH SERVICES, INC. Ph: 513-475-5680	Cincinnati 45206	Adults Molested as Children, Child Physical Abuse, Child Sexual Abuse, Domestic Violence, Survivors of Homicide	Youth Service Center	Crisis Counseling, Crisis Hotline Counseling, Follow-up Contact, Group Therapy, Information and Referral, Personal Advocacy, Shelter/Safe House, Telephone Contacts, Therapy, Assistance in Filing Compensation Claims, Criminal Justice Support Advocacy
SEVEN HILLS NEIGHBOR-HOOD HOUSES, INC. Ph: 513-632-7106	Cincinnati 45214	Adult Sexual Assault, Adults Molested as Children, Assault, Child Physical Abuse, Child Sexual Abuse, Domestic Violence, DUI/DWI Crashes, Elder Abuse, Robbery, Survivors of Homicide	Shelter/ Comm-unity Services	Crisis Counseling, Crisis Hotline, Emergency Financial Assistance, Emergency Legal Advocacy, Follow-up Contact, Support Groups, Information and Referral, Personal Advocacy, Shelter/Safe House, Telephone Contacts, Assistance in Filing Compensation Claims, Criminal Justice Advocacy
YWCA BATTERED WOMEN'S SHELTER Ph: 513-361-2137	Cincinnati 45202	Domestic Violence	Shelter	Crisis Counseling, Crisis Hotline Counseling, Emergency Financial Assistance, Follow-up Contact, Group Therapy, Information and Referral, Personal Advocacy, Shelter/Safe House, Telephone Contacts, Assistance in Filing Compensation Claims

DOMESTIC VIOLENCE CENTER PO BOX 5466 Ph: 216-651-8484	Cleveland	Adult Sexual Assault, Adults Molested as Children, Assault, Child Physical Abuse, Child Sexual Abuse, Domestic Violence, Non-Violent Crimes	Shelter	Crisis Counseling, Emergency Legal Advocacy, Follow-up Contact, Support Groups, Information and Referral, Personal Advocacy, Telephone Contacts, Assistance in Filing Compensation Claims, Criminal Justice Support Advocacy
THE CENTER FOR THE PREVENTION OF DOMESTIC VIOLENCE Ph: 216-831-5440	Cleveland 44122	Domestic Violence	Victim Resource Center	Assistance in Filing Compensation Claims, Information and Referral, Personal Advocacy, Telephone Contacts
CHOICES FOR VICTIMS OF DOMESTIC VIOLENCE PO BOX 06157 Ph: 614-258-6080	Columbus	Domestic Violence	Shelter	Crisis Counseling, Support Groups, Information and Referral, Shelter/Safe House, Therapy, Assistance in Filing Compensation Claims
OHIO HISPANIC COALITION Ph: 614-840-9934	Columbus 43229	Domestic Violence	Shelter	Assistance in Filing Compensation Claims, Follow-up Contact, Information and Referral, Personal Advocacy, Telephone Contacts

Oklahoma

| DOMESTIC VIOLENCE INTERVENTION SERVICES, INC.

Ph: 918-585-3163 | Tulsa 74135 | Domestic Violence | Shelter | Assistance in Filing Compensation Claims, Criminal Justice Support Advocacy, Follow-up Contact, Information and Referral, Personal Advocacy, Telephone Contacts |
| FAMILY SHELTER OF SOUTHERN OKLAHOMA

PO BOX 1408
Ph: 580-226-6424 | Ardmore | Adult Sexual Assault, Adults Molested as Children, Child Physical Abuse, Child Sexual Abuse, Domestic Violence, Elder Abuse | Shelter | Crisis Counseling, Crisis Hotline Counseling, Follow-up Contact, Information and Referral, Personal Advocacy, Shelter/Safe House, Telephone Contacts, Assistance in Filing Compensation Claims, Criminal Justice Support Advocacy |

ROGERS COUNTY COMMUNITY SERVICES CENTER, INC. PO BOX 446 Ph: 918-341-1424	Claremore	Adult Sexual Assault, Adults Molested as Children, Assault, Child Physical Abuse, Child Sexual Abuse, Domestic Violence, Elder Abuse	Social Services	Crisis Counseling, Crisis Hotline Counseling, Emergency Financial Assistance, Emergency Legal Advocacy, Follow-up Contact, Group Therapy, Information and Referral, Personal Advocacy, Shelter/Safe House, Telephone Contacts, Therapy, Assistance in Filing Compensation Claims, Criminal Justice Support Advocacy
MARIE DETTY YOUTH & FAMILY PO BOX 408 Ph: 580-250-1123	Lawton	Adult Sexual Assault, Adults Molested as Children, Assault, Child Physical Abuse, Child Sexual Abuse, Domestic Violence, Elder Abuse, Survivors of Homicide	Rape Crisis	Crisis Counseling, Crisis Hotline Counseling, Follow-up Contact, Group Therapy, Information and Referral, Personal Advocacy, Shelter/Safe House, Telephone Contacts, Therapy, Assistance in Filing Compensation Claims, Criminal Justice Support Advocacy
MARIE DETTY YOUTH & FAMILY PO BOX 408 Ph: 580-248-0171	Lawton	Adult Sexual Assault, Adults Molested as Children, Assault, Child Physical Abuse, Child Sexual Abuse, Domestic Violence, Elder Abuse, Survivors of Homicide	Rape Crisis	Crisis Counseling, Crisis Hotline Counseling, Follow-up Contact, Group Therapy, Information and Referral, Personal Advocacy, Shelter/Safe House, Telephone Contacts, Therapy, Assistance in Filing Compensation Claims, Criminal Justice Support Advocacy
MARIE DETTY YOUTH & FAMILY SERVICES PO BOX 408 Ph: 580-248-0171	Lawton	Adult Sexual Assault, Adults Molested as Children, Assault, Child Physical Abuse, Child Sexual Abuse, Domestic Violence, Elder Abuse, Survivors of Homicide	Rape Crisis	Crisis Counseling, Crisis Hotline Counseling, Emergency Legal Advocacy, Follow-up Contact, Group Therapy, Information and Referral, Personal Advocacy, Shelter/Safe House, Telephone Contacts, Therapy, Assistance in Filing Compensation Claims, Criminal Justice Support Advocacy

| NEW DIRECTIONS, INC.

PO BOX 1684
Ph: 580-255-8726 | Lawton | Adult Sexual Assault, Adults Molested as Children, Child Sexual Abuse, Domestic Violence, Survivors of Homicide | Rape Crisis Shelter | Crisis Counseling, Crisis Hotline Counseling, Emergency Legal Advocacy, Follow-up Contact, Group Therapy, Information and Referral, Personal Advocacy, Shelter/Safe House, Telephone Contacts, Therapy, Assistance in Filing Compensation Claims, Criminal Justice Support Advocacy |

Oregon

BRADLEYANGLE HOUSE PO BOX 14694 Ph: 503-232-7812	Portland	Domestic Violence	Shelter	Crisis Counseling, Crisis Hotline Counseling, Emergency Financial Assistance, Emergency Legal Advocacy, Follow-up Contact, Group Therapy, Information and Referral, Personal Advocacy, Shelter/Safe House, Telephone Contacts, Assistance in Filing Compensation Claims, Criminal Justice Support Advocacy
OREGON HUMAN DEVELOPMENT CORPORATION - HISPANIC ACCESS CENTER Ph: 503-232-4448 Ph: 503-236-9670 Fax: 503-234-9074	Portland 97214	Child Physical Abuse, Domestic Violence	Human Service/ Social Services Agency	Crisis Counseling, Crisis Hotline Counseling, Crisis Prevention, Emergency Financial Assistance, Follow-up Contact, Group Therapy, Information and Referral, Safety Plans (DV), Criminal Justice Support Advocacy
PORTLAND WOMEN'S CRISIS LINE PO BOX 42610 Ph: 503-872-8627	Portland	Adult Sexual Assault, Domestic Violence, Non-Violent Crimes	Shelter	Information and Referral, Shelter/Safe House, Telephone Contacts
RAPHAEL HOUSE PO BOX 10797 Ph: 503-222-6507	Portland	Child Physical Abuse, Child Sexual Abuse, Domestic Violence	Shelter	Crisis Counseling, Information and Referral, Personal Advocacy, Shelter/Safe House

SALVATION ARMY PO BOX 2398 Ph: 503-224-7718	Portland	Adult Sexual Assault, Adults Molested as Children, Assault, Child Physical Abuse, Child Sexual Abuse, Domestic Violence	Shelter	Crisis Counseling, Crisis Hotline Counseling, Emergency Financial Assistance, Emergency Legal Advocacy, Follow-up Contact, Group Therapy, Information and Referral, Personal Advocacy, Shelter/ Safe House, Telephone Contacts, Therapy, Assistance in Filing Compensation Claims, Criminal Justice Support Advocacy
VOLUNTEERS OF AMERICA- FAMILY CENTER Ph: 503-771-5503	Portland 97214	Adult Sexual Assault, Domestic Violence	Shelter	Crisis Counseling, Crisis Hotline Counseling, Emergency Financial Assistance, Follow-up Contact, Group Therapy, Information and Referral, Personal Advocacy, Telephone Contacts, Assistance in Filing Compensation Claims
YWCA PO BOX 19178 Ph: 503-535-3274	Portland	Adult Sexual Assault, Adults Molested as Children, Assault, Child Physical Abuse, Child Sexual Abuse, Domestic Violence, Elder Abuse	Shelter	Crisis Counseling, Crisis Hotline Counseling, Emergency Financial Assistance, Emergency Legal Advocacy, Follow-up Contact, Group Therapy, Information and Referral, Personal Advocacy, Shelter/ Safe House, Therapy, Assistance in Filing Compensation Claims, Criminal Justice Support Advocacy

Pennsylvania

DAUPHIN COUNTY VICTIM/ WITNESS ASSISTANCE PROGRAM 2 South Second Street, 4th Floor Ph: 717-780-7075 Fax:717-780-7079	Harrisburg 17102	Adult Sexual Assault/Rape Aggravated Battery, Arson, Child Physical Abuse, Child Sexual Abuse, Domestic Violence, Fraud, Gang Violence, Human Trafficking, Identity Theft,		Robbery, Stalking, Survivors Of Homicide, Terrorism, Disabled Victims Prosecutor- Based County Victim/ Witness Assistance Program Crisis Counseling, Crisis Hotline, Emergency Financial Assistance, Emergency Legal Advocacy, Fraud Investigation, Group Therapy, Identity Theft Counseling , Safety Plans (DV), Shelter/Safe House, Supervised Visitation, Transportation, Assistance in Filing Compensation Claims, Cell Phones (911), Court Advocacy

PENNSYLVANIA OFFICE OF THE VICTIM ADVOCATE 1101 S. Front Street Ph: 1-800-563-6399 Fax:717-787-0867	Harrisburg 17104	Adult Sexual Assault/Rape, Aggravated Battery, Arson, Child Sexual Abuse, Domestic Violence, Fraud, Gang Violence, Human Trafficking, Identity Theft, Robbery, Stalking, Survivors Of Homicide, Terrorism Corrections		Criminal Justice Support Advocacy, Victim/Witness Case Notification, Victim Services, Advance Notice to Victims of Release or Furloughs of Violent Offenders
PINNACLE HEALTH AND HOSPITALS 17 South Market Square Ph: 717-782-2467	Harrisburg 17101	Adult Sexual Assault, Child Physical Abuse, Child Sexual Abuse, Domestic Violence	Hospital	Crisis Counseling, Domestic Violence Screening and Assessment, Sexual Assault Crisis Team, Follow-up Contact, Information And Referral, Telephone Contacts, Assistance in Filing Compensation Claims, Court Advocacy
YWCA OF GREATER HARRISBURG Ph: 717-234-7931	Harrisburg 17103	Adult Sexual Assault, Adults Molested as Children, Child Sexual Abuse, Domestic Violence	Shelter	Crisis Counseling, Crisis Hotline Counseling, Emergency Financial Assistance, Follow-up Contact, Group Therapy, Information and Referral Shelter/Safe House, and Court Advocacy
CONGRESO DE LATINOS UNIDOS, INC. Ph: 215-763-8870	Philadelphia 19133	Domestic Violence	Shelter	Crisis Counseling, Crisis Hotline Counseling, Follow-up Hotline Counseling, Follow-up Contact, Group Therapy, Information and Referral , Personal Advocacy, Shelter/Safe House, Telephone Contacts, Assistance in Filing Compensation Claims

WOMEN AGAINST ABUSE, INC., Box 13758 Ph: 215-386-7777 or 215-386-1280	Philadelphia	Domestic Violence	Shelter	Crisis Counseling, Information and Referral, Emergency Shelter, Transitional Housing, Welfare Advocacy, Legal Advocacy, Court Advocacy
WOMEN IN TRANSITION Ph: 215-751-1111 or 215-564-5301	Philadelphia 19107	Domestic Violence	Shelter	Crisis Counseling, Crisis Hotline Counseling, Follow-up Contact, Group Therapy, Information and Referral, Shelter/Safe House, Assistance in Filing Compensation Claims, Court Advocacy
CRISIS CENTER NORTH Inc. PO BOX 101093 Ph: 412-364-5556 or 412-364-6728	Pittsburgh	Adult Sexual Assault, Adults Molested as Children, Child Physical Abuse, Child Sexual Abuse, Domestic Violence	Shelter	Crisis Counseling, Crisis Hotline Counseling, Emergency Financial Assistance, Emergency Legal Advocacy, Group Therapy, Referrals, Shelter/Safe House, Individual Therapy, Court Advocacy
PITTSBURGH ACTION AGAINST RAPE Ph: 412-431-5665	Pittsburgh 15203	Adult Sexual Assault, Adults Molested as Children, Child Sexual Abuse, Domestic Violence	Rape Crisis Center	Crisis Counseling, Crisis Hotline Counseling, Emergency Legal Advocacy, Follow-up Contact, Group Therapy, Information and Referral, Personal Advocacy, Therapy, Court Advocacy
THE CENTER FOR VICTIMS OF VIOLENCE AND CRIME 900 FIFTH AVE Ph: 412-350-1975	Pittsburgh 15219	Adult Sexual Assault, Adults Molested as Children, Assault, Child Physical Abuse, Child Sexual Abuse, Domestic Violence, DUI/DWI Crashes, Elder Abuse, Robbery, Survivors of Homicide	Victim Services and Victim Ad-vocacy Center	Crisis Counseling, Crisis Hotline Counseling, Emergency Legal Advocacy, Follow-up Contact, Group Therapy, Information And Referral, Individual Therapy, Victim Notification of Early Release of Violent Offenders, and Court Advocacy

WOMAN'S CENTER & SHELTER OF GREATER PITTSBURGH PO BOX 9024 Ph: 412-687-8005 or 877-338-TALK	Pittsburgh	Child Sexual Abuse, Domestic Violence	Shelter	Crisis Counseling, Crisis Hotline, Childcare, Emergency Legal Advocacy, Follow-up Contact, Group Therapy, Information and Referral, Therapy, Court Advocacy

Rhode Island

CAPITAL CITY COMMUNITY CENTERS Ph: 401-455-3880	Providence 02908	Adult Sexual Assault, Assault, Child Physical Abuse, Child Sexual Abuse, Domestic Violence, DUI/DWI Crashes, Elder Abuse, Non-Violent Crimes, Robbery, Survivors of Homicide	Human Service Agency	Crisis Counseling, Crisis Hotline Counseling, Emergency Financial Assistance, Emergency Legal Advocacy, Follow-up Contact, Information and Referral, Personal Advocacy, Shelter/Safe House, Telephone Contacts, Assistance in Filing Compensation Claims, Criminal Justice Support Advocacy
CHILD & FAMILY SERVICES OF NEWPORT COUNTY Ph: 401-849-2300	Newport 02840	Adult Sexual Assault, Assault, Domestic Violence, Elder Abuse, Non-Violent Crimes, Robbery	Family Service Agency	Crisis Counseling, Crisis Hotline Counseling, Emergency Financial Assistance, Emergency Legal Advocacy, Follow-up Contact, Information and Referral, Personal Advocacy, Shelter/Safe House, Telephone Contacts, Assistance in Filing Compensation Claims, Criminal Justice Support Advocacy

South Carolina

MY SISTER'S HOUSE PO BOX 5341 Ph: 843-747-4069	Charleston	Domestic Violence	Shelter	Crisis Counseling, Crisis Hotline Counseling, Emergency Financial Assistance, Emergency Legal Advocacy, Follow-up Contact, Group Therapy, Information and Referral, Personal Advocacy, Shelter/Safe House, Telephone Contacts, Therapy, Assistance in Filing Compensation Claims, Criminal Justice Support Advocacy

SISTER CARE, INC. PO BOX 1029 Ph: 803-926-0505	Columbia	Domestic Violence	Shelter	Crisis Counseling, Group Therapy, Information and Referral, Personal Advocacy, Telephone Contacts, Assistance in Filing Compensation Claims, Criminal Justice Support Advocacy
SISTERCARE, INC. PO BOX 1029 Ph: 803-926-0505	Columbia	Domestic Violence	Shelter	Crisis Counseling, Group Therapy, Information and Referral, Personal Advocacy, Shelter/Safe House, Assistance in Filing Compensation Claims
SAFE HARBOR IN PO BOX 174 Ph: 864-467-1177	Greenville	Adult Sexual Assault, Adults Molested as Children, Assault, Child Physical Abuse, Child Sexual Abuse, Domestic Violence, DUI/DWI Crashes, Elder Abuse, Non-Violent Crimes, Robbery, Survivors of Homicide	Shelter	Crisis Counseling, Crisis Hotline Counseling, Emergency Financial Assistance, Emergency Legal Advocacy, Follow-up Contact, Group Therapy, Information and Referral, Personal Advocacy, Shelter/Safe House, Telephone Contacts, Therapy, Assistance in Filing Compensation Claims, Criminal Justice Support Advocacy

South Dakota

CATHOLIC FAMILY SERVICES Ph: 605-333-3375	Sioux Falls 57105	Adult Sexual Assault, Adults Molested as Children, Assault, Child Physical Abuse, Child Sexual Abuse, Domestic Violence, DUI/DWI Crashes, Elder Abuse, Non-Violent Crimes, Robbery, Survivors of Homicide	Religious Social Service Agency Shelter	Crisis Hotline Counseling, Emergency Financial Assistance, Emergency Legal Advocacy, Follow-up Contact, Group Therapy, Information and Referral, Personal Advocacy, Shelter/Safe House, Telephone Contacts, Therapy, Assistance in Filing Compensation Claims, Criminal Justice Support Advocacy, Crisis Counseling

RAPE AND DOMESTIC ABUSE CENTER Ph: 605-339-0116	Sioux Falls 57102	Adult Sexual Assault, Adults Molested as Children, Child Sexual Abuse, Domestic Violence	Rape Crisis Shelter	Crisis Hotline Counseling, Emergency Financial Assistance, Follow-up Contact, Personal Advocacy, Shelter/Safe House, Assistance in Filing Compensation Claims, Criminal Justice Support Advocacy, Crisis Counseling
WOMEN AGAINST VIOLENCE, INC. PO BOX 3042 Ph: 605-341-3292	Rapid City	Adult Sexual Assault, Adults Molested as Children, Child Sexual Abuse, Domestic Violence	Shelter	Crisis Hotline Counseling, Emergency Legal Advocacy, Follow-up Contact, Group Therapy, Personal Advocacy, Shelter/Safe House, Assistance in Filing Compensation Claims, Criminal Justice Support Advocacy
MISSOURI SHORES DOMESTIC VIOLENCE CTR PO BOX 398 Ph: 605-224-0256	Pierre	Adult Sexual Assault, Adults Molested as Children, Assault, Child Physical Abuse, Child Sexual Abuse, Domestic Violence, Elder Abuse, Non-Violent Crimes, Survivors of Homicide	Shelter	Crisis Counseling, Crisis Hotline Counseling, Emergency Financial Assistance, Emergency Legal Advocacy, Follow-up Contact, Group Therapy, Personal Advocacy, Shelter/Safe House, Assistance in Filing Compensation Claims, Criminal Justice Support Advocacy

Tennessee

CASE MANAGEMENT Ph: 901-821-5600	Memphis 38122	Adult Sexual Assault, Assault, Domestic Violence, DUI/DWI Crashes, Elder Abuse, Non-Violent Crimes, Robbery, Survivors of Homicide	Mental Health Agency Shelter	Crisis Counseling, Crisis Hotline Counseling, Emergency Financial Assistance, Emergency Legal Advocacy, Follow-up Contact, Group Therapy, Information and Referral, Personal Advocacy, Shelter/Safe House, Telephone Contacts, Therapy, Assistance in Filing Compensation Claims, Criminal Justice Support Advocacy
YWCA OF GREATER MEMPHIS Ph: 901-323-2211	Memphis 38111	Domestic Violence	Shelter	Crisis Counseling, Crisis Hotline Counseling, Emergency Financial Assistance, Follow-up Contact, Information and Referral, Shelter/Safe House, Therapy, Criminal Justice Support Advocacy

S.A.V.E. (Survivors Against Violent Environments) Ph: 615-256-1330 Ph: 615-202-5252 Fax: 615-256-1330	Nashville 37204	Domestic Violence	Victims Service Centers, Shelter	Crisis Counseling, Crisis Hotline Counseling, Crisis Prevention, Emergency Financial Assistance, Emergency Legal Advocacy, Follow-up Contact, Fraud Investigation, Group Therapy, Identity Theft Counseling, Information and Referral, Personal Advocacy, Safety Plans (DV), Shelter/Safe House, Supervised Visitation, Telephone Contacts, Therapy, Transportation, Assistance in Filing Compensation Claims, Cell Phones (911), Criminal Justice Support Advocacy
UJIMA HOUSE PO BOX 280365 Ph: 615-242-5297	Nashville	Domestic Violence	Shelter	Crisis Counseling, Crisis Hotline Counseling, Follow-up Contact, Group Therapy, Information and Referral, Shelter/Safe House
YWCA OF NASHVILLE AND MIDDLE TENNESSEE Ph: 615-242-1070	Nashville 37215	Domestic Violence	Shelter	Crisis Counseling, Crisis Hotline Counseling, Emergency Legal Advocacy, Group Therapy, Information and Referral, Shelter/Safe House, Telephone Contacts, Assistance in Filing Compensation Claims, Criminal Justice Support Advocacy
WRAP Ph: 731-668-0411	Jackson 38305	Domestic Violence	Shelter	Crisis Counseling, Crisis Hotline Counseling, Emergency Financial Assistance, Emergency Legal Advocacy, Follow-up Contact, Group Therapy, Information and Referral, Personal Advocacy, Shelter/Safe House, Telephone Contacts, Therapy, Assistance in Filing Compensation Claims, Criminal Justice Support Advocacy

Texas

TRAVIS CO DOM VIO/ SEXUAL ASSAULT SURVIVAL CENTER PO BOX 19454 Ph: 512-356-1554	Austin	Adult Sexual Assault, Adults Molested as Children, Child Physical Abuse, Child Sexual Abuse, Domestic Violence	Rape Crisis Shelter	Crisis Counseling, Crisis Hotline Counseling, Emergency Financial Assistance, Emergency Legal Advocacy, Follow-up Contact, Group Therapy, Information and Referral, Shelter/Safe House, Telephone Contacts, Therapy, Assistance in Filing Compensation Claims, Criminal Justice Support Advocacy
THE FAMILY PLACE PO BOX 7999 Ph: 972-243-1611	Dallas	Domestic Violence	Shelter	Crisis Counseling, Emergency Legal Advocacy, Group Therapy, Information and Referral, Telephone Contacts, Assistance in Filing Compensation Claims, Criminal Justice Support Advocacy
AMISTAD FAMILY VIOLENCE AND RAPE CRISIS CENTER PO BOX 1454 Ph: 830-775-961	Del Rio	Adult Sexual Assault, Adults, Molested as Children, Child Physical Abuse, Child Sexual Abuse, Domestic Violence	Rape Crisis Shelter	Crisis Counseling, Crisis Hotline Counseling, Emergency Legal Advocacy, Follow-up Contact, Group Therapy, Information and Referral, Shelter/Safe House, Telephone Contacts, Therapy, Assistance in Filing Compensation Claims, Criminal Justice Support Advocacy
HOUSTON AREA WOMEN'S CENTER DIRECT SERVICES Ph: 713-528-6798	Houston 77019	Adult Sexual Assault, Adults Molested as Children, Child Physical Abuse, Child Sexual Abuse, Domestic Violence	Rape Crisis Shelter	Crisis Counseling, Crisis Hotline Counseling, Follow-up Contact, Information and Referral, Shelter/Safe House, Telephone Contacts, Assistance in Filing Compensation Claims, Criminal Justice Support Advocacy
NORTHWEST ASSISTANCE MINISTRIES FAMILY VIOLENCE CENTER Ph: 281-885-4673	Houston 77090	Adult Sexual Assault, Adults Molested as Children, Assault, Child Physical Abuse, Child Sexual Abuse, Domestic Violence, Elder Abuse	Shelter	Crisis Counseling, Crisis Hotline Counseling, Emergency Financial Assistance, Follow-up Contact, Group Therapy, Information and Referral, Telephone Contacts, Therapy, Assistance in Filing Compensation Claims, Criminal Justice Support Advocacy

| VICTIM ASSISTANCE CENTRE, INC. Ph: 713-755-5625 | Houston 77002 | Adult Sexual Assault, Adults Molested as Children, Assault, Child Physical Abuse, Child Sexual Abuse, Domestic Violence, DUI/ DWI Crashes, Elder Abuse, Non-Violent Crimes, Robbery, Survivors of Homicide | Victim Assist- ance | Crisis Counseling, Witness Case Notification, Emergency Financial Assistance, Emergency Legal Advocacy, Court Advocacy, Follow-up Contact, Group Therapy, Information and Referral, Coordination with Shelter/ Safe House, Telephone Contacts, Therapy, Assistance in Filing Victim Compensation Claims, Criminal Justice Support Advocacy |

Utah

MURRAY POLICE DEPARTMENT Ph: 801-284-4203	Salt Lake City 84105	Adult Sexual Assault, Assault, Child Physical Abuse, Child Sexual Abuse, Domestic Violence, Elder Abuse, Non- Violent Crimes, Survivors of Homicide	Law Enforce- ment Agency	Crisis Counseling, Emergency Financial Assistance, Emergency Legal Advocacy, Follow-up Contact, Group Therapy, Information and Referral, Referral to Shelter/Safe House, Telephone Contacts, Therapy, Assistance in Filing Compensation Claims, Criminal Justice Support Advocacy
SALT LAKE CITY POLICE DEPARTMENT Ph: 801-799-3747	Salt Lake City 84111	Adult Sexual Assault, Assault, Child Physical Abuse, Child Sexual Abuse, Domestic Violence, Elder Abuse, Non- Violent Crimes, Robbery, Survivors of Homicide	Law Enforce- ment Agency	Crisis Counseling, Emergency Financial Assistance, Follow-up Contact, Information and Referral, Personal Advocacy, Referral for Shelter/Safe House, Telephone Contacts, Assistance in Filing Compensation Claims, Criminal Justice Support Advocacy
YWCA OF SALT LAKE Ph: 801-537-8600	Salt Lake City 84111	Domestic Violence	Shelter	Crisis Counseling, Emergency Financial Assistance, Group Therapy, Information and Referral, Personal Advocacy, Shelter/Safe House, Telephone Contacts, Assistance in Filing Compensation Claims

CAPSA PO BOX 3617 Ph: 435-753-2500	Logan	Adult Sexual Assault, Domestic Violence	Shelter	Crisis Counseling, Emergency Financial Assistance, Emergency Legal Advocacy, Follow-up Contact, Group Therapy, Information and Referral, Personal Advocacy, Shelter/Safe House, Telephone Contacts, Assistance in Filing Compensation Claims, Criminal Justice Support Advocacy
CHILD & FAMILY SUPPORT CENTER Ph: 435-752-8880	Logan 84341	Adults Molested as Children, Child Physical Abuse, Child Sexual Abuse, Domestic Violence	Family Service Agency Shelter	Crisis Counseling, Follow-up Contact, Group Therapy, Information and Referral, Personal Advocacy, Shelter/Safe House, Telephone Contacts, Therapy, Assistance in Filing Compensation Claims, Criminal Justice Support Advocacy
CENTER FOR WOMEN & CHILDREN IN CRISIS PO BOX 1075 Ph: 801-374-9351	Provo	Adult Sexual Assault, Adults Molested as Children, Child Physical Abuse, Child Sexual Abuse, Domestic Violence, Elder Abuse, Non-Violent Crimes	Family Service Agency	Crisis Counseling, Emergency Financial Assistance, Follow-up Contact, Group Therapy, Information and Referral, Personal Advocacy, Shelter/Safe House, Telephone Contacts, Therapy, Assistance in Filing Compensation Claims, Criminal Justice Support Advocacy
PROVO CITY CORPORATION PO BOX 1849 Ph: 801-852-6251	Provo	Adult Sexual Assault, Assault, Child Physical Abuse, Child Sexual Abuse, Domestic Violence, Elder Abuse, Robbery, Survivors of Homicide	Shelter	Crisis Counseling, Emergency Financial Assistance, Emergency Legal Advocacy, Follow-up Contact, Information and Referral, Personal Advocacy, Shelter/Safe House, Telephone Contacts, Assistance in Filing Compensation Claims, Criminal Justice Support Advocacy

SAFESPACE PO BOX 158 Ph: 802-863-0003	Burlington	Adult Sexual Assault, Adults Molested as Children, Assault, Domestic Violence, Non-Violent Crimes	Shelter	Crisis Counseling, Crisis Hotline Counseling, Emergency Financial Assistance, Emergency Legal Advocacy, Follow-up Contact, Group Therapy, Information and Referral, Personal Advocacy, Shelter/Safe House, Telephone Contacts, Therapy, Assistance in Filing Compensation Claims, Criminal Justice Support Advocacy
WOMEN HELPING BATTERED WOMEN PO BOX 1535 Ph: 802-658-3131	Burlington	Domestic Violence	Shelter	Shelter/Safe House
WOMEN'S RAPE CRISIS CENTER PO BOX 92 Ph: 802-864-0555	Burlington	Adult Sexual Assault, Adults Molested as Children, Child Sexual Abuse, Domestic Violence, Elder Abuse	Rape Crisis Shelter	Crisis Counseling, Crisis Hotline Counseling, Emergency Financial Assistance, Emergency Legal Advocacy, Follow-up Contact, Group Therapy, Information and Referral, Personal Advocacy, Shelter/Safe House, Telephone Contacts, Assistance in Filing Compensation Claims, Criminal Justice Support Advocacy
BATTERED WOMEN'S SERVICES AND SHELTER PO BOX 828 Ph: 802-223-0023	Montpelier	Domestic Violence	Shelter	Crisis Hotline, Emergency Shelter/Safe House, Child Care program, Criminal Justice Support Advocacy, and Financial Assistance
VERMONT NETWORK AGAINST DOMESTIC VIOLENCE & SEXUAL ASSAULT PO BOX 405 Ph: 802-223-1302	Montpelier	Child Physical Abuse, Child Sexual Abuse, Domestic Violence	Coalition of Shelters	Legislative Advocacy, Crisis Hotline Counseling, Follow-up Contact, Support Groups, Information and Referral, Personal Advocacy, Shelter/Safe House, Telephone Contacts, Assistance in Filing Compensation Claims, Criminal Justice Support Advocacy

| WOMEN'S CRISIS CENTER PO BOX 933 Ph: 802-257-7364 | Brattleboro | Adult Sexual Assault, Domestic Violence | Rape Crisis | Crisis Counseling, Crisis Hotline Counseling, Emergency Legal Advocacy, Group Therapy, Information Group Therapy, Information and Referral, Personal Advocacy, Shelter/Safe House, Telephone Contacts, Assistance in Filing Compensation Claims, Criminal Justice Support Advocacy |

Virginia

SAMARITAN HOUSE Ph: 757-430-2642 23452	Virginia Beach	Domestic Violence	Shelter	Crisis Counseling, Crisis Hotline Counseling, Emergency Legal Advocacy, Follow-up Contact, Group Therapy, Information and Referral, Personal Advocacy, Shelter/Safe House, Assistance in Filing Compensation Claims
VA BEACH Ph: 757-427-4875	Virginia Beach 23456	Adult Sexual Assault, Adults Molested as Children, Assault, Child Physical Abuse, Child Sexual Abuse, Domestic Violence, DUI/DWI Crashes, Elder Abuse, Non-Violent Crimes, Robbery, Survivors of Homicide	Shelter	Crisis Counseling, Crisis Hotline Counseling, Emergency Legal Advocacy, Follow-up Contact, Group Therapy, Information and Referral, Personal Advocacy, Shelter/Safe House, Telephone Contacts, Assistance in Filing Compensation Claims, Criminal Justice Support Advocacy
NORFOLK Ph: 757-664-4850	Norfolk 23510	Adult Sexual Assault, Adults Molested as Children, Assault, Child Physical Abuse, Child Sexual Abuse, Domestic Violence, DUI/DWI Crashes, Elder Abuse, Non-Violent Crimes, Robbery, Survivors of Homicide	Shelter	Crisis Counseling, Crisis Hotline Counseling, Emergency Legal Advocacy, Follow-up Contact, Group Therapy, Information and Referral, Personal Advocacy, Shelter/Safe House, Telephone Contacts, Assistance in Filing Compensation Claims, Criminal Justice Support Advocacy

YWCA OF SOUTHAMPTON ROADS Ph: 757-625-4248	Norfolk 23510	Domestic Violence	Shelter	Crisis Counseling, Crisis Hotline Counseling, Emergency Legal Advocacy, Follow-up Contact, Group Therapy, Information and Referral, Personal Advocacy, Shelter/Safe House, Assistance in Filing Compensation Claims
SALVATION ARMY PO BOX 1631 Ph: 540-343-5335	Roanoke	Domestic Violence	Social Service Agency Shelter	Crisis Counseling, Crisis Hotline Counseling, Emergency Legal Advocacy, Group Therapy, Information and Referral, Personal Advocacy, Shelter/Safe House, Assistance in Filing Compensation Claims
TOTAL ACTION AGAINST POVERTY PO BOX 2868 Ph: 540-343-6781	Roanoke	Domestic Violence	Social Services	Crisis Counseling, Crisis Hotline Counseling, Emergency Legal Advocacy, Follow-up Contact, Group Therapy, Information and Referral, Personal Advocacy, Shelter/Safe House, Assistance in Filing Compensation Claims

Washington

| ADWAS/DV

Ph: 206-726-0093 | Seattle 98102 | Child Physical Abuse, Domestic Violence | Shelter | Crisis Counseling, Crisis Hotline Counseling, Emergency Legal Advocacy, Follow-up Contact, Group Therapy, Information and Referral, Personal Advocacy, Shelter/Safe House, Telephone Contacts, Assistance in Filing Compensation Claims, Criminal Justice Support Advocacy |
| DAWN/DV

PO BOX 88007
Ph: 206-000-0000 | Seattle | Domestic Violence | Shelter | Crisis Counseling, Crisis Hotline Counseling, Emergency Legal Advocacy, Follow-up Contact, Group Therapy, Personal Advocacy, Shelter/Safe House, Assistance in Filing Compensation Claims, Criminal Justice Support Advocacy |

FREMONT PUBLIC ASSN/ BROADVIEW/DV PO BOX 31151 Ph: 206-622-3108	Seattle	Domestic Violence	Shelter	Crisis Counseling, Crisis Hotline Counseling, Emergency Legal Advocacy, Follow-up Contact, Group Therapy, Personal Advocacy, Shelter/Safe House, Assistance in Filing Compensation Claims, Criminal Justice Support Advocacy
NEW BEGINNINGS/DV PO BOX 75125 Ph: 206-522-9474	Seattle	Domestic Violence	Shelter	Crisis Counseling, Crisis Hotline Counseling, Emergency Legal Advocacy, Follow-up Contact, Group Therapy, Personal Advocacy, Shelter/Safe House, Assistance in Filing Compensation Claims, Criminal Justice Support Advocacy
SALVATION ARMY/CBH/DV PO BOX 20128 Ph: 206-325-8517	Seattle	Domestic Violence	Social Service Agency Shelter	Crisis Counseling, Crisis Hotline Counseling, Emergency Legal Advocacy, Follow-up Contact, Group Therapy, Personal Advocacy, Shelter/Safe House, Assistance in Filing Compensation Claims, Criminal Justice Support Advocacy
YWCA OF SEATTLE/KING COUNTY/DV Ph: 206-461-4876	Seattle 98101	Domestic Violence	Shelter	Crisis Counseling, Crisis Hotline Counseling, Emergency Legal Advocacy, Follow-up Contact, Group Therapy, Personal Advocacy, Shelter/Safe House, Assistance in Filing Compensation Claims, Criminal Justice Support Advocacy
EASTSIDE DOMESTIC VIOLENCE PROGRAM/DV PO BOX 6398 Ph: 206-562-8840	Bellevue	Domestic Violence	Shelter	Crisis Counseling, Crisis Hotline Counseling, Emergency Financial Assistance, Emergency Legal Advocacy, Follow-up Contact, Group Therapy, Personal Advocacy, Shelter/ Safe House, Assistance in Filing Compensation Claims, Criminal Justice Support Advocacy

PUYALLUP TRIBE OF INDIANS Ph: 253-573-7939	Tacoma 98421	Adult Sexual Assault, Adults Molested as Children, Assault, Child Physical Abuse, Child Sexual Abuse, Domestic Violence, DUI/ DWI Crashes, Elder Abuse, Non-Violent Crimes, Robbery, Survivors of Homicide	Crime Victim Services	Crisis Counseling, Crisis Hotline Counseling, Emergency Financial Assistance, Emergency Legal Advocacy, Follow-up Contact, Group Therapy, Information and Referral, Personal Advocacy, Shelter/ Safe House, Telephone Contacts, Therapy, Assistance in Filing Compensation Claims, Criminal Justice Support Advocacy
YWCA OF PIERCE COUNTY/DV Ph: 206-383-2593	Tacoma 98402	Domestic Violence	Shelter	Crisis Counseling, Crisis Hotline Counseling, Emergency Legal Advocacy, Follow-up Contact, Group Therapy, Personal Advocacy, Shelter/Safe House, Assistance in Filing Compensation Claims, Criminal Justice Support Advocacy

West Virginia

YWCA RESOLVE FAMILY ABUSE PROGRAM Ph: 304-340-3554	Charleston 25301	Adult Sexual Assault, Adults Molested as Children, Assault, Child Physical Abuse, Child Sexual Abuse, Domestic Violence, Elder Abuse	Shelter	Crisis Counseling, Crisis Hotline Counseling, Emergency Legal Advocacy, Follow-up Contact, Group Therapy, Information and Referral, Personal Advocacy, Shelter/Safe House, Telephone Contacts, Assistance in Filing Compensation Claims, Criminal Justice Support Advocacy
TASK FORCE ON DOMESTIC VIOLENCE, INC. PO BOX 626 Ph: 304-367-1100	Fairmont	Adult Sexual Assault, Adults Molested as Children, Assault, Child Physical Abuse, Child Sexual Abuse, Domestic Violence, Elder Abuse	Shelter	Crisis Counseling, Crisis Hotline Counseling, Emergency Financial Assistance, Emergency Legal Advocacy, Follow-up Contact, Group Therapy, Information and Referral, Personal Advocacy, Shelter/ Safe House, Telephone Contacts, Therapy, Assistance in Filing Compensation Claims, Criminal Justice Support Advocacy

BRANCHES DOMESTIC VIOLENCE SHELTER PO BOX 403 Ph: 304-529-2382	Huntington	Domestic Violence	Shelter	Crisis Counseling, Crisis Hotline Counseling, Emergency Legal Advocacy, Follow-up Contact, Group Therapy, Information and Referral, Personal Advocacy, Shelter/Safe House, Telephone Contacts, Therapy, Assistance in Filing Compensation Claims, Criminal Justice Support Advocacy
FAMILY SERVICES: A DIVISION OF GOODWILL INDUSTRIES PO BOX 7365 Ph: 304-525-7034	Huntington	Adult Sexual Assault, Adults Molested as Children, Assault, Child Physical Abuse, Child Sexual Abuse, Domestic Violence, Non-Violent Crimes, Survivors of Homicide	Family and Social Service Agency	Vocational Training and Job Placement, Emergency Financial Aid, Crisis Counseling, Family Counseling, Social Services, Follow-up Contact, Group Therapy, Information and Referral, Personal Advocacy, Telephone Contacts, Criminal Justice Support Advocacy

Wisconsin

SOJOURNER TRUTH HOUSE, INC. PO BOX 080319 Ph: 414-643-1777	Milwaukee	Domestic Violence	Shelter	Crisis Counseling, Emergency Shelter/Safe House, Follow-up Contact, Information and Referral, Assistance in Filing Compensation Claims, Criminal Justice Support Advocacy
DANE COUNTY DISTRICT ATTORNEY'S OFFICE Ph: 608-267-8875	Madison 53703	Adult Sexual Assault, Adults Molested as Children, Assault, Child Physical Abuse, Child Sexual Abuse, Domestic Violence, DUI/DWI Crashes, Elder Abuse, Non-Violent Crimes, Robbery, Survivors of Homicide	Victim Assist-ance	Crisis Counseling, Victim/Witness Case Notification, Emergency Legal Advocacy, Transportation to Court, Court Advocacy, Childcare while in Court, Group Therapy, Information and Referral, Coordination with Shelter staff, Telephone Contacts, Therapy, Assistance in Filing Compensation Claims, Criminal Justice Support Advocacy

DOMESTIC ABUSE INTERVENTION SERVICES PO BOX 1761 Ph: 608-251-1237	Madison	Domestic Violence	Shelter	Crisis Counseling, Crisis Hotline Counseling, Emergency Financial Assistance, Emergency Legal Advocacy, Follow-up Contact, Group Therapy, Information and Referral, Personal Advocacy, Telephone Contacts, Assistance in Filing Compensation Claims, Criminal Justice Support Advocacy
NEW HORIZONS SHELTER PO BOX 2031 Ph: 608-791-2604	Lacrosse	Adult Sexual Assault, Domestic Violence	Shelter	Crisis Counseling, Follow-up Contact, Group Therapy, Information and Referral, Personal Advocacy, Assistance in Filing Compensation Claims, Criminal Justice Support Advocacy

Wyoming

CHEYENNE POLICE DEPARTMENT VICTIM ASSISTANCE PROGRAM Ph: 307-637-6507	Cheyenne 82001	Adult Sexual Assault, Adults Molested as Children, Assault, Child Physical Abuse, Child Sexual Abuse, Domestic Violence, DUI/DWI Crashes, Elder Abuse, Non-Violent Crimes, Robbery, Survivors of Homicide	Law Enforce-ment Agency	Assistance in Filing for Protective Order, Emergency Financial Assistance, Follow-up Contact, Information and Referral, Personal Advocacy, Referral, Personal Advocacy, Transportation to Shelter/ Safe House, Telephone Contacts, Assistance in Filing Victim Compensation Claims, Criminal Justice Support Advocacy
CHEYENNE SAFEHOUSE/ SEXUAL ASSAULT SERVICES, INC. PO BOX 1885 Ph: 307-635-2888	Cheyenne	Adult Sexual Assault, Domestic Violence, Non-Violent Crimes	Shelter	Crisis Counseling, Crisis Hotline Counseling, Emergency Financial Assistance, Emergency Legal Advocacy, Follow-up Contact, Group Therapy, Information and Referral, Personal Advocacy, Shelter/Safe House, Telephone Contacts, Assistance in Filing Compensation Claims, Criminal Justice Support Advocacy

DIVISION OF VICTIM SERVICES Ph: 307-777-7200	Cheyenne 82002	Adult Sexual Assault, Adults Molested as Children, Assault, Child Physical Abuse, Child Sexual buse, Domestic Violence, Elder Abuse, Non-Violent Crimes, Robbery, Survivors of Homicide	Victim Assist-ance Agency	Crisis Counseling, Crisis Hotline Counseling, Emergency Financial Assistance, Emergency Legal Advocacy, Follow-up Contact, Information and Referral, Personal Advocacy, Shelter/Safe House, Telephone Contacts, Assistance in Victim Filing Compensation Claims, Criminal Justice Support Advocacy
SELF HELP CENTER Ph: 307-235-3119	Casper 82601	Adult Sexual Assault, Child Physical Abuse, Child Sexual Abuse, Domestic Violence, Elder Abuse, Non-Violent Crimes	Resource Center	Crisis Counseling, Crisis Hotline Counseling, Emergency Financial Assistance, Emergency Legal Advocacy, Follow-up Contact, Group Therapy, Information and Referral, Personal Advocacy, Educational materials on DV, Telephone Contacts, Therapy, Assistance in Filing Compensation Claims, Criminal Justice Support Advocacy
HOPE CENTER PO BOX 824 Ph: 307-864-4673	Thermopolis	Adult Sexual Assault, Adults Molested as Children, Domestic Violence, Elder Abuse	Sexual Assault and Do-mestic Violence Services	Crisis Counseling, Individual and Group therapy, Emergency Legal Advocacy, Follow-up Contact, Information and Referral, Referral to Shelter/ Safe House, Criminal Justice Support Advocacy
HOT SPRINGS CRISIS LINE PO BOX 824 Ph: 307-864-4673	Thermopolis	Adult Sexual Assault, Child Physical Abuse, Child Sexual Abuse, Domestic Violence, Elder Abuse Crisis	Hotline Services	Crisis Counseling, Crisis Hotline Counseling, Information and Referral, Referral to Mental Health Services, Domestic Violence Programs, Addiction Services, or Family Counseling

Index

abandonment, 18
Abarbanel, Gail, 156
Abbey, Alice, 156
acquaintance rape, 155–71, 173
action plan, 135–36
adjourn, definition of, 173
adjournment in contemplation of
	dismissal, 173
administrative law, 173, 183
affidavit of service, 173
Alabama, 188
Alaska, 188
alcohol. *See* drinking
Alcoholics Anonymous, 7
anger
	control, 6–7, 20, 35
	of victim, 134
	as warning sign, 19
anxiety, 35–37, 55–56, 77–79
Arizona, 188
Arkansas, 188
arraignment, 316
arrest, 145–46, 149, 174
Asbury Park Press, 109
assault, 149–50, 174

bail, 174
bars, 5, 162
battering. *See* male batterers
benzodiazepines, 162
binge drinking, 5, 20
birth defects, 15, 87
booking, 174
Burgess, Ann Wolbert, 181

California, 188
case law, 174
CDC. *See* Centers for Disease Con-
	trol and Prevention

cell phones, 115–16, 136, 152, 174
Centers for Disease Control and Pre-
	vention (CDC), 4, 97
charge, criminal, 174
child abuse, 29, 45, 46, 61–67,
	83–86, 100–101
Child Abuse, Domestic Violence,
	Adoption and Family Services
	Act (1992), 141, 177
chronic abuse, 81–95, 120–21, 123–27
	background of victims, 81–83
	critical incidents in early life of
		victims, 83–86
	first incidents of, 86–88
	future plans of victims, 94–95
	seeking help for, 93–94
	worst incidents of, 88–93
civil court, 148–49, 174, 177
civil law, 174–75, 183
Clinton, Bill, 186
club drugs, 5
coalitions against domestic violence,
	175, 187–92
cocaine, 31, 34, 91–92, 99
cognitive mastery, 136
college students, 5, 19, 39–41, 178
Colorado, 188
command unit/precinct, 175
communication, 132
complainant, 175
complaint, 175
concurrent jurisdiction, 175
Connecticut, 188
conviction, 175
coping skills, 6, 135
corporal punishment, 46
counseling, 6–7
couples counseling, 6–7
court intake hearing, 175